Mental Toughness for Runners

This book provides you with an astounding piece of knowledge, a tool, and the personal experiences of an extraordinary ultra-distance runner and sport psychologist. With this book, Michele Ufer has added another milestone to the existing literature on running.

Prof. Dr. Oliver Stoll
Martin-Luther University Halle-Wittenberg, Germany

You will learn much about yourself and our sport. Whether theorist or practitioner, you will definitely put it to use!

Jochen Schmitz
Chief editor, RUNNING magazine

MICHELE UFER

MENTAL TOUGHNESS for RUNNERS

A COMPLETE GUIDE

Meyer & Meyer Sport

British Library Cataloguing in Publication Data

A catalogue record for this book is available from the British Library

Originally published as *Mentaltraining für Läufer*, © 2016 by Meyer & Meyer Verlag

Mental Toughness for Runners

Maidenhead: Meyer & Meyer Sport (UK) Ltd., 2019

ISBN: 978-1-78255-161-4

© 2019 by Meyer & Meyer Sports (UK) Ltd.

Aachen, Auckland, Beirut, Dubai, Hägendorf, Hong Kong, Indianapolis, Cairo, Cape Town, Manila, Maidenhead, New Delhi, Singapore, Sydney, Teheran, Vienna

Member of the World Sports Publishers' Association (WSPA)

Printed by C-M Books, Ann Arbor, MI

ISBN: 978-1-78255-161-4

Email: info@m-m-sports.com

www.thesportspublisher.com

CONTENTS

PROLOGUE

PROLOGUE BY PROF. DR. OLIVER STOLL, SPORT PSYCHOLOGIST

This book provides you with an astounding piece of knowledge, a tool, and the personal experience of an extraordinary ultra-distance runner and sport psychologist. With this book, Michele Ufer has added another milestone to the existing literature on running.

What makes this book so exceptional? On the one hand, it is the rock-solid technical foundation presented in language even the psychological layperson is able to understand, and on the other hand, it is the extremely candid treatment of sport psychology techniques, which he not only describes, but also presents via actual exercises in this book. And he did not leave out an opportunity for self-diagnosis.

A book like this can only be successful if the author can bring quite a bit of personal experience in distance running to the table. This, along with his own sport psychology training and his ability to build a network during his time as an active athlete, can validate his personal experience or allow him to process it with a book like this. In addition to world-class ultra-runners like Florian Reus, we also hear from scientists who do cutting-edge research (e.g., exercise addiction).

I do not know of any previous sport psychology book about running that bundled not only the author's experience, but also that of his colleagues—or rather other runners—and made it available to the public in this way.

This book is also not a purely celebratory book, stating that mental training is the only and exclusive key to success; Michele Ufer also impressively points out the limits of mental training and addresses the so-called *dark side of running*. Michele thus demonstrates his ability to have a more differentiated view of his passion. In addition to his role as a runner, Michele Ufer is clearly also a practical sport psychologist and scientist.

Although I am an experienced sport psychologist and runner myself, I was able to personally benefit from the content of this book. I can only imagine how much more beginning runners and athletes who are less knowledgeable about sport psychology can learn from this publication. I wish all of you many hours of productive reading and lots of fun trying out the techniques, and most of all continued joy in running and achieving your personal goals.

Dr. Oliver Stoll
Leipzig, Germany
August 8, 2016

PROLOGUE BY JOCHEN SCHMITZ, CHIEF EDITOR OF RUNNING MAGAZINE

Dear Readers,

A few years ago, a previously unknown athlete appeared out of nowhere on the German ultra-running scene. This person caught our attention when we saw impressive photos in the editorial department of *RUNNING* Magazine that showed the athlete at a 250 km stage race in the Atacama desert, which he went on to finish seventh overall. I, of course, had to get to the bottom of this thing and picked up the telephone. In the end, I got Michele Ufer on the phone. He was the new guy, the athlete in the photos, and he told me how he came to participate so successfully in the aforementioned race with some physical—but lots of mental—training. This conversation was followed by many more, some remarkably long, and my curiosity about Michele's approach and the subject of sport psychology continued to grow.

As a result of these discussions, we decided not to deny our readers this subject matter and created the series of articles called "Mental training in practice," a column in our magazine which continues to be very popular. Thus it seemed only a matter of time until Michele would publish a book on his field of expertise. You are holding it in your hand.

During my time at university, I was able to take several semesters of psychology, and in my capacity at *RUNNING* Magazine I am in daily contact with athletes of various performance levels for whom sport psychology is an important factor. Moreover, as a runner, I have gained insight into my mental potential and myself. Based on this experience, I highly recommend this book. You will learn much about yourself and our sport because this is a hands-on book with lots of tests as well as examples that invite active participation or imitation. It also satisfies the science- and theory-oriented reader via cross-references, sources, and a long list of references. Whether theorist or practitioner, you will definitely make use of it.

And now some personal information about Michele: He is a true jack-of-all-trades! Next to his professional activities, he is always working to increase his knowledge and, of course, balances that part of his life with regular running. And on top of all that, he organizes a trail event by the name of *Traildorado*. Michele usually has a smile on his face and possesses a mischievous sense of humor (which you will see that now and then in the book).

In this spirit, I hope you will gain many insights from what follows.

Jochen Schmitz
Berlin, Germany
January 13, 2016

IT ALL BEGINS WITH AN UNUSUAL RUNNING STORY

Man cannot discover new oceans unless he has the courage to lose sight of the shore.

—André Gide

If you want something you never had, then do something you never did.

—Nossrat Peseschkian

1 IT ALL BEGINS WITH AN UNUSUAL RUNNING STORY

Imagine the following: You have a friend who was an ambitious soccer player in his youth, but never stood out for exceptional athletic performances, especially for running or endurance sports. This friend has never run a marathon, a half-marathon, or even an official 10K, and he knows nothing about the sport of running or the running scene. He has never really been interested. But one night, you meet up at your favorite pub and, over a beer, he cheerfully tells you that he just signed up for a 250 km ultra-marathon at one of the earth's most hostile places! Surely this news would cause you to at least sit up and take notice.

1.1 THE ATACAMA EXPERIMENT: PERFORMANCE THAT DEFIES THE IMAGINATION

Now let's listen to what this guy has to say. This race consists of six stages over a distance of 250 km through the driest desert in the world, the famous Atacama in Chile, during which runners compete at an altitude of 2,500-3,500 m. This South American desert is said to be 50 times drier than the infamous Death Valley in the United States, with some areas recording zero precipitation since the beginning of weather records. Moreover, the race is organized as a self-supported run; in other words, runners must carry all of their personal items during the entire race. Filled with the mandatory personal gear (e.g., sleeping bag, ground pad, extra clothes, First Aid kit, provisions, headlamp), the running backpack weighs 7-10 kg (15-22 lbs.). Drinking water is supplied every 10-15 km during the race and at the target location at the end of each stage. Simple group tents that sleep 10-15 people are provided at the end of each stage. Participants run through deep sand, hilly terrain, and rocky canyons that sometimes require some climbing. The route travels through dried-up salt lakes, across razor-sharp scree, and sometimes even through mountain streams in deeply carved canyons. And it all takes place in a completely surreal landscape that is surrounded by snow-covered volcanoes that stand more than 6,000 m high.

When your novice-runner friend goes on to tell you with a cheerful smile that there isn't much time to prepare because the race takes place in four months, what would you think? Maybe something like:

a)   "He's nuts! Impossible! Much too dangerous! Crazy! He'll never be able to do it!"

Or preferably:

b)   "Wow, awesome! What an adventure! What courage! Why not? He might be able to do it."

Most people would agree with the first reaction, wondering what in the world your friend could be thinking. But the novice runner was not deterred by any of it. He was completely focused on the challenge.

As you might suspect, that novice runner was me, and in 2011, as part of an extreme self-test, I wanted to experience and demonstrate the increase in athletic performance the human body is capable of with the targeted use of mental training and sports hypnosis. And now that the cat is officially out of the bag, I can openly admit that my foolhardy goal was really just one thing: to somehow make it from stage to stage in spite of my lack of experience and very short preparation time. But onsite everything turned out much different than planned, and in fact much better.

Instead of just struggling through the desert day after day and arriving in one piece or somehow managing to make it across the finish line, I relatively quickly ran my way into the top ten much to everyone's surprise, including my own. And I got better every day. Of course I also made a number of mistakes and had some crazy experiences, but I was nevertheless able to secure an unbelievable seventh place finish overall, with my daily best being a fourth-place finish. And with that I left some experienced and semi-professional runners in the dust. It was an incredible experience and result. The organizers and many participants I talked to could not believe that I had never previously participated in an official race and had never run more than 29 km (18 miles) during the entire four-month preparation period. It was a perfect sensation. I was on a total emotional high and the psychological experiment was a complete success. In my book *Flow Jäger (Flow Hunter)*, I offer a more detailed account of my experiences at the Atacama race.

Now you might think there was a lot of luck involved, too, and I agree completely. Of course we always need a little luck in life, particularly for such adventurous undertakings, that's for sure! But it's also good to know how one can help that luck along a little. And so, after my adventure, people often asked me precisely how I did it, how I trained, and especially which mental techniques I used.

Michele at the Atacama Crossing

MY MENTAL TOOLBOX

How did I do it? In addition to four moderately hard running units per week based on the principle of training smart rather than (too) hard prior to the race, I worked intensively on my goals, imagining myself reaching them as specifically and acutely as possible. And I especially imagined how I wanted to achieve them. Intense and vivid mental images emerged. I experienced emotions. You might say I built a wonderful memory of the future inside my head that I would remember again and again along with all the corresponding emotions. Despite the fact that it can be incredibly motivating, in my experience, it is surprisingly often neglected.

Neuroscientists have long known that new synapses are created that allow the desired result to become more probable. First, I extrapolated concrete challenges as well as abilities I would need in order to master the challenges on the path to my goals. Then I thought of past situations—in sports and in other areas of my life—in which I was successful and during which I had already demonstrated these strengths. This allowed me to access positive, performance-enhancing emotions and unconscious knowledge of how I had accomplished something in the past. And since it is possible to purposefully talk oneself into or out of something, I embellished the entire thing with strategies to turn negative thinking into positive thinking.

I created a set of emotions, internal images, self-talk, and inner monologues that helped me achieve my goals. I then mentally and physically embedded these sets or equipped them with triggers so they would be activated in certain situations, either unconsciously or consciously, to let their positive effect unfold. Such triggers can be images, symbols, music, small movements, or words, but also stimuli like the starting signal, lacing your shoes, or positioning your foot. I also occasionally used little subtle scenarios to positively impact seemingly automatic processes, like, for instance, the sensation of pain, movement coordination, metabolism, and regeneration. That's the quick version.

I often didn't have the time for a detailed explanation of my approach. And some people justifiably commented that things that worked for me don't necessarily work for other athletes. And I agree wholeheartedly. However, in recent years, I had the wonderful opportunity to share my approaches with many running athletes. In 2012, I received an inquiry from Jochen Schmitz, the chief editor at *RUNNING Magazine*, asking if I would write an article on the topic of motivation and health.

After initial hesitation, I declined and offered a counter-proposal. I did not want to discuss this topic in such a limited way because I thought the risk of it turning into just another factoid story about motivation was just too high. Instead, I suggested a series of articles, each featuring a well-defined sport psychology topic presented in a realistic way. The suggestion was well received. The series of articles, "Mental training in practice," was born and has been a feature in every issue since (beginning in 2016). The feedback on the published articles has been very positive. Time and again, readers or runners tell me that the suggestions are helpful and also inspire self-reflection.

Because lots of material had accumulated over the years, in 2015, the idea was to make a selection of previous articles available to a greater audience in a bundled and expanded form. Of course, this was also an opportunity to include my practical experience in coaching runners, as well as more detailed explanations of my approach during the Atacama experiment. That was the idea. You are holding the result in your hand. Enjoy!

1.2   THE BOOK'S CHARACTER AND STRUCTURE: HOW IT WORKS

This book is not a textbook that offers a comprehensive overview of sport psychology. It's also not a scientific book. The use of technical language has been reduced to a minimum in favor of everyday language. For a more immersive experience, simply refer to the bibliographical references. I also won't offer you any secrets to success or open up a box of tricks. Such a title might sell better, but that would be deceptive marketing.

HONESTY IS THE BEST POLICY:
WHAT THIS BOOK CAN AND CANNOT DO

I want to be honest. You may find that you are already doing many of the things in this book unconsciously in your everyday life, and that's good! It means this material will justify or confirm all the things that have already worked or have proven to be helpful. Continue to use them in the future and spread the word! Other strategies have been used for hundreds of years in many cultures around the world, but many have been forgotten. Or they may just not get the necessary attention in your busy everyday life, even though they can be powerful tools. So it is good to be reminded. And some suggestions are based on current research findings from the areas of psychology, medicine, and neuroscience. They offer information on how you could change something to achieve your goals better, faster, more easily, or more reliably, regardless of whether they involve motivation, performance, or health and general well-being. Nothing more, but also nothing less.

EXPERIENCE STRAIGHT TO THE POINT

The contents of this book were gained by experience. They were successfully tested around the world by myself and other athletes during various races in more or less extreme conditions. Moreover, they were tried and tested on recreational and high-performance athletes during different coaching processes that lasted from one intensive hour to multi-day seminars, as well as over an extended period of time as part of comprehensive personal and career development. The contents and methods are presented succinctly and simply so you can get started as quickly as possible without first having to labor through pages and pages of explanatory theory.

DO IT!

You are holding a workbook in your hands. It can effectively help you to ... work on yourself. But only if you really want to, and actually do it! Only by using the presented strategies will the true value of the book reveal itself, will you acquire a taste for it. Thus I would be honored if you were to really put this book to work. Grab a pencil and underline the passages that are most important to you, circle places in the text, take notes, and try the exercises and strategies. This book is a utilitarian object and wants your personal additions. Only then will it be complete, if that is even possible.

WHO IS THIS BOOK FOR?

This book is for **runners of all performance levels**, from beginners to old hands, regardless of whether their preferred running terrain is trail, street, mountain, desert, rainforest, tartan track, urban forest, or whatever. **Triathletes, cross-country skiers, expedition participants** will also be able to find many suggestions that go beyond running. And anything that is helpful to athletes might possibly be of interest to those who accompany and support athletes in their sport, such as **running coaches, personal trainers, (sport) psychologists, mental trainers,** or **significant others**. The strategies presented here are also very well suited for challenges outside the running sport. So it is possible that some non-runners—corporate leaders, executives—will also enjoy reading this book. And then we could think of running as a symbol for things running smoothly, professionally and privately, because after all: "Life is like an ultra-marathon."

FIND YOUR PERSONAL TREASURES

Since our motivation, personality, past experiences, and goals can be very different, it is likely that not all contents will be equally relevant to all readers. You should therefore choose those things that are currently of particular interest to you. That might be the entire book, or a particular suggestion or exercise that will make the difference in the future or that initiates an important change. And periodically pick up the book again because we always continue to change and evolve. Over time, things can become more important and interesting even if they weren't before.

THE PERFECT SIX-WEEK PLAN TO HAPPINESS?

We can draw the following conclusion from what has been said so far: Although you would probably like to be given a plan that tells you exactly when you have to do what how many times per week, I cannot do you that favor.

Every person is different. Mind games that help one individual might drive someone else crazy. A training rhythm that works fabulously well for one person might make someone else feel pressured. Training content that might fit one person's current situation perfectly may well be completely wrong for another. For this reason I would like to invite you to use the presented material to develop your very own plan that meets your actual needs. Mental training becomes most effective when it is specifically adapted to your situation. That means fine-tuning: experiment, experience, reflect, and if necessary, adapt again. You can start by working your way through the exercises, and then build on them to develop your own creations.

THE BOOK'S STRUCTURE

◆ In chapter 2, we take a critical look at typical everyday training for runners, shine a light on the different ways the mind can influence and affect the body, and consider which possibilities mental training can offer us.

◆ Next, we make a sound determination of our current situation (GPS), based on which we will define the current status quo as well as future target states. We will then be able to deduce our personal developmental goals. Moreover, determining our current location via our personal GPS is an excellent way to evaluate the goal achievement processes.

◆ In chapter 4, we will address a topic that is often given surprisingly little attention and, possibly for that very reason, can lead to unnecessary motivation problems. We will answer the question of how we should structure and manage goals so they are truly effective. And we will also learn which attitudes are helpful or impedimental in overcoming challenges.

◆ One core element of mental training is working with mental images and thoughts. Chapter 5 outlines many opportunities for the use of so-called visualizations to create memories of a successful future and magic moments.

◆ In chapter 6, we will address how we can activate, develop, and, in critical moments, use or access our (to some extent unconscious) abilities, strengths, and resources.

◆ Since everything isn't always going smoothly in life, in chapter 7 we take a look at how we can constructively deal with injuries, failure, crises, and exercise addiction.

And we will frequently look at concrete application examples of the presented strategies within the context of practical examples and the explanations for the Atacama project. Now and again we will add a brief look at research.

As you read you will notice that some topics seem to repeat themselves. That is indeed the case and it is intentional. Just like in any good cookbook, there are some ingredients that we use again and again, in different variations and combinations depending on what it is we are preparing or trying to achieve.

Since the first publication of this book, I have received numerous messages from readers about their experiences and successes with my methods. I was very happy about—often touched by—every single one of them. I had the idea to let some readers share their success stories in this book because that could motivate and encourage others to apply the presented strategies. I am very happy that some readers agreed to share their experiences with us. To read these success stories, see the section at the end of the book.

I am really curious to see which suggestions you will find most valuable and what changes and improvements you will notice after their implementation. 3, 2, 1, go!

Focus is important. Here Michele is shown running across razor-sharp crusts of salt. One misstep, and they puncture the bottom of your shoe.

HOW MUCH OF YOUR HEAD IS IN YOUR FEET?

The largest undiscovered part of the world lies between our ears.

—William O'Brian

2 HOW MUCH OF YOUR HEAD IS IN YOUR FEET?

Soon after I had successfully finished the Atacama experiment, I received a phone call from two journalists. Only a few days later, two big articles about my story appeared in different daily newspapers. I was flattered that major athletes took a backseat, at least in this one edition. But what was most interesting was the title. Although two different journalists had conducted the interviews, and two completely different publishers had published the articles, the titles were identical: "As far as your feet will carry you." When I read that, I had to smile, and I immediately thought, "Your feet will carry you as far as your head wants them to." I then gave a subsequent presentation with the following slightly more provocative title: "How much of your head is in your feet? Running a 250-km race through the driest desert in the world with mental strength." I like that question very much, but does that make me an ardent proponent of mind over matter? No!

In this chapter you will learn about the intelligent connection between mind and body, the partly puzzling effects the mind can have on the body (and vice versa), the exact meaning of mental training, and the extent to which mental training can be used to achieve goals and increase performance more elegantly. Or in plain English: The head and body are two sides of a coin and they are inextricably linked. To ignore this fact in everyday training would be downright negligent.

2.1 ANTIQUATED EVERYDAY TRAINING: IS THE EARTH STILL FLAT?

Sparrows will never understand why eagles fly higher than cherry trees grow.

—Russian proverb

In elite sports performance, density at the top tends to be very high. When two athletes with the same talent, the same training conditions, and the same general level of fitness and health compete against each other, the one who has the edge at the critical moment will be the one with the stronger mind. While materials-based, biomechanical, and athletic training-related approaches have increasingly exhausted their potential, the largest developmental resources lie within the brain. And how is it in recreational and popular sports? It's actually pretty similar. We can train as hard as we want, run tons of miles, but if we're mentally not in a good place on the big day, we might not achieve our goal. And so it is no surprise that this realization is also gaining ground in recreational sports.

Whenever you ask an athlete if the mind is important for athletic success, the answer is: "Yes, of course!" And that is true regardless of the type of sport. By now, everyone knows that success and failure are somehow also a matter of the mind. Some say it is a matter of attitude or character, while others say it's a matter of motivation or willpower. Even in the running world everyone agrees that achieved results and successes are also a matter of the mind. Nevertheless, the question remains of how exactly to manage it, or rather how to optimally tune the brain muscle to be able to reliably access its performance at the critical moment and achieve precisely the successes or changes one desires. Or how to train more appropriately and holistically by using forms of mental training, thereby achieving goals more elegantly, more joyfully, or faster, with less effort.

Here suggestions are mostly perfunctory and largely anecdotal, the standard advice we hear all the time. In practice it isn't very helpful because it is not followed by concrete information on how to improve motivation or how to develop willpower.

Of course, I don't know how many hours a week you train. Is it an average of 3, 5, 10, or 20 hours? And at top times, how many more hours does that add? Granted, that depends on your personal circumstances, ambitions, and goals, but, be honest, how much of your average training time do you devote to mental training? Probably less? The good news is that many athletes already unconsciously use a number of approaches without being aware of it. They visualize competitions, plan progressions ahead of time, and know how to motivate themselves during difficult moments. You can learn and train your mental abilities just like you can systematically learn, train, and refine physical abilities. And the investment pays off, as you will see later on.

The sport of running is a worldwide mass phenomenon. There is probably no other sport for which more books, service providers, and internet sites with detailed training plans for all different distances and target times are offered. The plans are eagerly traded, intensely debated, offer training orientation, and are very helpful if one knows how to choose wisely. But why do these training plans still include so little information on mental training, on integrating the mind in the performance development process?

2.2   POWER OF THE MIND

While some runners are convinced that everything is somehow mental, others consider psychology and mental training wishy-washy or irrelevant hocus-pocus. Let's take a look behind the scenes to form a more differentiated and, most of all, a well-founded opinion on our psyche and mental training.

By now, the effects of the mind on the body have been scientifically very well documented. For our purposes I would like to first share a few well-known research results. You can find detailed information and supplementary explanations in the following chapters.

◆ It is regularly confirmed that certain personality traits, attitudes, and deportments have a positive effect on physical processes, the immune system, and overall health, as well as overall success and satisfaction, not just in sports, but also in life overall.

◆ A substantial piece of evidence from the area of sports medicine suggests that the performance-limiting factor in endurance performance appears to be primarily a matter of the brain.

◆ Sport psychology research reveals many positive links between the use of mental or sport-psychology techniques during training and competition and general performance level, the situational athletic performance, and health.

◆ Research on hypnosis and studies on the influence of trance processes in extreme athletes, fakirs, and Shaolin monks has given us impressive insights, providing suggestions on how to cleverly integrate the use of concentration techniques like the power of thought, mental imagery, and autosuggestion to positively influence largely automatic and uncontrollable physical processes such as pain, fatigue, stress reaction, metabolism, post-sports injury regeneration, and healing, among others.

◆ Sports hypnosis results in extensive positive, health-enhancing physiological changes. The impressive results of a recent study even showed that objectively identical physical performance and effort performed during a state of trance can considerably reduce the amount of subjectively felt exertion and actual muscle activity, compared to a normal alert state.

OUR AUTOPILOT

Let's take it a step further. A large portion of our behavior is automated and unconscious. Experts say 90-95%. While you are reading this book, your breathing until just this moment most likely proceeded fairly unconsciously. Until now, without your being aware of it, your muscles have also largely made sure that everything moves the way it should, no matter where you are right now and regardless of whether you are standing, sitting, lying down, or walking, and without your having to permanently think about which muscle groups to contract how much at what ratio in order to achieve a desired position or movement as you turn the pages. It is precisely this autopilot that allows us to function, unburdening our everyday consciousness. It makes sure that lots of things function as quick as lightning or without having to think about them. That's good, as long as we get the desired results.

But what happens when we sometimes aren't satisfied? When we don't achieve the desired performances, are unmotivated or lethargic, when there are ingrained habits, fears, or other obstacles that seem to stand in our way? If that unconscious autopilot controls a large portion of our thoughts, feelings, and behavior, would it not make sense to involve that autopilot in our training, in our personal development? But *how* can we bring our subconscious mind onboard and thereby make our athletic training more modern and more successful, accelerate our personal development, or make it possible in the first place?

In view of the fact that the mind influences the body, does it not make sense to work more on mental processes as part of the training structure that has proven to dramatically improve performance capacity, performance efficiency, heath, and well-being? Yes, absolutely. Let's do it!

And in case you are still not quite convinced, I urge you to carefully read the following segment

2.3   THE MIND'S ASTOUNDING EFFECTS ON THE BODY: LEARNING TO CONTROL THE UNCONTROLLABLE?!

DOES RUNNING STRENGTHEN OR WEAKEN THE IMMUNE SYSTEM? IT DEPENDS!

It is no longer a secret that running is good for your health and, among other things, can effectively boost the immune system. However, it can also have the opposite effect. We are more susceptible to infection after major athletic exertion, such as a marathon. Our immune system appears to be weakened temporarily due to physiological changes, which means we may catch a cold more easily. In the fall of 2015, the German Ultramarathon Association's (DUV) magazine *ULTRAMARATHON* published an interesting article written by an esteemed fellow runner. In "Not just 'mental': ultrarunning and immune defense," biologist Verena Liebers reported on a current sports medicine study about the effects of running on infection-relevant messengers (Liebers, 2015; Gill et al, 2015).

At a 24-hour run in Scotland, a team of researchers studied the effects of the competition on bodyweight, perceived gastro-intestinal discomfort, and other physiological parameters, like the quantity of certain messengers in the blood that play a role in infections. For comparison, blood samples were taken from the subject group immediately before and after the race. The results showed that nearly all of the tested messengers (interleukin-6/-8/-10/-1/-beta, tumor necrosis factor, interferon gamma, C-reactive protein) had considerably increased after the race. Moreover, 75% of participants complained of gastro-intestinal discomfort or nausea, whereby a link was established between the gastro-intestinal problems and the increased presence of two messengers (interleukin-8/-10).

But this link could not be substantiated during a follow-up study (Gill et al., 2015) at a multi-day ultramarathon in Spain. However, here, too, considerably higher levels of infection-relevant messengers were detected. This means runners react to the physical exertion by producing more messengers that can also be found during infections or inflammation. Physiological changes take place that far exceed the phenomenon of weight loss. While the body immediately takes regulating measures, an increased susceptibility to infection remains for a certain amount of time.

Experts call this the *open window theory.* While according to Liebers these studies do not provide concrete information for practical purposes, she wanted to at least start a conversation and remind those ultrarunners who always say that everything is mental, "that even for an ultrarunner not everything is 'strictly mental.' Anyone who is willing to undergo such exertion must be aware that he places his body under stress" (Liebers, 2015, pg. 120).

On the one hand, I was pleased that the DUV's association magazine *ULTRAMARATHON* published an article on such an exciting topic in layman's terms. On the other hand, I had to ask myself if it did not come up short because, in my opinion, one significant aspect was not taken into account, at least if one takes a more holistic view of the human being: What effects could our mind, our personality, and the conscious and unconscious use of certain strategies potentially have on infection-relevant blood values and gastro-intestinal sensitivity? Or in other words: When two athletes possess the same physical qualifications, are equally well trained and healthy, couldn't it be possible that their values differ depending on their individual attitudes and the mental strategies they use?

A RUN IS NOT LIKE A RUN, IS NOT LIKE A RUN: EXTERNAL STRESS VS. INTERNAL (PHYSIOLOGICAL AND PSYCHOLOGICAL) STRAIN

Staying on the topic of stress and gastro-intestinal complaints for the moment, we are probably all familiar with one of the following situations in our everyday lives or that of our friends, acquaintances, and colleagues: Just before a college exam, driving test, important company presentation, a job interview, or an important competition we consider a major highlight, we react with relaxed anticipation or with anxiety and stage fright. The night before the big event, some sleep soundly while others toss and turn accompanied by a queasy stomach. They are experiencing stress.

We all know and experience it again and again, that people often react differently to identical situational demands. Some are stressed. Others are not.

In stress research as well as in sport science—specifically in training theory and sport psychology—we therefore differentiate between *stress* and *strain* or rather *internal* and *external stress.*

External stress refers to the situational demands that are objectively the same for everyone (for instance, completing a half-marathon). Strain or internal stress refers to a person's individual physiological, biochemical, and psychological reactions to a specific external stress factor.

Of course circulatory, respiratory, and thermoregulation, as well as muscle metabolism also depend on the physical condition and general state of health. However, they can significantly differ even with the same strain and physical condition, and cause different levels of stress. It is also indisputable and universally known that physiological stress is inextricably linked to mental and emotional factors. For instance, anxiety and fear always result in an elevated heart rate, shallower breathing, increased perspiration, and altered muscle tone—and often also in a queasy stomach. Surely none of this is conducive to a good performance.

Now the critical question remains: Can we control mental factors so they can have a desirable or beneficial effect on the strain, and if so, how?

Verena Liebers' title is slightly provocative: "Not just mental." Of course she is right. Anything we do has a mental and a physical component. And by simply imagining ourselves running a fast 10K through the woods this afternoon, we still haven't even covered 1 m. However, body and mind, physiological and mental processes are inextricably linked. They complement each other and impact each other, positively and also negatively. Here are a few exciting and educational examples on the subject.

STRONG CHARACTER?
THE MIND'S EFFECT ON OUR IMMUNE DEFENSES

Psychoneuroimmunology deals with the interactions between the mind and the nervous and immune systems, and is currently one of the most important areas in medical research. The knowledge that many mental factors have an important positive and negative effect on immune defenses is increasingly gaining acceptance (Schubert, 2011; Pressman & Cohen, 2005).

Personality traits such as optimism, self-esteem, and self-efficacy, along with social relationships and activation of positive emotions in everyday life, have a beneficial effect on the immune system, and verifiably lead to faster healing after injury or surgery. If the mind has such a powerful effect on our health and even on healing after injuries or surgeries, is it not reasonable to think that the mind also affects temporary inflammatory responses and metabolic processes during and after athletic activity, and thereby can positively impact individual stress levels and recovery times?!

PLACEBOS AND NOCEBOS: FAITH CAN MOVE MOUNTAINS INSIDE THE BODY, IN PART WITH DRAMATIC RESULTS

Medical placebo research is an extremely exciting, still relatively new area of research. It addresses the following question: Which mechanisms are at work when sick, suffering people are treated with placebos and get well? The success rate in large-scale controlled studies is astoundingly high.

But it gets even more mind-boggling: Have you heard of placebo operations? It works like this: A recommendation of surgery is made to a patient with, for instance, knee complaints. Everything proceeds exactly like a regular operation. There is a comprehensive pre-surgery briefing, anesthesia is discussed, and at some point the patient ends up in the OR and is anesthetized. But instead of a regular orthoscopic surgery to, for example, remove part of the meniscus, two superficial cuts are made. That's it! The knee is otherwise left untouched. The patient wakes up half an hour later, and it appears that he has had knee surgery. Post-op procedures also take their usual course.

Ordinarily one would think that nothing has changed since no real intervention took place and nothing on the knee has been changed. But lo and behold, even with placebo surgeries the rate of success is astoundingly high. Postoperatively some patients have fewer or no symptoms at all (Siegmund-Schultze 2008). Both strategies have one thing in common: An intensive healing process occurs even though no medically effective chemical or operative intervention takes place.

But it can also work the opposite way, and in extremely dramatic fashion. *Nocebos* refers to the circumstance when preparations that don't contain therapeutic agents, due to personal expectations, are unhealthy and even cause illness. In 2006, a 26-year

old man was told by his then significant other, that she planned to leave him. The young man's lovesickness was so severe that he wanted to end his life. Since he had previously participated in a medical study for a new medication, he had in his possession 29 tablets of a highly effective medication. He swallowed the entire contents of the container. Shortly afterwards, his medical condition deteriorated dramatically and he was admitted to a local hospital. The doctors fought for his survival. The man's blood pressure was dangerously low. As part of the treatment, one doctor contacted the director of the medical study to find out which ingredients were in the medication. The director of the research project took a look at the files and replied: "None!"

The man had been part of the control group and had only taken a placebo medication without any therapeutic agents. Just the belief that he had swallowed a highly effective, large dose of a deadly medication put the man in serious danger. The moment the man was told that he had merely been part of the control group and had been administered a non-effective placebo preparation consisting only of starch and lactose, his dire medical condition improved within a short amount of time and he was discharged from the hospital free of complaints (Merlot, 2008).

Conclusion: Fervently believing in healing (or illness) alone greatly activates one's own power to heal (or destroy) and causes positive (or negative) changes in the body or brain entirely without external or conscious help. In the future, wouldn't it be interesting to control these powers a little more systematically before, during, and after major stresses and strains? At least the positive ones? But what and how should we believe during those moments, what should we focus our attention on?

ABOUT DEEP DIVERS, ICE MEN, FAKIRS, MONKS, MIRACLE RUNNERS, AND PEOPLE LIKE YOU AND ME: ALTERED STATES OF CONSCIOUSNESS AND CLEVER WAYS TO FOCUS ATTENTION FOR EXTRAORDINARY PERFORMANCES

Up to now we have received valuable information about the fact that our mind—meaning our personality traits, attitudes, and expectations—broadly and constantly affect our bodies without us consciously controlling these processes. But we are also able to specifically influence physical processes that are completely automatic and appear to not be deliberately controllable. To preempt: Yes, we can do so, and it might represent one of the greatest and most valuable opportunities for personal development and improved performance.

The famous lemon experiment is a wonderful example of how our conscious thoughts and mental imagery affect our bodies in a minimum of time.

EXERCISE: THE LEMON EXPERIMENT

Imagine holding an already peeled lemon in your hand. It is a plump, early-ripening, and therefore particularly sour lemon. Imagine what the lemon's surface feels like as you turn it over and move it around in your hand. And now imagine raising your arm and passing the lemon under your nose to smell it. You begin to notice a pleasant, fresh lemon scent. The longer you hold the lemon in your hand, look at it, and sniff it, the stronger the lemon's fresh scent becomes. And now imagine bringing the lemon to your lips, opening your mouth, and taking a big bite.

For many people, this exercise works particularly well with their eyes closed. The more intense and detailed the attention that is focused on the mental image, the more senses or cognitive channels are activated, and generally the more significant is the immediate physical reaction. Some people literally shudder when they imagine themselves biting into the sour lemon. Others' facial muscles contract or they experience a spontaneous increase in saliva production.

We can purposefully use such mechanisms to put ourselves into desired positive states. Even just remembering positive experiences (e.g., particular successes or pleasant moments) also results in positive physical reactions. But whenever we focus our attention on negative memories, it inevitably results in perceptible negative physical reactions or the respective symptoms of stress. And even if those effects are so minimal that we are not conscious of them, they can still have a decisive impact on whether or not we achieve our goals as desired (also see chapter 6.1).

VIRTUAL PAIN MANAGEMENT: PAIN-FREE ON THE ROAD TO BECOMING A MIRACLE RUNNER?

It doesn't matter what distances you run; there comes that point for every runner when not just the legs begin to hurt. It might be the occasional unpleasant twitch of this or that muscle. Other times it feels like the legs, the lungs, and just plain everything is about to explode. Runners have the critical ability to tolerate this pain for as long as possible and still keep running. That requires a certain amount of willpower and is essential to any endurance runner's success. But what would happen if we could manage this pain or even tune it out? Wouldn't that be a huge help to personal performance development?

ANESTHESIA? NO, THANK YOU!

Sometimes, when you see a dentist, you might need a little work, and to make sure the whole process is as pleasant as possible for the patient, you generally get an injection to numb the area to be treated. Dental hypnosis, a practice that is being offered by many dentists in the USA, is now gaining popularity in Germany (Schmierer, 2009). Instead of resorting to a chemical hammer, the patient is guided or supported by dental hypnosis so he won't feel any pain during the procedure without the use of classic anesthesia (i.e., chemical pain relievers or narcotics). Many scientific findings show that this approach is considered much more pleasant and has fewer side effects for the patient.

Since the results are exceedingly positive, there are now well-educated, innovative physicians practicing conventional medicine, who use hypnosis during surgical procedures. Depending on the patient and the type of surgery, a severe sports injury and even larger open wounds can be treated either completely without classic anesthesia, or with significantly lower doses of anesthesia due to a combination of hypnosis and conventional anesthesia. The amazing thing is that healing processes after surgeries with accompanying hypnosis often proceed considerably better and faster than those in which conventional anesthesia was used (Bejencke, 2009; Schmierer, 2009; Wicks, 2009).

NO MORE PAIN, WOULDN'T THAT BE WONDERFUL?

Now one might tend to think that not feeling any pain would be a wonderful thing and would open up all sorts of new possibilities. On your way to becoming a super-runner without any pain? Be careful! We all know that pain can also have a positive function that protects us from overuse and damage to our body, and ignoring this protective mechanism can result in major complications. For example, a few years ago, I attended a conference on mental strength. One of the participants talked very openly and self-critically about the case of a top female German athlete who had suffered a muscle strain. But instead of taking it down a notch, she proceeded, full steam ahead, through a rather meaningless competition. And you might have already guessed how the whole thing ended. The slight, easily treatable muscle strain turned into a full-blown torn muscle, which inevitably forced the athlete to take a prolonged break during a critical phase in her season. Not good!

The moral of the story: Of course it is good, and often helpful, to handle pain constructively, to turn it off in some situations and at least tolerate it better and more calmly in others. We can use this ability very nicely to help ourselves and should do so. At the same time, this last example in particular shows us that we should always pay attention to our body to avoid a short-term injury, as well as long-term damage that often isn't noticeable while running until many years later. The mind is very powerful, but so is the body. And just as wise and precious! Happy is the man who can establish effective body-mind teamwork in which both areas cooperate equally with each other to facilitate healthy short- and long-term performance development.

"THE BODY DOMINATORS – PEOPLE PUSHING THE LIMITS OF WHAT IS PHYSICALLY POSSIBLE": EXCEPTIONAL ATHLETES, THEIR STRATEGIES, AND WHAT WE CAN LEARN FROM THEM

In late 2012, there was an exciting episode from the documentary series *Terra X*, titled "The Body Dominators – People pushing the limits of what's physically possible" (Staudenmayer, 2014). It featured several people that achieve extraordinary performances in very different areas. The question they tried to answer was to what extent each of us has similar hidden talents.

FREEDIVERS

Herbert Nitsch is one of the most successful freedivers of all time. He can dive to a depth of 214 m without an oxygen tank and with only one breath. Nitsch is able to control the blood distribution in his body via intense concentration or meditation so the body's outer regions (i.e., the limbs) receive as little blood as possible, which results in considerably lower oxygen consumption. He is also able to resist the natural breathing reflex, and can achieve an extremely calm, focused physical and mental state in spite of the extreme diving depth and the associated high risks. It reduces his energy consumption to the absolute essential, allowing him to make perfect use of the available oxygen to achieve extremely sustained dives that feel like an eternity at an unbelievable depth.

FAKIRS AND ATHLETES WITH FAKIR QUALITIES

Fakirs and other people that stick needles and other decorative objects through their nose, ears, cheeks, etc., as part of religious and cultural rituals, also use these abilities. What's astounding: There is usually no blood flowing during these activities, nor do the participants seem to be in pain.

A sport psychologist in the United States did a similar experiment with a number of athletes (Liggett, 2004). After briefly introducing the topic *self-hypnosis* and the use of focusing techniques, each athlete had two tiny holes poked a few millimeters apart in the back of their hands with a fine needle. What do you think happened with the wounds?

Maybe I should add the following information: The test subjects were first divided into two groups. The first group was told to focus on blood coming out of only the right hole. The second group's task was to focus on blood coming out of only the left hole.

The athletes were speechless when they noticed that the results matched each group's instructions. One athlete initially confused the psychologist, causing him to think the experiment had failed because no blood appeared at all. But then he was equally surprised when the test subject revealed that he had initially imagined no blood flowing at all, and only several seconds later did blood flow from the desired hole.

THE ICEMAN AND TUMMO MEDITATION

Wim Hof's achievements are similarly puzzling. By using focusing or meditation techniques, the so-called *Iceman* is able to control his body temperature even under extreme conditions. He develops an unbelievable ability to stay in deadly cold temperatures for very long periods of time, and he also does things that would usually cause death very quickly in humans. For instance, he dives a distance of 80 km nude under an ice floe during the artic winter, or stays trapped inside a large ice cube for more than an hour. Of course it seems natural to try to explain this performance capacity and endurance under extreme conditions by believing that Wim Hof might possess a certain abnormal genetic predisposition or special physical qualifications.

But a study done at the University of Minnesota showed that this is not the case, and that the extraordinary achievements are related to a special form of meditation Wim Hof uses called *Tummo meditation*. It is a Buddhist meditation practice whose objective is the controlled raising of the body temperature to consciously direct energy from the inside to the outside and thereby eliminate negative thoughts, stressors, etc. by burning them away. Several scientific studies confirm the temperature-regulating effects of Tummo meditation and suggest that practitioners have learned to be more aware of their body's internal processes, and then purposefully influence them (Benson et al., 1982; Lutz et al., 2007).

The second part of the program featured the world-famous Shaolin monks in China. Shaolin monks are known for their remarkable martial arts and dancing, their muscle strength, speed, and imperviousness to extreme endurance tests. They cultivate their unbelievable abilities over years of intense physical training and with special meditation techniques and breathing exercises. These outstanding physical abilities are based on the so-called *internal power of Chi*. It is said that the power of one's Chi is greatest when body and mind are in perfect harmony. Interestingly, the Shaolin monks believe that this energy doesn't originate inside the fighter but rather from nature, and only flows through him when, as previously mentioned, body and mind are in harmony!

All those briefly introduced here, as well as the other adventurers, extreme athletes, and exceptional talents presented in the *Terra X* program have one thing in common: They all mentioned again and again that during their extraordinary top-performances they were in a kind of trance, a state of consciousness apart from the normal waking consciousness, during which attention is focused to the extreme. Getting back to running, we received the same feedback from the *Lung-Gom-Pa runners* in Tibet, also monks. These *trance runners* are able to run hundreds of kilometers at a fast pace through the Tibetan highlands (Ufer, 2013) without any physical training, using primarily the power of the mind and special breathing techniques.

PRACTICE MAKES PERFECT

All of these exceptional athletes have something else in common: They did not just drop from the sky. Their extraordinary performances are based on years of intensive training, whereby they paid particular attention to the intensive development and training of their mind and their mental abilities. Now you might think that those are all great, exciting stories. But does one have to practice mediation for years to be able to achieve exceptional performances or be able to influence automatic processes? The answer is yes and no. On the one hand, every good or extraordinary endurance performance requires a certain developmental process. That also applies to mental abilities.

(You can find information on the topic of expertise in sports and the possibilities and limits of mental training in chapter 2.4). On the other hand, we can all relatively quickly learn to purposefully influence our body without many years of meditation or mental training. But the more we immerse ourselves in it and practice it, the more possibilities arise. The following examples illustrate this impressively.

One effective way to influence the vegetative nervous system is the purposeful use of certain breathing techniques. Just taking a deep breath followed by a slow exhale has an immediate regulating effect on the activity of the sympathetic and parasympathetic nervous system. This technique can easily be used for stress management to reduce mental stress within seconds while also providing long-term health benefits (you can find more specific information on this topic in chapter 6.7 on relaxation.)

The interaction between the sympathetic and parasympathetic nervous system is also a key topic in *heart rate variability* (HRV) research. You may already know from training theory that HRV is helpful in managing training and training load by reliably identifying phases of overtraining and fatigue. It allows you to more accurately adapt your training stimulus to your current situation. It also offers information on how we can achieve a hugely positive impact on our physical and mental performance by synchronizing our breathing and heart rhythm (Servan-Schreiber, 2006). There is an enormous similarity to the Shaolin monks, who reason that their extraordinary performance capacity is based on the effects of harmonizing. However, learning such coherency of breath and heartbeat is not that difficult and is a rewarding practice.

FROM RESEARCH

During a study at Michigan State University, 16 test subjects (students) were tasked with influencing the behavior of their endogenous *granulocytes* through intense concentration. Granulocytes are *white blood cells* and part of our immune defense system. As *phagocytes*, they attack pathogens to render them harmless. The number of granulocytes in the blood increases with infections in order to combat them. Since we are not able to feel our granulocytes, one would think we would not be able to deliberately influence something on such a small and abstract physical level. That makes the result all the more astounding. All of the test subjects were able to change the number of white blood cells just by intensely focusing on physical changes. Some even managed to improve their ability to adhere to the blood vessels (Kretschmar & Tzschaschel, 2014). Bongarzt (1996) also confirms these effects within the context of his studies on the use of relaxation hypnosis.

Isn't this fantastic? And to circle back to the introductory study about the immune defense of ultrarunners, what interesting practical possibilities present themselves when we once again complete a long, hard workout or competition and can feel the effects of temporary inflammation in our body? And of course there are a number of other physical processes relevant to our athletic activity that we can deliberately influence.

FROM SPORTS MEDICINE: IS THE BRAIN THE PERFORMANCE-LIMITING FACTOR IN ENDURANCE PERFORMANCES?

90% of running is a matter of the mind. The rest is mental.

In 2006, Hollmann and colleagues (2006) from the Institute for Circulatory Research and Sports Medicine as well as the Institute for Motor Function and Kinetics at the German Sport University in Cologne authored a highly interesting survey article on the role of the brain in endurance exercise for the *German Journal of Sports Medicine*. They prefaced the article by pointing out that "the effects of motivation and hypnosis on strength performance have been known since the 1960s." By contrast, with respect to endurance performance, the cardiopulmonary system and metabolism (cardiac cycle, respiration, muscle metabolism) are still considered the performance-limiting factors. Is this notion still up to date and tenable?

The results from many experiments provide impressive proof of a central fatigue component in addition to a local fatigue component. As part of a study, healthy male test subjects were given the task of rhythmically contracting their hands for as long as possible with the aid of a hand ergometer. Of course the ability to contract diminishes after a while due to fatigue, and at some point the test subjects were no longer able to contract their hands at all. But when electrical impulses were used to stimulate the motor nerves responsible for hand contraction, the original contractile force was briefly restored and a few more repetitions were possible. After the values plummeted again, electrical impulses were administered once again, this time directly to the relevant working muscles. Afterwards, the test subjects were again able to complete several contractions. This study demonstrates very memorably that central fatigue of the brain or central nervous system takes place before fatigue of the local musculature.

According to Noakes (2002), the brain as a *central governor* has a crucial function in managing the training load. An area in the prefrontal cortex, a region of the brain located behind the forehead, receives lots of information from all body regions as well as vital organs, such as the heart and the brain itself. Based on this information, the central governor protects the central nervous system from overload. There might be the perceived "I-can't-do-it-anymore" reaction, although objectively—and from a purely physiological standpoint—the performance limit has not been reached yet. The assumption is that additional performance reserves can be mobilized with a special effort of will (or, as we have seen, with clever experiments). According to Ikai and colleagues (1967), that would indicate that the mind is the performance-limiting factor.

Jones and Kilan (2002) confirm that it is time to part with previous perceptions of performance limits on a hemodynamic and metabolic basis, and instead pay more attention to the brain's performance-limiting role. And in the course of their studies, during which the opioid system in the brain was blocked during athletic performance to manipulate emotional effects, Sgherza and colleagues (2002) concluded that performance was limited by how individual test subjects felt and not by the objective physiological findings.

Neuroscience studies have shown that the brain's plasticity can be immediately altered with meditation and hypnosis (Halsband, 2009). So it is no surprise that exceptional athletes rely on self-hypnosis, meditation techniques, and other forms of mental training (in addition to their physical training) to purposefully impact performance and relevantly influence brain function and emotions.

Since we can purposefully influence our mind and emotions with our body, it is impossible to separate body and mind. It is impossible to avoid a holistic view. As long as this isn't reflected in our training, we must consider our training as suboptimal at best.

2.4   MENTAL TRAINING AS THE MAGIC BULLET? POSSIBILITIES AND LIMITS

So what exactly is *mental training* and how does it work? First of all, it's trendy. And it is a vague expression to boot. Nowadays, when you start surfing the Internet, the key word *mental training* will yield countless results. The terms *mental training*, *mental coaching,* or *mental trainer* are not trademarked terms. It is therefore no surprise that we are presented with such a broad and colorful range of topics under the label of mental training. Everything from sport-psychology offers to leadership, management, and team training, seminars to improve your luck, health, creativity, speed-reading ability, learning and memorizing techniques, and flirting strategies, to manipulation of the opposite sex, to offers for dementia and Alzheimer's patients, all the way to esoterically tinged quests for meaning and self-realization, and much, much more. For this reason, and in order to distinguish it from other approaches, I would like to briefly present my definition of mental training based on scientific sport psychology.

MENTAL TRAINING IN THE ORIGINAL, NARROWER, AND BROADER SENSES

THE ORIGINS

The term *mental training* originated in sport psychology and refers to a process used to optimize athletic movement sequences, along with physical training. In its original sense, mental training purely meant that we imagined ourselves repeating movements before our mind's eye without actually performing them (Eberspächer, 2012). The intensive mental simulation of movements alone can have an extremely positive effect on actual real movement sequences. To do so, the following mechanism is used.

Even just intently imagining a movement results in the activation of participating nerves and muscles just like they would during an actual movement. While it is less than during a real movement, it can still be measured and is effective. Only the execution is arrested. It might sound simple, but anyone who has ever done truly intensive and systematic mental training knows that it can be quite strenuous.

We have seen this, for instance, when bobsledders prepare and optimally tune in for the high-speed run through the ice tunnel just before their race. by letting the course pass in front of their mind's eye, extremely focused and with eyes closed, and their bodies seem to follow their thoughts through the various banked turns, possibly even swaying along. For very complex movements, such as high diving and artistic gymnastics, repeated mental imagery is considered a basis for sensible physical training, because without having a concrete mental image of a movement, its satisfactory execution will hardly be feasible. Runners can use mental training in its original sense to, for example, improve their personal running style or to improve their hurdling technique so they can be more relaxed, faster, and conserve energy. Or they want to be able to put less stress on their joints and the rest of the locomotor system to stay healthy long term. Do you have an idea—a detailed mental image—of what YOUR perfect running style would look like?

MENTAL TRAINING IN THE NARROWER SENSE
Mental training is now not just used to optimize movements, but also during athletic movement sequences in general. To get ready for an important race, you can do a mental run-through of the entire competition—or certain key situations as well as possible problems—to be better prepared. You create important mental routines and automatisms because you already know precisely—and without having to think about it for long—what you need to do in certain situations or at particular times. This mental rehearsal also helps remove some of the dread of certain difficulties. You develop problem-solving approaches in anticipation and then have them ready when needed.

This mental simulation of action sequences is also being successfully implemented outside of sports and is used systematically in, for instance, pilot training and by other professional groups, so they can confidently access complex action sequences in critical situations and under extreme stress without having to think about what to do. Or in other words: So every movement during an emergency is automatic.

We usually rehearse certain actions in our mind so we can achieve the desired result later. But what should that result look like? Are we able to experience it in front of our mind's eye and actually feel it with our body? It is a question that is neglected or negated surprisingly often. Intensely imagining possible positive results and goals is an essential part of mental training. Attractive objectives push our behavior in the right direction and provide the necessary motivation, at least as long as they are a good fit. In difficult moments or when the legs hurt and the lungs burn, imagining yourself successfully achieving your objective can be extremely helpful and unleash the necessary strength to keep trying.

Moreover, we can use mental training not just to prepare our future actions via mental simulation, but also to better guide our experiences and behavior in the present. We are able to access mental images and perceptions in the here and now that that can help us in one way or another. We can develop routines to replace negative images and perceptions with positive, productive ones and are thereby able to exert influence over our current experiences.

We already use the option of mentally simulating difficult, important situations based on the motto "What do I do if...," before we actually put ourselves in that situation and prove ourselves. In this respect, mental training in the narrower sense may not be new to you. However, the question remains, to what extent can you make these processes a little smarter to better achieve your goals? And as we saw in the previous chapter, we can also systematically use our mental images and perceptions to influence autonomously occurring physical processes or induce them, which, for athletes, is not insignificant.

In summary, mental training in its original and narrower sense means purposefully exerting constructive influence over our emotions, physical processes, and actions through mental imagery (i.e., a type of training inside the head). You could also call it deliberate head cinema.

MENTAL TRAINING IN THE BROADER SENSE
To me, mental training in the broader sense means the systematic development and improvement of attitudes and psychological abilities that help us manage specific challenges, be it in sports or in our professional or personal lives. Depending on the specific challenges, these abilities and their manifestations can be very different. Someone completing a 250 km run through the desert needs slightly different mental qualities than someone who wants to be one of the world's fastest 100 m runners.

GOALS AND EFFECTIVENESS OF MENTAL TRAINING

It is basically about improving one's self-leadership or self-regulation abilities. It is about increasing the likelihood of actually achieving the things we intend to do as planned, regardless of which specific goals we may be pursuing.

Some may wish to make their movements smoother to conserve energy. Others wish to work on their motivation; on better balancing their job, family, and running; eliminating dysfunctional behaviors; to better handle the stress of competitions; increase self-confidence; accelerate post-injury rehab; achieve a new best time; embark on a special running expedition; stay happy and healthy (or become so again); or whatever! And as varied as these athletic and private goals are, so too are the characters behind the goals and the stories behind the characters. It is much like training running. Mental training is most effective when the individual circumstances are consistently taken into account, meaning when it is a systematic developmental process geared to a specific person, their goals, and parameters.

FINE TUNING

Isolated, short stimuli—for instance a simple mental exercise—can provide extraordinarily helpful support and result in immediate improvements if you know what you are doing. At the same time, the benefits of mental training are most effective, and comparable to physical training, when the techniques are used regularly and not just read over or tried once. Because when it comes to the mind, it is about fine tuning, finding your own way, and being able to use strategies appropriately and with some level of experience. Some things we do correctly intuitively. Or we do them incorrectly. And that's why it's sometimes just like running: Only when I look in a mirror via a video analysis am I able to see the way I really run, independent of my own self-perception. This new information helps me to purposefully improve my running style. And it could be just as beneficial to use new information for psychological improvements such as recognizing blind spots and developmental potential that previously might not have been used in the best possible or most sensible way.

POSSIBILITIES AND LIMITS

Simply put: Even in mental training, you can't turn a hotdog into a steak!

"You can achieve anything if you just put your mind to it" is one of the many slogans on the psychology market. I can wish (and truly want) to be able to run the 100 m at a new record time of 8.9 seconds next year. But if I am realistic, it probably won't happen. Next to a slight multi-year lack of sport-specific training, my muscles and biomechanical leverage ratios will set natural limits. Is the picture I am painting here a slight exaggeration?

There are a number of confident mental trainers that promise their potential clients pie in the sky, often with dubious results or even dangerous consequences (more on that in chapter 7.1). Admittedly, mental training can be a very valuable and powerful tool. Very often people credit their use of mental techniques for their successes or breakthroughs. Systematic and customized mental training can be extremely beneficial to performance and personal development. But ...

With all the justified euphoria, we should still always be aware of the following: While mental training increases the likelihood of being able to better access your inherent abilities and potential and apply them in everyday life, which allows you to achieve your desired successes and results more reliably or calmly, it cannot perform miracles. Except may be if you gained access to the secret knowledge of the amazing Tibetan Lung-Gom-Pa runners (I'm working on it, but then it would no longer be secret knowledge.). Until then, we runners will just have to console ourselves with the fact that even mental training does in a way require great diligence, and next to working on physical fitness and general lifestyle, it is only one of several components. An often neglected and extremely powerful one (maybe even the most powerful), but nevertheless only one.

ARE THERE SHORTCUTS TO SUCCESS? TRAINING VS. COACHING

There is a famous number in expertise research, which focuses on the prerequisites under which people from very different spheres achieve top-performances: 10,000. No, that's not quite right. There is another number or rather a rule of thumb: 10. Again and again, it is apparent that people who have acquired a certain expert status spent approximately 10,000 hours or 10 years educating themselves, practicing, and working extremely diligently (Hagemann et al., 2007). Whether they are chess grandmasters, top athletes, or professional musicians, anyone who wants to be good must put in the time. Someone who wants to get really good has to invest lots of time in developing his abilities. Aside from a few exceptions, there is generally no shortcut to success.

But what if you already reached a certain level, and still have not achieved the desired success? What if you technically could achieve certain things but just can't get it done? Let's assume that, based on his training results and performance diagnostics, a really good runner on a regular basis doesn't perform as well as he should at competitive races. Would more or less intense physical training make sense here? Or should the athlete try more frequent and intensive mental imaging of his movements and runs? More physical training would most likely not yield the desired results and may even have the opposite effect: over-training or burnout.

And instead of training physical or mental abilities, it can of course also be advisable to resort to coaching for solutions to certain, often unconscious blocks, motivational lows, and so on. Valuable positive changes can certainly happen here within a very short period of time as long as you can find the right parameters. Sometimes these positive changes are downright dramatic, and sometimes they are rather small and at first glance not spectacular, but they are very significant and powerful because they represent an initial spark followed by a considerable, long-term positive domino effect. And sometimes all we need is a helpful suggestion to gain a new, different perspective on things.

CONCLUSION AND OUTLOOK

Body and mind are two sides of the same coin and are inextricably linked. Anyone who trains one-sidedly by focusing only on the body misses out on a great opportunity. There is lots of evidence—some of it astounding—of the impact of the mind or mental techniques on physical processes, and using them can be very advantageous. Many yet unforeseen, untapped opportunities lurk here. That means people who want cutting-edge and integrated training also invest time into training the brain in addition to the body. After all, it's an important part of the body. Integrating mental training into your everyday life improves the optimal interplay between body and mind or the general ability of confident self-leadership. This in turn increases the likelihood of achieving desired goals faster and easier, or sometimes just achieving them at all.

The following chapters will show how you can, by using tried and proven mental strategies, make your training more cutting edge, more integrated, and thus more effective, or make the athletic aspects of your life smoother and more satisfying over all.

You may have the occasional "aha!" moment or you might achieve astonishing results. Or maybe it will be the small, quiet, subtle changes and shifts that will create a valuable long-term effect for you, and here and there facilitate constant positive changes. Just pay attention to what happens.

POSITION FIXING: STARTING MY PERSONAL NAVIGATION SYSTEM

Look inside yourself. There is the wellspring of good that never stops bubbling if you never stop digging.

—Marc Aurel

Only the smartest people use their acumen not just to judge others, but to also judge themselves.

—Marie Baroness of Eber-Eschenbach

3 POSITION FIXING: STARTING MY PERSONAL NAVIGATION SYSTEM

We can compare the start of mental training to using a navigational system similar to what most of us use in our cars. Initially, two pieces of information matter: the destination and your current location.

When I do live coaching with my clients, we tend to start by working very intensively on the topic of *destinations*. "Where do I want to go and what is the best way for me to get there?" are the key questions. A personal *position determination* is often virtually built-in if the process requires it. In real life, things are often highly interconnected. Since a book has a slightly different format and I can only present important facts one at a time, I would like to first give you some tools to perform a valid personal position determination. Being aware of this information can affect your choice of goals and can prove to be critical to your success during the ongoing process of reaching your goal. Because just like a navigation system we can only determine an optimal path when, in addition to having a clear picture of where the journey is going, we take into account where we are starting. We can also use the tools to control developmental processes and evaluate their effectiveness. Or, to stay with our example of a navigational system: While on the road, we need to check to make sure we're still on the right track and the right path, and when we have reached our goal.

3.1 "I'M GOING TO RATE MYSELF": IMPORTANT TOPICS IN A NUTSHELL

Scientists enjoy working with sophisticated survey tools. They ideally provide valuable information on psychological issues. This chapter will include such scientifically sound surveys on the topics of mental strengths and running motivation. Some people don't like this more academic approach that often includes quite a bit of reading and analyzing. They prefer a more informal approach. And since I am an avowed pragmatist, I would like to first tell you about a very simple, effective, and absolutely viable way of quickly ascertaining current statuses, that I personally use all the time in my coaching practice: working with *scales* (Ufer, 2014).

SCALES TO ASCERTAIN CURRENT STATUSES

This approach is extremely easy: Simply choose topics that are important to you and rank the current or desired future state on a scale from 1 to 10. Depending on the question, the scale's two corner values can of course vary. For example:

◆ 1 = a little, 10 = a lot
◆ 1 = never, 10 = always
◆ 1 = not at all, 10 = absolutely
◆ 1 = miserable, 10 = excellent
◆ 1 = ☺, 10 = ☹

EXAMPLE:
On a scale from 1 (not at all) to 10 (absolutely), how satisfied are you currently?

◆ With your life overall?
◆ With your job?
◆ With your relationship?
◆ With your athletic presence?

◆   With your current competition results?
◆   With your level of motivation?

On a scale from 1 (not at all) to 10 (absolutely), how satisfied am I currently with ...			
My work-life balance?	1	5	10
My current competition results?	1	5	10

How good is my current ...		
Contact with my sponsor?	☹	☺
Overall energy level?	☹	☺

How often do I currently use the following strategies during a competition?			
Remembering past successes	1 (never)	5	10 (always)
Using a thought-stop technique	1 (never)	5	10 (always)

Figure 1 Sample scales.

Much like a thermostat, the scale provides us with quick and effective information regarding current statuses in important areas. We can integrate these scales into our training journal, or even create an Excel file to analyze data over time. We can take the survey spontaneously on our own, with a teammate, or on the fly with our coach, and quickly generate some topics of conversation.

GOALS FOR WORKING WITH SCALES
◆   Ascertain current statuses
◆   Become aware of resources
◆   Deduce possible goals
◆   Align perceptions of multiple people
◆   Show progress (with repeated use)

POSSIBLE ANALYSES

◆ Resource orientation: If the value is not 1, but higher, what does work well (sometimes)? Which abilities and specific behaviors are already being used to make the value higher than 1?

◆ Goal orientation: Which specific steps must I take to improve by 1-2 points? How would others recognize that I have improved by 1 or 2 points?

◆ Conflict potential and blind spots: When a scale is filled out by two or more people, and the ratings are different, why are these ratings different?

The scope is unlimited. Possible topics are:

◆ How is the atmosphere within the running group?
◆ How would you rate your current state of health?
◆ What is your current energy level?
◆ How often do you use XYZ ability during a competition?
◆ How appealing is goal X?
◆ How well did your last month of training go?

FURTHER EXAMPLES FOR THE USE OF SCALES

EXERCISE: MY SOURCES OF STRENGTH

Which activities and things give you strength, do you enjoy doing, and are good for you? Make a list and scale it by

a) How much they benefit you, how valuable they are when you experience them, regardless of whether that is currently the case, and

b) how often you are currently actually doing them.

Often you'll find yourself thinking, "Oops, actually I would like to do more of this or that, but I'm not doing it." Why? Maybe this scaling exercise will help us pay more attention to certain aspects of our lives and reprioritize things?

EXERCISE: VALUES — COORDINATES OF OUR ACTIONS

What are the important values in my life? For example: family, fair play, adventure, money, and so on? Compile a list. Choose the five values currently most important to you and scale them by how much you currently implement them. This exercise can uncover conflict potentials that could possibly lead to performance blocks.

For instance, Amler and Colleagues (2009) refer to a young athlete who always ended important competitions below his performance potential. It turned out that he was about to be accepted into an athletic training facility some distance away which would considerably reduce his contact with family and friends. Some of his values (performance and athletic success) were conflicting with other values (family and friends). Once he was made aware of this, a mutually agreeable solution was found.

3.2   WHERE AM I RIGHT NOW?

Who do you think knows you best? Someone at work? Someone from your sports club or team? Close friends or family? Did I forget anyone? Of course, it's you! Usually no one knows us better than we do. We should take advantage of that fact. Be your own coach! Imagine being your own advisor. The following exercises will help you pause during your hectic daily life and check in with yourself to see if everything is going the way you want.

EXERCISE: TODAY I'M GOING TO PAY MYSELF A VISIT

This is very well suited for casting a frequent critical eye on our current life situation to see if things are going the way they are supposed to go. It is also a good source of material for the subsequent, rather analytical, self-coaching exercise.

◆ **Relaxation**
Take some time and find a quiet place (turn off your phone). Close your eyes, take a few deep breaths. Inhale, then exhale slowly while consciously relaxing your body and your muscles.

◆ **Visual imaging exercise**
Now imagine paying yourself a visit. It is odd, I know, but do it anyway. You approach your house or apartment, ring the doorbell, and as an outsider you take note—like a kind of neutral doppelganger or camera—of everything you see. How does the place make you feel? How do you like the entrance? If it were to send a message, what would it be? When the door opens and you appear, how do you perceive yourself? What do you look like (body language, facial expression, gestures, clothing)? What do you sound like? What effect does this person have on you? Is he or she alone? When you enter, what do you see, what do you notice?

Now accompany this person (i.e., yourself) through a typical day at home, at work, with family, with friends, during leisure time, and while exercising. Take a close look at yourself and watch as intently as possible. Exactly how do you perceive the person and the overall situation? Is he or she content and happy? In the right place? With the right partner? Working in the right job? Was the current situation planned? Do any of the observations you make from a distance surprise you?

Take your time with this exercise. Just like in sports, it sometimes takes a while to warm up to this exercise. After a little practice, you can also enter a typical problem situation your daily life, training, or competition, and observe.

◆ **Analysis**
What did you notice? What did you like particularly well? What were you satisfied with? What was less satisfactory? Where do you see the beginnings of changes or improvements? On a scale from 1 (miserable) to 10 (perfect), how would you describe your current situation? How could you raise the score by 1-2 points? What concrete action could you take?

EXERCISE: HELICOPTER COACHING

It is easier to provide wisdom to others than to ourselves.

—Francois de la Rouchefoucauld

We are often able offer advice to others that we should really take ourselves. We can take advantage of that ability. In this exercise (Meiss, 2009), you again observe yourself with the emotional distance of a neutral observer, and answer the following questions.

◆ **What is this person's issue?** What exactly is going on and what, if anything, impedes him? What is the problem or challenge?

◆ **If there is a deep-seated issue, what could it be?** What bubbles below the surface? What is it that bothers this person? What should he concentrate on? What is truly important in a solution?

◆ **In your opinion, which problem-solving approaches will definitely fail?** What has he tried before that didn't work? What is something you should not suggest? What diverts him from his actual goal?

◆ **What resources does this person have?** How can he apply all of his strengths, resources, experiences, and other options to reach his goal? Exactly how can those resources help him if he uses them?

◆ **What resources can this person still generate?** Where does he still have development potential? Where is he definitely able to evolve? Precisely what can he do to acquire certain strengths? And after he has developed them in the future, how will he have changed? What will he do differently? How will others recognize the change?

◆ **What attitudes and insights would be helpful?** What insights does he require to get ahead? What attitudes might be counterproductive? What is important for him to recognize?

◆ **What could help him?** What would be particularly helpful? What would really help him get ahead? What specifically could he do himself?

◆ **What advice would you give this person?** What suggestions would be useful and which ones would he accept?

These exercises work just like all those training plans. Briefly reading about when you should complete which number of interval units and long runs at what speed is very different from investing the time and actually doing it.

3.3   PERSONAL PERFORMANCE PROFILE

There are always movies on television and at the movie theater about gifted profilers with extraordinary analytical abilities, a good understanding of relationships, and a sensitive antenna for people. Due to their intuition regarding not very obvious or hidden strengths and powers, they are able to shed light on certain dark circumstances and develop solutions in the most difficult cases. The good news is that we don't have to be exceptionally talented profilers with secret service background to complete a psychological profile of which we are the target. The *performance profiling* method (Butler & Hardy, 1992) can be implemented without prior knowledge and serves us well during mental training, personal development, or while preparing for particular challenges. The method is very simple and is often used at the Olympic champion level. Weston and colleagues (2010, 2011) confirm that performance profiling of athletes (and their coaches) is routinely used as a valuable and an extremely helpful tool in the field.

Performance profiling
◆ strengthens athletes' self-confidence;
◆ identifies mental strengths and weaknesses;
◆ directs the focus to the things that should be addressed;
◆ is motivating and helps formulate self-imposed developmental goals; and
◆ evaluates actual states and monitors developmental processes.

			Actual			Target				
Trait or strength 1			○			×				
Trait or strength 2				○			×			
Trait or strength 3					○	×				
Trait or strength 4			○				×			
Trait or strength 5				○			×			

Figure 2a Performance profiling example.

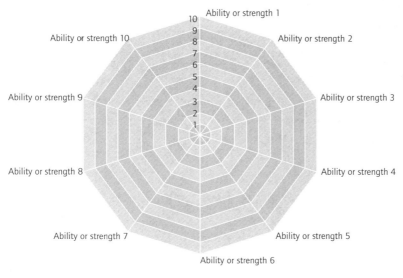

Figure 2b Another performance profiling example.

EXERCISE: PERFORMANCE PROFILING

The purpose of performance profiling is to identify your important mental training goals as well as increase your motivation to implement mental training, meaning developing mental abilities and strengths in everyday life and deploying them long term.

Process

◆ Think about what strengths, abilities, traits, and strategies an excellent runner possesses or requires to achieve your specific goal (e.g., running a marathon in 2.48 hours; becoming the most relaxed, happiest recreational runner in the world; or getting back in shape after a serious injury). Make a list of your answers. You can categorize them if you like.

◆ To what degree do you already possess these right now? Draw a spider web or a bar graph. Rank the level of development on a scale from 1 (currently doesn't exist at all or not used at all) to 10 (currently very highly developed or used regularly) and mark your evaluation with a circle.

◆ Which value would be ideal or which value could you realistically achieve by a given date (e.g., national championships, first marathon, return to your sport)?

◆ For visualization purposes, add the results to a chart or diagram (see figure 2). This will give you an excellent visual overview of your strengths and areas of development.

◆ What are the most important topics and what specific steps can you take to improve in the identified areas?

The advantage of performance profiling is that you are creating a system for evaluation and development that is in line with your specific needs and that reflects your specific situation.

3.4   DIAGNOSING MY MENTAL STRENGTHS

Our ability to reliably access our existing abilities at critical moments is extremely important to our success. With respect to performance, in this context we often refer to *mental strength*. However, the term is vague and is often used in very different ways.

Does it mean something like willpower? Or stress resistance? Resilience*? Motivation? Perseverance? The ability to concentrate? You can see that sweeping buzzwords are not very helpful if we want to work with mental processes and their development more systematically. Of course many scientists have worked more systematically on the question of what makes an athlete more successful from a psychological point of view.

WHAT ARE THE NECESSARY INGREDIENTS FOR BECOMING MORE MOTIVATED AND POWERFUL?

A number of strategies emerged that consistently show major links to athletic success. Of course the relevance of certain strategies always depends on the demands of the respective sport and the athlete's goals. Someone who strives to achieve a national marathon record or the extension of a sponsorship deal will approach his training units and competitions differently than a recreational runner who wants to cross the marathon finish line in 4 hours. Short-distance runners face other challenges and have different psychological demands than ultra-marathon runners. Psychological strategies should therefore always be viewed and developed in the right context.

The individual development of relevant strategies during training and competitions can be assessed via the *Test of Performance Strategies (TOPS)* (Hardy et al., 2010). The questionnaire is one of the world's most-used diagnostic tools in sport psychology (Weinberg & Gould, 2015). I applied a slightly revised and translated German version (Ufer, 2015)—based on Schmid & Colleagues (2010)—with several hundred runners for my research project on the topic of self-leadership, flow, and peak performance, and have consistently received positive feedback regarding its usefulness. Would you like to know how highly developed these strategies are in you? Great, because the following exercise will allow you to make a scientifically sound diagnosis of your mental strengths.

Resilience is the psychological power of resistance, the ability to withstand difficult situations in life without lasting damage.

QUICK AND EASY:
ONLINE QUESTIONNAIRE INCLUDING AUTOMATIC PERSONAL EVALUATION

The website www.running-psychology.com offers broad sport psychology diagnostics, which I used during a research project with runners from many different countries and still use to advance the research. In addition to gathering information regarding your training and background experience and personality characteristics, it also uses questionnaires on mental skills, running motivation, resilience, and general self-leadership. It is simple, saves time, and has the advantage of providing you with a personal evaluation in graphic form without your having to do the math.

EXERCISE: DIAGNOSIS OF MY MENTAL STRENGTHS

This questionnaire measures the use of mental strategies in sports. Since athletes have different approaches to their sport and one sport's demands can sometimes be vey different from those of another, it can be expected that the answers will also be very different. There is no right or wrong answer. The more honest you are with your answers, the more reliable the evaluation will be.

EXPLANATIONS

Some of the terms used here will have different meanings to different people. We therefore included brief definitions of these terms with the aid of specific examples.

◆ *Visualization* refers to the process of consciously imagining movements and conditions while engaging all the senses. Example: A runner uses this type of mental imagery to memorize a running route or he imagines a smooth run or a successful finish.

◆ *Self-talk* is the thoughts directed at ourselves. Often it is a way to tell ourselves what we need to do. Example: When a runner is tired, he says to himself, "Now stay on the heels of the runner in front."

◆ *Relaxation* is the systematic reduction of mental and physical tension, for instance via progressive muscle relaxation, breathing techniques, quiescent images, etc.

◆ *Activation* is the opposite of relaxation, meaning that mental and physical tension is built up deliberately. Example: Prior to his competition, a sprinter feels sluggish. To build up tension, he slaps his thighs with his hands.

◆ *Emotional control* means the capacity to regulate negative emotions.

◆ The term *performance* can refer to the result of your actions, meaning the training or competition result, as well as the process of how you achieved the result, meaning the execution of your movements or your technique.

Listed below are statements about the use of mental skills. Please indicate how frequently you use these or draw on them during everyday training or competitions by making a checkmark in the appropriate column.

Table 1 Use of mental strategies during training and competition.

Item #	Use of mental strategies during training and competition	1 Never	2 Rarely	3 Some-times	4 Often	5 Always
1	I can get my intensity levels just right for competition.					
2	I can control my emotions when things are not going well at practice.					
3	*I have difficulty with my emotions at competitions. (R)*					
4	I set realistic but challenging goals for practice.					
5	In competition, I am sufficiently prepared to be able to perform on automatic pilot.					
6	I motivate myself to train through positive self-talk.					
7	I am able to control distracting thoughts when I am training.					

(continued)

Table 1 (continued)

Item #	Use of mental strategies during training and competition	1 Never	2 Rarely	3 Some-times	4 Often	5 Always
8	I imagine my competitive routine before I do it at a competition.					
9	I am able to perform skills at practice without having to consciously think about them.					
10	I can get myself "up" if I feel flat at practice.					
11	My self-talk during competition is negative.					
12	I manage my self-talk effectively during competition.					
13	I have very specific goals for practice.					
14	I use practice time to work on my relaxation technique.					
15	During competition I set specific result goals for myself.					
16	During practice, I visualize successful past performances.					
17	I use relaxation techniques during competitions to improve my performance.					
18	I set personal performance goals for a competition.					
19	I have specific cue words or phrases that I say to myself to help performance during competition.					
20	At practice, when I visualize my performance, I imagine watching myself as if on a video replay.					
21	*I have difficulty getting into an ideal performance state during training. (R)*					
22	*I keep my thoughts positive during competition. (R)*					
23	I can get myself "up" if I feel flat at a competition.					

Item #	Use of mental strategies during training and competition	1 Never	2 Rarely	3 Some-times	4 Often	5 Always
24	I say things to myself to help my practice performance.					
25	At practice, I can allow the whole skill or movement to happen naturally without concentrating on each part.					
26	At competitions, I rehearse the feeling of my performance in my imagination.					
27	*My emotions keep me from performing my best during practice. (R)*					
28	I imagine screwing up during a competition.					
29	*I don't set goals for practices, I just go out and do it. (R)*					
30	I say things to myself to help my competitive performance.					
31	I rehearse my performance in my mind before practice.					
32	I can allow the whole skill or movement to happen naturally in competition without concentrating on each part.					
33	*I have difficulty controlling my emotions if I make a mistake at competitions. (R)*					
34	I relax myself before competition to get ready to perform.					
35	I evaluate whether I achieve my competition goals.					
36	I talk positively to myself to get the most out of competitions.					
37	*I have trouble maintaining concentration during long practices. (R)*					
38	I can get myself ready to perform when I am at competitions.					

(continued)

Table 1 (continued)

Item #	Use of mental strategies during training and competition	1 Never	2 Rarely	3 Some- times	4 Often	5 Always
39	I manage my self-talk effectively during practice.					
40	I am able to trust my body to perform skills in competition.					
41	I practice using relaxation techniques at workouts.					
42	*My attention wanders while I am training. (R)*					
43	*I get frustrated and emotionally upset when practice does not go well. (R)*					
44	I can psych myself to perform well in competitions.					
45	I talk positively to myself to get the most out of practice.					
46	I set very specific goals for competition.					
47	If I'm starting to "lose it" at a competition, I use a relaxation technique.					
48	I am able to perform skills at competitions without having to consciously think about them.					
49	*My emotions get out of control under the pressure of competition. (R)*					
50	I use workouts to practice relaxing.					
51	I can psych myself to perform well in practice.					
52	During competition I have thoughts of failure.					
53	I visualize my competition going exactly the way I want it to go.					

Item #	Use of mental strategies during training and competition	1 Never	2 Rarely	3 Some-times	4 Often	5 Always
54	*My practice performance suffers when something upsets me at training. (R)*					
55	*I need to monitor all the details of each move to successfully execute skills in practice. (R)*					
56	During practice, I can perform automatically without having to consciously control each movement.					
57	I use relaxation strategies as a coping strategy at competitions.					
58	I can get my intensity levels just right for practice.					
59	During practice I focus my attention effectively.					
60	I set goals to help me use practice time effectively.					
61	At practice, when I visualize my performance, I imagine what it will feel like.					
62	*My emotions keep me from performing my best at competitions. (R)*					
63	During training sessions, I use relaxation techniques to improve my performance.					
64	I rehearse my performance in my mind at competitions.					

EVALUATION

Since some items are positive and others are negative, the items printed in *italics* should first be switched over or reversed (it is also called recoding, hence the (R) behind those respective items) using the following pattern: 1 = 5, 2 = 4, 3 = 3, 4 = 2, 5 = 1. The value 1 becomes 5, 2 becomes 4, 3 remains 3, 4 becomes 2, and 5 becomes 1.

Calculate the respective averages for strategies at competitions or training by figuring out the sum of the respective item values and dividing them by 4.

Competition:	Training:
◆ Self-talk: 12, 19, 30, 36 ◆ Emotional control: 3, 33, 49, 62 ◆ Automaticity: 5, 32, 40, 48 ◆ Goal-setting: 15, 18, 35, 46 ◆ Visualization: 8, 26, 53, 64 ◆ Activation: 1, 23, 38, 44 ◆ Relaxation: 17, 34, 47, 57 ◆ Negative Thinking: 11, 22, 28, 52	◆ Self-talk: 6, 24, 39, 45 ◆ Emotional control: 2, 27, 43, 54 ◆ Automaticity: 9, 25, 55, 56 ◆ Goal-setting: 4, 13, 29, 60 ◆ Visualization: 16, 20, 31, 61 ◆ Activation: 10, 21, 51, 58 ◆ Relaxation: 14, 41, 50, 63 ◆ Attention control: 7, 37, 42, 59

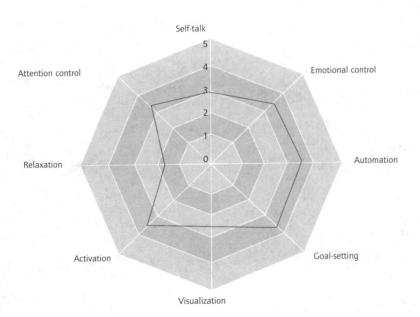

Figure 3a TOPS evaluation for the training area.
(The line stands for the average value.)

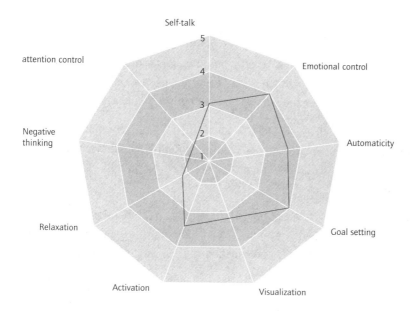

Figure 3b TOPS evaluation for the competition area.
(The line stands for the average value.)

Enter the values into the overview. This will give you a good general view of the current status quo.

INTERPRETATION

Much like a successful diagnosis made by a physician, a valid database allows you to identify the mental skills needed to overcome certain challenges that you might be able to purposefully improve.

Many studies show that using mental strategies is key to top athletic performance. There are also significant differences when comparing athletes at different performance levels (e.g., national top athletes and Olympic champions). For instance, the latter post considerably higher values in the areas of goal setting, activation, relaxation, emotional control, and focus. In addition, multiple and unique international title winners differ in their mental strengths. A link between flow experiences, resilience, and the use of mental techniques was also detected. And the more mental strategies an athlete uses in training, the more successful he feels during a competition (Frey et al., 2003; Jackson et al., 2001; Krane & Williams, 2010, Ufer, 2018).

Here is a suggestion for how to handle the data:

1.   Be aware that, while attention control is only measured for training, negative thinking, meaning self-talk and thoughts about giving up or failure, are only collected in the area of competition. The lower the score is on the negative thinking scale, the better.

2.   Which areas are not very well developed in comparison to others? You could increasingly refine these as part of your mental training. Think about how an improvement in these areas could affect your athletic performance and how you would like to accomplish this improvement.

3.   Where do you see definite differences between training and competition? In the future you should increasingly use and develop areas in training that tend to be less well developed in training than they are in competitions. How would you go about that?

4.   How does your own profile differ from the average value (i.e., the orange line)? Be aware that other runners might have interpreted the test items differently and that the average value is simply a rough guide based on more than 400 runners to date, and does not support any conclusions on "good" or "bad" runners (Ufer, 2015).

Have fun with your ongoing development and the optimal use of your mental skills!

3.5   WHY DO I RUN? WHAT DRIVES ME?

Most athletes confirm that, while running, the following aspects matter most to them in varying degrees of importance: socializing, relaxation, mental and overall health, weight management, clearing of the head, problem-solving, enjoying nature, exploring personal limits, self-improvement, and proving something. Of course, some runners are also competitive and love to compete with others.

But in any case it is good to know what drives us to run and why running is so important to us. Because, and we will see this over the course of the book, sometimes runners lose sight of their original motivations, which can have a negative effect. You might want to record your important motivations during the following exercise. The questionnaire *Motivations of Marathoners (MOMs)* was originally developed by Ogles and Masters (1993) and was later translated into German by Stoll (1998). Please note that the questionnaire can be applied to all running distances (i.e., you don't have to be a marathon runner).

EXERCISE: MOTIVATION FOR RUNNING

Please assess your current reasons for running by referring to the following list. They can vary from person to person and can also change over time. If an assertion does not at all apply to you, please mark it with a 1 (not important at all). If the assertion is highly applicable, please mark it with a 7 (very important).

Table 2 Reasons for running.

Item:	1	2	3	4	5	6	7
1. To help control my weight							
2. To compete with others							
3. To earn the respect of my peers							
4. To reduce my weight							
5. To improve my running speed							
6. To earn the respect of people in general							
7. To socialize with other runners							
8. To improve my health							
9. To compete with myself							
10. To become less anxious							
11. To improve my self-esteem							
12. To have something in common with other people							
13. To add a sense of meaning to life							
14. To prolong my life							

(continued)

Table 2 (continued)

Item:	1	2	3	4	5	6	7
15. To feel less depressed							
16. To meet people							
17. To become more physically fit							
18. To distract myself from daily worries							
19. To make my family or friends proud of me							
20. To make my life more purposeful							
21. To look leaner							
22. To run faster							
23. To feel more confident about myself							
24. To participate with my family or friends							
25. To make myself feel whole							
26. To reduce my chance of having a heart attack							
27. To make my life more complete							
28. To improve my mood							
29. To improve my sense of self-worth							
30. To share a group identity with other runners							
31. To create a positive emotional experience							
32. To feel proud of myself							
33. To visit with friends							
34. To feel a sense of achievement							
35. To push myself beyond my current limits							

Item:	1	2	3	4	5	6	7
36. To have time alone to sort things out							
37. To stay in good physical condition							
38. To concentrate on my thoughts							
39. To solve problems							
40. To see how high I can place in races							
41. To feel a sense of belonging in nature							
42. To stay physically attractive							
43. To get a faster time than my friends							
44. To prevent illness							
45. To make people look up to me							
46. To see if I can beat a certain time							
47. To blow off steam							
48. To bring me recognition							
49. To have time alone with the world							
50. To get away from it all							
51. To make my body perform better than before							
52. To beat someone I've never beaten before							
53. To feel mentally in control of my body							
54. To get compliments from others							
55. To feel at peace with the world							
56. To feel like a winner							

EVALUATION

The individual items can be combined into the following categories. As you do so, add up the values of the respective items and divide the total by the number of items. Afterward, you can enter the values on the chart.

Physical Health Motives
◆ General Health Orientation: (8, 14, 17, 26, 37, 44) / 6
◆ Weight Concern: (1, 4, 21, 42) / 4

Achievement Motives
◆ Competition: (2, 40, 43, 52) / 4
◆ Personal Goal Achievement: (5, 9, 22, 35, 46, 51) / 6

Social Motives
◆ Recognition: (3, 6, 19, 45, 48, 54) / 6
◆ Affiliation: (7, 12, 16, 24, 30, 33) / 6

Psychological Motives
◆ Psychological Coping: (10, 15, 18, 28, 36, 38, 39, 47, 50) / 9
◆ Self-Esteem: (11, 23, 29, 31, 32, 34, 53, 56) / 8
◆ Life Meaning: (13, 20, 25, 27, 41, 49, 55) / 7

INTERPRETATION

People can have very different reasons for running. They can also change over time. Many people choose to begin running for exercise and for their health, and then become increasingly performance-focused. Others have had a performance-oriented career and are more interested in the social aspect. Some just want to unwind and clear the head. And of course this sport and all its trappings offer a great opportunity to get recognition and increase self-worth. Surprisingly, these last two items are rarely acknowledged to the extent that their outward appearance might suggest.

Here is a suggestion for handling the data:

◆ Ultimately, when it comes to incentives, there is no good or bad, no right or wrong; it is still always a matter of dosage.

◆ Losing sight of one's original motives can become problematic. There are lots of examples: runners that put too much emphasis on some areas due to societal norms and group pressure and in the process may focus too much on things that aren't really in line with their other incentives. That can lead to frustration, demotivation, and performance blocks.

Table 3 Evaluation of running motivation.

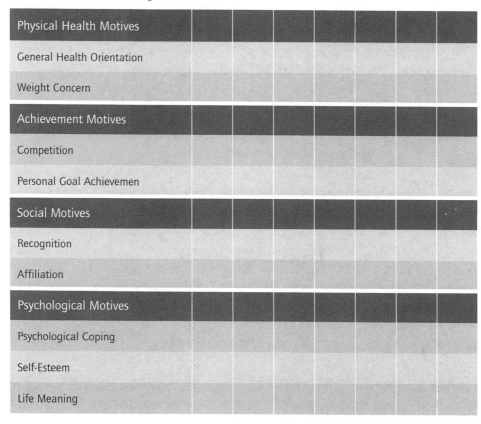

Physical Health Motives								
General Health Orientation								
Weight Concern								
Achievement Motives								
Competition								
Personal Goal Achievemen								
Social Motives								
Recognition								
Affiliation								
Psychological Motives								
Psychological Coping								
Self-Esteem								
Life Meaning								

Table 4 Implicit, unconscious wants.

Affiliation Striving for:	Power Striving for:	Achievement Striving for:
◆ Closeness ◆ Security ◆ Friendship ◆ Affection ◆ Family ◆ Partnership Intimacy	◆ Influence ◆ Control ◆ Dominance ◆ Status ◆ Money	◆ Success ◆ Recognition ◆ Progress ◆ Development ◆ Fulfillment ◆ Self-realization

◆ It is important to remember to periodically stop and listen to your inner voice to find out what is *truly* important to you and also what is *good for you*.

◆ You can complete this questionnaire again to really be able to see any changes.

A MONKEY WRENCH IN THE WORKS: IMPLICIT VS. EXPLICIT MOTIVES

One of the problems with the above questionnaire is that it merely captures our conscious (i.e., explicit) motives that we ascribe to ourselves. But our unconscious (i.e., implicit) motives are just as important, if not more so. Next to biological motives such as breathing, hunger, sex, warmth, and sleep, we can differentiate three categories of implicit motives: *affiliation, power, and achievement.*

These unconscious motives emerge early in life and they vary from person to person. Whenever we feel really good about achieving a certain goal, we can assume that we are acting in accordance with our unconscious motives. If we feel less good, it is a sign that our goals aren't in line with our unconscious motives. For instance, someone who sets ambitious athletic goals, but whose achievement motive isn't particularly distinct, will have problems. In view of this fact, the topic of *motivational problems* can quickly acquire a new and interesting meaning, as we will see in chapter 4. If you choose goals that don't match your motives, you will have trouble keeping at it when things get tough. This is just a teaser for why we should pay attention to our feelings and bring them onboard with us whenever we embark on a journey.

THE ATACAMA EXPERIMENT: MOTIVATIONAL BLOCK DUE TO INCONSISTENT GOALS

Lighting zigzags, too, but it also strikes!   —French proverb

After the thought of doing the Atacama run had become manifest in my head over the years and once plans finally began to firm up, I completed a performance diagnostics test administered by an experienced national trainer for mid-distance runners. The results weren't exactly outstanding, but there was a certain foundation, and that was fine. During the evaluation session, the trainer mentioned that it would make sense to train for a marathon first. Yes, setting my sights on a 42 km marathon as an intermediate goal for a subsequent 250 km run sounded absolutely reasonable.

So far so good. And what do you think happened next? Nothing! I did not prepare for the marathon. On the contrary, I felt like my running enthusiasm had hit rock bottom. I lost sight of the project and, to stick with the topic of position fixing, I had stopped dead in my tracks. Months later, I asked myself why I had not started to prepare. Here is the trivial answer: I simply was not interested in typical marathons.

I thought about what is truly important to me in life, about what the values are that I want to live by, in sports and training, too. And it turns out adventure, travel, discovering new territory, and expeditions are at the top of the list. A typical marathon generally doesn't offer these things, which is likely why my motivation completely faded away.

Only after I freed myself from the advice that I should first diligently train for a marathon with an elaborate training plan did I feel better and my interest in running was renewed. What exactly changed? I redefined my training runs and saw them as a kind of micro-expedition. That made it possible for me to look forward to going on a discovery tour during my little running expeditions, to discover new things about my environment (and about myself), for example beautiful little stream courses, beer gardens, gulches, and overlooks, that I had not previously known about. I rediscovered the joy in running and the approach, the path, was in line with my inner needs.

MOTIVATION AND GOALS: FUELING AND GUIDING PRODUCTIVE ENERGY

Success is not the key to happiness. Happiness is the key to success. If you love what you do, you will be successful.

—Albert Schweitzer

Strong reasons bring about strong performances.

—William Shakespeare

4 MOTIVATION AND GOALS: FUELING AND GUIDING PRODUCTIVE ENERGY

The topic of motivation is one of the psychological evergreens. Week after week, we come across motivational tips in countless print and online media. It would be difficult to avoid them even if you wanted to. Given that huge amount of advice, one would think that after reaching a certain age and thus having been exposed to all those tips, we would all be true motivational experts, but somehow that's not always the case. Is it the quality of the advice? Is it our ability to grasp and implement it? What could the problem be? Again and again, I see—and a number of my colleagues confirm this—that systematic goal setting by athletes is often surprisingly perfunctory and less systematic, even though they are a key element of our actions and the basis of success. For this reason, the goals that have been set often aren't as effective as they could be.

As an introduction to this chapter, I'm going to use a slightly unusual approach to the topic of motivation and goals. What would happen if we had a slightly more constructive approach to problems, thereby eliminating them almost automatically or using them for our conscious ongoing development? How can we take advantage of the full psychological and motivational potential of goals? What is it that drives us? What pitfalls await as we set our personal goals and how can we set goals that are multi-dimensional and appropriate for our brain so they will burn into our minds and help us get through difficult times?

4.1 EVERYDAY SELF-SABOTAGE, OR: FUCK YOU, PROBLEM!

You cannot tailor-make the situations in life, but you can tailor-make the attitudes to fit those situations.

—Zig Ziglar

WHAT CAN RUNNERS LEARN FROM SKIERS?

A recurrent science-focused continuing-education conference for sports medicine physicians was held in the summer of 2014. The event took place in a well-known Alpine ski resort. Technical lectures were held in the morning and during the evening hours, and attendees could ski in between. Anyone who wished could join a guided group that included a skiing class. Since some attendees had mentioned that they, as physicians of sports medicine, would like to hear or learn something on the topic of sport psychology and mental training, I was asked to hold one or two lectures as part of the week's events.

Since the conference took place in the mountains and the topic of high-altitude medicine was on the agenda, we decided to open the event with our award-winning documentary *Marathon at Mount Everest: The Highest 42,195 km in the World*, along with some comments on the mental challenges that such a sporting event presents. The presentation generated a lively debate, but also enthusiasm. The attendees were impressed to see what people who weren't necessarily top athletes—average runners like you and I, those who might have already suffered some misfortunes, or who were much older than 70—could accomplish when they believe in themselves and their abilities, set challenging goals for themselves, and muster the courage to pursue them even in the face of adversity.

Interest in the second lecture was piqued. I titled it "Motivation and Goals: Guide to Self-Sabotage." During the 30-minute presentation, I intended to provide the attendees with specific knowledge they could apply directly during the afternoon's ski practice to test its effectiveness. The results were astounding and again generated lively conversations. After my lecture, many attendees noticed positive changes during the subsequent ski lesson; they reported skiing a little better and more confidently, that they were less afraid or uncertain and were focused and thereby more self-assured, which in turn affected their athletic performance. What did the participants change and what can we runners learn by watching skiers? It's quite simple. I showed them how we can hugely affect our thinking, emotions, and actions with the type of language we choose and the way we focus our attention.

SELF-SABOTAGE MADE EASY: THE POWER OF LANGUAGE

How do we dramatically increase the likelihood of getting precisely what we don't really want? How do we manage to trip up ourselves as well as others and sabotage our goal attainment (or at least make it more difficult) with our choice of language, and what lessons do we learn from doing so?

Language is ubiquitous. Language is at once easy and difficult. Language can energize people and manipulate them. Again and again studies show that communication is a key issue in sports clubs, corporations, teams, friendships, or partnerships. Language is also a form of communication, and a powerful one at that. Sports language also has a positive or negative effect on our performance and goal attainment. That's why it makes sense to know some hacks and useful communication strategies, regardless of whether you wish to communicate with your charges as a coach, as an athlete with your running buddies, or with yourself to boost your performance.

Regardless of the type of sport or running discipline we engage in—whether we listen to trainers, the well-intended suggestions from our sports friends, or our own internal voice when it tells us what we should or should not do—we constantly listen to instructions, suggestions, and objectives based on the following pattern:

◆ Don't put so much pressure on yourself.
◆ Don't allow yourself to be provoked.
◆ Don't be so stressed.
◆ Don't arch your back so much.
◆ Don't stiffen up when you run.
◆ Don't …

Or, to come back to the skiing students who, in the heat of the moment, tell themselves:

◆ Don't hit the snow gun.
◆ Don't ski straight at another skier.
◆ Don't let your legs get rigid.
◆ Don't be afraid.

Does that sound familiar? I think it does, and it's probably not uncommon. All of those verbalizations are well intended, yet have their pitfalls and often lead to precisely the behavior we wish to avoid. Why is that?

YOU WILL MOVE IN THE DIRECTION YOU FOCUS ON!

Countless centers in our brain are working together to enable us to understand language. And there are additional centers devoted to cognition, image processing, movement control, etc. The relevant centers are in constant communication with each other. As a result, complex networks of neuronal activity form. Our brain works associatively, permanently linking a huge amount of information. This generally also includes visual imagery of facts and circumstances. However, the difficulty is that there are no images in our heads for concepts that include denials; that is, by trying *not* to imagine something, we inevitably imagine precisely that which we should not imagine.

The instruction: "Don't think about a delicious serving of ice cream with whipped cream on top" results in our brain correctly understanding this command from a linguistic standpoint, but at the same time, our brain is already creating a visual (ice cream with whipped cream on top) that must then be denied or deactivated. Such mixed messages cause confusion. Our brain requires considerably more computing power and processing time for denials. But since athletic training is designed to optimize processes it would be illogical to waste time and resources, particularly with respect to the control center between our ears.

For example, say someone tells you, "Don't put so much pressure on yourself," "Don't arch your back so much," "Don't stiffen up when you run." In terms of brain psychology, the following happens: In order to understand what is going on, what is being talked about, the brain, in addition to activating many speech centers, very quickly retrieves an entire network of stored mental images, experiences, emotions, and physical sensations on the topics of pressure, your back, or running stiffly. But then you have to deny—or rather deactivate—them during a second step, whereby your attention has already been directed in a corresponding, and unfortunately wrong, direction. Having to then deny all of this again requires the brain to expend computing power and resources that are scarcely or not at all available during a time of major strain, when we are already at our limit or when the brain is already very busy working on something new or difficult.

There are wonderful examples from the field for that. I am thinking of a world championship boxing match in which two boxers returned to their corners completely drained and in a trance at the end of a round. Exhausted, they collapse onto their stools. That's not what being fresh and fully conscious looks like. The coach of one of the boxers instructed him, among other things, to absolutely not drop his guard, while the other boxer was told to find the gap for a hard right. Moments later, the inevitable happened. The bell sounded for the next round. The boxers stood up, moved toward each other, bobbed and weaved a little. And then it happened: One boxer let down his guard and the other one found the gap for his hard right. Bam! The fight was over.

Here is another example you can try out yourself. The command: "Don't think about the pope in a pink bathrobe," immediately conjures up this image before our mind's eye. As you can see, trying not to think about something leads precisely to that thought. In this case, something that is purposefully used as part of systematic mental training—namely the medically proven fact that mentally simulating movements will result in the corresponding muscular reactions—can prove to be our undoing. The lightning-fast inner representation or image of the unwanted behavior (e.g., running stiffly) leads to the activation of corresponding neuronal networks and to automatic muscle contractions that correspond to the unwanted behavior.

Conclusion: Language that focuses on mistakes leads to results that we actually wish to avoid.

FOCUSING ON GOALS INSTEAD OF MISTAKES

Theoretically, the solution sounds as mundane as it does simple. But unfortunately, it is difficult to implement because we are culturally predisposed to using lots of negations and to focus on problems and deficiencies.

Systematically focus on what you want to achieve in the future, not on what you no longer want. In other words, whenever you catch yourself formulating *"away from"* goals, suggestions, and instructions, stop yourself and rephrase them as *"towards"* goals. How does it work? It's simple! Use the magic word *instead*. Ask yourself what specifically you want to do, experience, and achieve instead.

Example:

"I want my job to be less stressful" or *"I don't want to be so nervous prior to the start"* are typical "away from" goals that focus on problem behaviors. We articulate quite vaguely what we don't want anymore, but the essential information is missing, namely what should happen instead. This results in a kind of goal and orientation vacuum (e.g., Where are we going and what are we focusing on?). This adage says it well: "If you don't know where you want to go, you can't be surprised when you arrive some place completely different."

With the question "What do I want instead?" we can turn the above statements into "towards" goals like "I want to appear calm and relaxed at important meetings" or "I want to feel confident, calm, and full of positive energy prior to the start."

EXERCISE: FOCUSING ON GOALS INSTEAD OF MISTAKES AND PROBLEMS

Write down five examples of "away from" suggestions, thoughts, or instructions from your daily training or competitions that you have heard or spoken recently, and turn them into "towards" goals.

Table 5 "Towards" goals instead of "away from" goals.

"Away from" goal	"Towards" goal
Don't allow teammate X to provoke you.	
I don't want to get stomach cramps.	
Don't get your feelings hurt so easily.	
...	

IMPLICATION OF RESOURCES AND SUCCESS

Now let's reach into our bag of tricks once more to find some effective self-coaching strategies. Which phrasing do you think is more productive?

◆ "Let's see how long it will take me to find my ideal running rhythm."

◆ "Let's see how quickly I can find my rhythm."

The first version basically implies that it will take a long time. If you want to effectively orient or instruct yourself or another athlete towards a specific goal or improvement, you should use positive speech patterns that imply that you or the other athlete will achieve your goal and possess the necessary abilities. These speech patterns can activate mental images of goal attainment as well as conscious or unconscious search processes for paths and means on the way to the goal.

AVOIDING ADDITIONAL PROBLEMATIC PHRASING

Again and again, words creep in that sometimes have a disastrous effect on our motivation and performance. The word *try* is such a word. It unconsciously implies that we can only achieve something with lots of effort. Better phrasing would be: "Allow yourself to run loosely and elegantly."

And finally the word *must.* The use of the word *must* creates pressure. It also leads to reactance, a conscious or unconscious type of resistance and the desire to do just the opposite. Better would be: "I will train today." My suggestion is to eliminate the word *must* from daily training and competitions.

Any constraint inhibits and squeezes nature and it is unable to express its beauty in all its charm.

—Wilhelm Heinse

If you can internalize this, you are well on your way! If you are able to emancipate yourself a little here and use negations only sparingly in the future, you are using a valuable approach to brain-appropriate thinking.

TWEAKING PROBLEMS OR MANIPULATING TALENTS? PROBLEMS AND WEAKNESSES VS. SOLUTIONS AND RESOURCES

WHAT IS MORE IMPORTANT: THE HOLES OR THE CHEESE?

Let's assume you enter a pitch-dark room but would like to be able to see. It would not occur to most people in this situation to find out why it is so dark in the first place. They would search for the light switch.

During a research project initiated by Steve de Shazer and Insoo Kim Berg in Milwaukee, USA in the 1980s, countless consultations and therapy sessions on very different topics were held over the course of several years. They always revolved around the handling of, in some cases, extremely difficult problems and the implementation of desirable change processes in everyday life. Here is what made this project special: The clients agreed to have experts sit behind a two-way mirror and record and analyze these sessions. The goal was to receive an answer to an extremely simple question: Which consulting methods work better or faster? Which strategies can be used to make the coaching process as effective as possible? How can we help people get a handle on their problems as quickly as possible and actually implement positive changes (Szabó & Berg, 2006, de Shazer & Berg, 1997)?

The results were astounding, challenged many a scientific consensus, and ensured the creation of a new, highly effective coaching method that made its way into corporations, schools, sports, and many other areas of life: *solution-focused short-term coaching*. Runners or their trainers can, of course, also use these findings.

ARE YOU A PROBLEM JUNKIE OR A SOLUTION SURFER?

Many people still believe that expertly solving psychological problems or difficulties requires explicit knowledge about their causes. They intuitively ask themselves how to solve a problem if they don't really understand it. However, the researchers found that focusing tons of attention on analyzing problems and their causes is often not necessary, even unproductive. It might be helpful to an auto mechanic fixing an engine, but isn't always the method of choice to quickly bring about desired changes or improvements in people.

The moment we intensively and comprehensively immerse ourselves in the problems and their causes, we activate precisely those problematic mindsets and behaviors (neuronal networks) that are supposed to be overcome in the first place, accompanied by negative feelings that come along with thinking about the problem.

Experts refer to this as entering a *problem trance*: You walk in circles, don't really get anywhere, and feel bad, sometimes even helpless. Problem-focused counseling methods therefore lead to more prolonged change processes. This quickly conjures up the stereotypical image of psychologists whose clients spend years on the couch, digging around in their past during a psychoanalysis without realizing any substantial changes in the present.

Albert Einstein once said, "We cannot solve our problems with the same thinking we used when we created them." Thus *solution-oriented coaching* focuses primarily on one thing: desirable objectives. Instead of analyzing problems, the focus is consistently on objectives. Instead of focusing our attention on negative facts and circumstances from the past that did not work well, we shift our energy to positive, future results. This triggers positive learning processes, and is more fun and more motivating.

The research project showed that when attention is directed to specific, desirable results and improvements as well as the necessary resources, when we consistently think about or discuss with others what exactly it would be like if a certain problem no longer existed or simply resolved itself and a specific goal was reached, progress is faster and long-term solutions are much more likely.

Instead of analyzing, we quickly enter an action phase because we talk about it or think about where we want to go and what specifically needs to be done next to get closer to a goal. This approach is very practical and hands-on. And most of the time it is also very effective.

EXERCISE: PROBLEM VS. SOLUTION AND RESOURCE ORIENTATION

ASCERTAINING THE CURRENT SITUATION
On a scale from 1 to 10, how satisfied are you currently with your life overall, whereby 1 would mean desperately unhappy and 10 would mean everything is perfect? Mark the place on the scale that is currently most accurate.

You can exchange these questions for countless other topics, depending on what your current interest might be (e.g., "How satisfied are you with your current performance?," "How successful were or are you in this or that area?," "How much of your performance potential are you currently able to tap into?," "What is your current stress level?").

On a scale from 1 (not at all) to 10 (very), how ...			
Satisfied with your current performance?	1	5	10
...	1	5	10

Let's assume you marked 6. It may continue like this:

Table 6 Problem orientation.

Question	Answer
Why did you not get a higher score on the scale?	
What exactly are the problem areas?	
What are the causes of these problems?	
What went or is going wrong?	
What is the reason and whose fault is it?	
How can you solve these problems?	

Table 7 Solution and resource orientation.

The fact that you marked a 6 means a lot of things are already working quite well.	
Specifically what has worked out well so far?	
What contributes to that success?	
Which qualities have helped you to be successful?	
Exactly what do you do and which specific behaviors do you exhibit?	
Which behaviors do you wish to continue, exhibit more often, or expand upon in which situations?	
Assuming you would move up one point on the scale, what would change? What would you do differently? How would you or others notice that something has changed?	

EVALUATION

If you take yourself as an example, which approach feels better immediately and motivates you more to keep reading? It is usually the solution-oriented version. It is much more appreciative of you and others, puts the focus increasingly on your own strengths, talents, and abilities, and promotes self-confidence. And it focuses on the present and the future. That is motivating because, in the end, we can only work on those.

It is about identifying ideal circumstances or goals and exploring possible ways to get there in the most efficient way. As you do so, let the following maxims guide you:

◆ Find out what works well and do more of that.

◆ Don't try to fix what already works.

◆ If something doesn't work well long term, stop and do something else.

You don't have to be an expert in solution-oriented short-term coaching. But someone who consistently cultivates an attitude and mindset focused on goals, strengths, and resources will have fewer problems, have more fun, and be more motivated on the way to achieving goals, often reaching the desired goals considerably faster (Grant, 2012). Along the way, several principles and methods on the subject of *goal attainment* have proven very helpful in increasing the likelihood of actually arriving where we want to go. We will take a look at this in chapter 4.3.

4.2 NEVER AGAIN, MOTIVATIONAL PROBLEMS! A BEAUTIFUL NEW WORLD OF ATHLETICS OR SOMETHING FROM THE PSYCHOLOGICAL BAG OF TRICKS?

Consciousness is just a PR campaign by your brain to make you think you actually have a say in something.
                                                                        —J.D. Haynes

The head is round so thought can change direction.
                                                                        —Francis Picabia

A great deal of our behavior is completely automatic and takes place outside of our conscious control. We are largely steered through life by our subconscious. The findings from brain research seem to be unequivocal. Any time we think we have made a conscious decision, those decisions have already been made in the depths of our brains for half an eternity (Soon et al, 2008).

While I don't want to have a controversial debate here about whether or not we possess free will, all experts at least agree that a significant portion of our behavior occurs unconsciously, meaning far from conscious thought and control. If we had to permanently make only conscious decisions, our brains would have barely enough computing capacity left to control our breathing.

THE NEW-YEAR'S RESOLUTION PHENOMENON: AND THE TRAP SNAPS SHUT AGAIN
We're all familiar with the New Year's resolution phenomenon. At the start of a new year or on our birthdays, we plan to do something new, to make changes, (e.g., get more exercise, train more consistently, eat healthier, be more relaxed, quit smoking, spend more time with our partner, start this or that, stop this or that, learn, and improve). We set goals we want to achieve, are sure of the positive results, and yet most resolutions fizzle among the chaos of everyday life. How does this happen?

TRAINING FRUSTRATION AND STRESS
Again and again I see recreational athletes who, when they first start running, simply enjoy running, and as the body adjusts to the physical effort relatively quickly, they

begin to set ambitious goals like, for instance, running a half-marathon in X amount of time, finishing a marathon, or whatever. That's great. Here is what's not great: In spite of the desire to improve and in spite of elaborate training plans, problems creep in here and there. Sometimes it is hard to get going. There are motivational lows before long runs. Frustration sets in because training units cannot be completed as planned due to professional or family obligations. We start to put pressure on ourselves. Particularly problematic is that thoughts and soliloquies like "Today I must ..." begin to creep in. We already explained why this is problematic.

WHEN YOU FIGHT AGAINST YOUR WEAKNESSES YOU FIGHT AGAINST YOURSELF
In situations like this, we refer to or debate how to fight the *inner couch potato* almost by default. Many of us may not be aware that the way we think about and talk to ourselves often has a surprisingly negative effect on us, at least when it is not meant to be humorous. I therefore recommend not fighting problems and aspects of your personality, but rather purposefully using them as valuable resources for very specific improvements. It is a method that has been very successful in coaching. Redirecting attention from problems to possible solutions creates a kind of relief and a more positive experience. We are more likely to think in terms of possibilities and resources that are available to us.

TACTICAL REFRAMING
What might that look like in practice? We use a tried and tested and extremely helpful approach that has proven successful in self-coaching: *reframing*. We assign a different, often opposite, interpretation to a situation or put it in a different context. Let's simply call it rethinking! Instead of fighting the inner couch potato, we can, for instance, begin thinking of it as an inner watchdog and bring it on board as a competent partner or trainer. Let's imagine that the motivational problem isn't really a problem but an intelligent signal from deep within the mouthpiece of our subconscious that pursues a positive intention and holds a valuable message. What might that message be? Maybe an inner voice pointing out that our goals are not consistent yet? Or that the specific paths leading to the goal should be improved?

Try it. Instead of feeling frustrated and fighting against yourself, you can remove the self-imposed pressure, relax, and open yourself up to constructive learning.

It is easy to set new goals, as the New Year's resolution problem shows. It appears to be less easy to set goals so they actually align our actions the way we want, optimally boosting our motivation and endurance to pursue our goals so we really stick with it in order to achieve the goals we have set. Usually it isn't a lack of understanding of the importance of the goals but rather a lack of specific advice on how to ideally structure goal-setting and goal-pursuit processes so they are effective.

4.3 BRAIN-APPROPRIATE GOAL MANAGEMENT: THE BASIS OF SUCCESS

A man without a goal is an arrow without a tip! —Sitting Bull

We must arrange for our goals to come our way. —Theodor Fontane

Setting goals is easy. So why devote an entire chapter to the subject? Although setting goals seems extremely easy, it is often done very superficially. Amazingly, runners and many other athletes often neglect this very important pillar of their success and happiness. In this context, sport psychologists refer to *goal-setting training*. Yes, this too, can be practiced and improved upon. I give it a slightly different name: *brain-appropriate goal management*. With brain-appropriate goal management, goals that fit one's personality and life situation are mentally and emotionally embedded in such a way that they release an optimal energy boost, permanently steer actions in the right direction, and promote motivation, even—and especially—when it gets difficult. This is a good time investment and an important part of mental training. Anyone who does this regularly is verifiably more successful, and not just in sports.

FROM RESEARCH: SELF-MOTIVATION AND PERFORMANCE INCREASE THROUGH INTELLIGENT GOAL SETTING

Does setting difficult goals increase performance more so than setting easy or no goals, or does an instruction like "Give it your best" possibly work better?

These are some of the questions countless scientists around the world have asked on the subject of goals and their effect on our behavior and performance. Instead of a laborious search for clues and the gathering of individual results in order to find valid answers to design effective mental training, there is an easier way: meta-analyses of the use and effectiveness of goal-setting processes in sports and vocation.

Meta-analysis refers to synoptic papers summarizing the results from different scientific studies that were executed independently of each other. The results are impressive and unequivocal. The use of goal-setting strategies works extremely well. More than 90% of studies in general psychology (far more than 500) done with more than 4,000 participants in more than 10 countries show that goal-setting techniques consistently had a very strong influence on behavior during the most diverse activities, regardless of whether the subjects were children, researchers, managers, warehouse workers, physicians, or any other group of individuals. And in sports? The situation looks very similar. By now, around 80% of sports science and sport psychology studies detect major positive effects (Burton & Weiss, 2008; Weinberg & Gold, 2015). It has been proven that goal-setting strategies are an extremely powerful tool for improving motivation and performance. However—and this is the significant limitation—only if it is done correctly.

PRINCIPALS OF SUCCESSFUL GOAL-SETTING PROCESSES

Let's take a look at which factors have a positive effect on the effectiveness of goal-setting and goal-attainment processes. And you can use these findings right away if you like.

THE CLASSIC: DO YOUR BEST VS. SMART GOALS

"Do your best" is probably the classic among motivational sayings. However, its effectiveness is limited compared to specific, measurable, behavior-based goals, particularly with respect to long-term development and improvement. Here the SMART formula has received quite a bit of attention. And rightfully so! Someone who sets SMART goals is more likely to achieve them. What exactly does SMART mean? It is essentially about being as specific as possible about one's goals. The general statement: "I want to lower my cholesterol" is less effective than: "I will lower my cholesterol from 290 to 200 by X date, by immediately forgoing that nightly portion of chips, and I will walk/run 3 times a week for at least X minutes. Yee-haw!"

THE SMART FORMULA IN DETAIL

◆ **Specific:** What exactly do I want to achieve? When, where, with whom, how often, how long, in which context? The phrasing of the goal should be as specific as possible. No vague wish, but a specific positive statement.

◆ **Measurable:** How exactly do I or others recognize that I have achieved my goal? Only if I have formulated specific success criteria will I be able to later verify my success or progress.

◆ **Attractive and action oriented:** What makes the goal attractive? What would I have gained athletically and in my life overall? Which important need would it satisfy? What could be the goals behind the goals? Does it fit into my overall life situation? If yes, which specific steps or actions are required to reach the goal? What exactly should be done? What can I do to get one step closer on the path to my goal?

◆ **Realistic:** Is it feasible? Is it an ideal challenge? Can the goal really be achieved independently? Goals should be achievable yet challenging, otherwise you will lose motivation.

◆ **Time dependent:** Precisely when—by what date—do I want to have reached my goal? Without this information, we tend to put things off. Also, without a specific date we are unable to verify success or any progress we have made.

EXERCISE: TURNING WISHY-WASHY GOALS INTO SMART GOALS

Turn the following example goals and other goals from your everyday life into smart goals.

Table 8 Wishy-washy goals and SMART goals.

Wishy-washy goals	SMART goals
Some day I would like to complete the 250 km Atacama Crossing run through the Chilean desert.	On June 3, 2011, after a fantastic week of competing, I will cross the finish line at the oasis village of San Pedro injury free and with my head held high, and will successfully end my psychological experiment. In order to achieve this and to also fully enjoy this adventure, I will train 4 times a week for the next 3.5 months, will acquire the necessary gear, plan my trip, and learn about ultra-marathons.
I want to improve my marathon time.	
I want to have more endurance.	
I want to lose weight.	
I want to be less nervous prior to the start of a competition.	
I want to become a champion.	

(continued)

Table 8 (continued)

Wishy-washy goals	SMART goals
I want to gain mental strength.	
…	
…	
…	

Success is achieving self-imposed goals. If we stick to this definition, the SMART formula provides us with a tried and tested tool to orient our behavior to specific goals and to measure and celebrate successes. This is important because achieved goals have an effect on our future motivation and self-confidence. It is also helpful to write them down, particularly for long-term goals. We are all familiar with the saying: "Out of sight, out of mind." When we can keep our goals before our eyes, they will remain ever present.

FINDING THE OPTIMAL GOAL DIFFICULTY

In your opinion, does it make sense to set particularly difficult, particularly easy, or moderately difficult goals? Or, putting it in slightly different terms, what do training, sex, and studying for an exam have in common? Any idea? Here is the answer: It is the *Inverted U-Model!* Let's take a look at the image below.

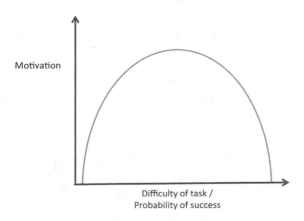

Figure 4 Relationship between goal difficulty and motivation.

Here it is again, the inverted u-model. This might bring back memories of math class. But don't worry if math wasn't your forte! This inverted u-curve applies to many different areas of activity, like, for instance, a well-designed training unit. At first, intensity is relatively low because you need to warm up. This is followed by the central workload, and afterwards there is usually an easy walk-run or cool-down.

If, by chance, you are currently training to become a physical therapist or are studying for an exam, your learning units should proceed as follows: Some light fare to start and warm up with, like, for instance, creating an overview and reviewing the previous learning unit and the learning unit structure. Next comes the main learning phase, during which content is worked out and committed to memory, and finally another relaxing activity like, for example, mentally reviewing the learning unit, tidying up documents, and planning the next unit.

This progression pattern also applies to good sex. First, you get each other in the mood with foreplay. Then you get down to business, followed by after-play, though all of us know that there can be exceptions to this. A really good dinner or menu also follows this pattern. We begin with one or more appetizers followed by the main course, and finally dessert.

This curve is also used in the areas of motivation and goal setting and offers us clues about the relationship between motivation and task difficulty. Imagine that the lower, horizontal axis represents the difficulty of a task and the vertical axis shows the level of motivation. The lowest values are shown at the bottom left, the highest values at the top right. The curve's shape shows that low-difficulty tasks are met with equally low motivation. Interest in such goals quickly fades away. Goals that require little or no effort are relatively mindless from a motivation psychology point of view. But goals that are too difficult to achieve can lead to frustration, decreased self-confidence, and low performance. Since one won't be able to reach the goal anyway, the motivation level is accordingly low. Goals have an optimal effect on our motivation and performance when they are moderately difficult. Or, in other words, when the likelihood of reaching our goal is around 50/50. So the trick is to find an optimal balance between a goal's challenge and the possibility of actually reaching it.

Sounds simple, but it can be quite tricky. Extremely success-oriented athletes automatically set very challenging yet realistic goals and generally reach them, which in turn affects their self-confidence and any future goals. It is different for people who are less driven by their hope for success, but rather by their fear of possible failure. They avoid setting challenging goals and instead tend to set very easy or difficult goals. This is of particular significance to trainers and course instructors who support other people and accompany them in their development. Less success-oriented athletes need to frequently be reminded of the importance of a realistic goal-setting strategy. It is important to be able to properly assess the abilities and personalities of one's charges to offer them the best goal-setting support.

CONVEYING DREAMS TO THE HERE AND NOW: COMBINING LONG AND SHORT-TERM GOALS

The longest journey begins with the first step.   —Lao Tse

Dreaming noble dreams and imagining them in all their glory is wonderful. But those dreams can fizzle if we don't derive short-term goals from the long-term goals. Research shows quite unequivocally that the synergy between short- and long-term goals is essential to success. Long-term goals offer the necessary direction and provide a global orientation. But someone who only focuses on long-term goals usually does not improve his performance (Kyllo & Landers, 1995).

Short-term goals are critical to success because they move us systematically, step-by-step towards our long-term goal while also providing a basis for our ability to monitor or evaluate our progress on the way to the desired long-term goal. Thus we are able to always take a look and see if we are still on the right track. Moreover, achieving short-term intermediate goals gives us a sense of achievement and maintains our motivation. Short-term goals should begin with an athlete's current performance and ability level, and difficulty levels should gradually increase in accordance with increases in ability or fitness level.

The following two methods have proven helpful in combining long- and short-term goals:

1. **The goal-setting ladder or the mountain top as a metaphor**
   Imagine a ladder, or maybe a mountain. The top rung or the top of the mountain represents the reaching of a desired long-term goal. The lowest rung or the foot of the mountain represents the current status quo (i.e., your abilities). Now you need to identify appropriate intermediate goals, step-by-step or rung-by-rung, that build on each other and will take you to your desired goal. Writing down, visualizing, and hanging up or displaying this personal path of development in an exposed location can be very helpful. This method seems so simple and yet it is extremely effective. It has proven successful in working with many athletes all the way to world and Olympic champions (Weinberg & Gould, 2015).

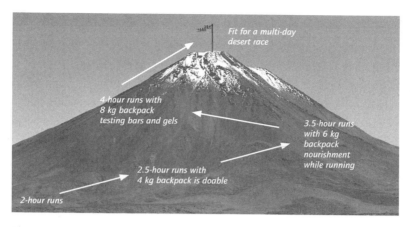

Figure 5 Goal-setting ladder using the Atacama experiment as an example.

2. Backward planning

A second method is borrowed from project management and served me incredibly well during my preparation for the Atacama Crossing in terms of approaching my goals systematically and maintaining my motivation during difficult moments. Admittedly, both versions yield the same results, so it is really just a matter of choice. But deadline-based backward planning might work well and create the necessary commitment for athletes who frequently find themselves putting things off.

FROM EXPERIENCE: ATACAMA EXPERIMENT: BACKWARD PLANNING

Since my preparation time of 3.5 months (or about 15 weeks) was very limited, I created a chart made up of 15 columns, one for each week. Then I earmarked different rows for a variety of things I had to get done because not only did I have to get my body in shape, I also had to get the necessary gear ready, plan the trip, the provisions, and the mental aspects, etc. Here are some examples of my approach to physical training, particularly the long runs.

Instead of starting with the current status quo and planning my preparations chronologically from the present into the future, similar to the goal-setting ladder, I planned backwards from the future to the present. I began planning my short-term intermediate goals with the question: What do I have to complete by the starting shot to be optimally prepared?

The answer: To be able to enter the race as fit as possible in March 2012, I must have completed a two-week tapering phase (i.e., a recovery phase). For the tapering to be as effective as possible, I should complete my final and longest run of four hours just prior to the tapering phase. In order to do well on that run, I should have completed a 3.5-hour run once a week for the previous three weeks, etc. This is how I was able to create a consistent series of intermediate goals. Whenever my motivation lagged and I found myself asking if I could just skip the day's unit, I remembered the backward planning and I knew that if I skipped or postponed this training unit, the entire timetable would shift and in the end I wouldn't be as fit on day X as I want to be.

I saw this before my mind's eye as a kind of timeline or measuring stick that floated above the calendar. You can push it back and forth, but only a little. If I push it too far, I sabotage myself or rather my goals. That thought made my little low disappear instantly, I put on my running pants, and cheerfully started out on my long run in freezing winter weather at 5 AM on a Monday morning.

Table 9 Backward planning for time-sensitive identification of intermediate goals.

	Week														
	1	2	3	4	5	6	7	8	9	10	11	12	13	14	15
Length of long runs			2.5			3			3.5			4-h-Run	Taper	Taper	Start
< Backward planning (from week 15 to week 14 to week 13, etc.)															

WHY WINNERS DON'T ALWAYS THINK ABOUT WINNING: RESULT, PERFORMANCE, AND PROCESS GOALS

RESULT GOALS

When children compete, they usually only think about one thing: winning. It is no different with top athletes. They compete to win, become world champions, get a medal, get a spot on the podium, finish a race in the top ten, outrun a certain opponent, win a certain place in the overall ranking or age group, etc. Of course, this also applies to less ambitious athletes. They focus their attention on the results that don't just depend on their own abilities but, during comparison competitions, that also depend on those of the respective opponents or competitors. Such results are, of course, very valuable, and they can be extremely motivating in the long run (e.g., winning the national championship).

However, there are also disadvantages. Excessive attention on result goals before or during a competition can build unnecessary pressure, lead to fear of failure, and shift the attention to negative thoughts (e.g., what if ...?) instead of staying in the moment. Most important is the optimal execution of actions. And interestingly, that is why winners in particular don't really think about winning before or during a competition, but instead focus on about bringing a good performance. And that takes us to the second type of goal.

PERFORMANCE GOALS

Next to result goals, which by definition always rank our performance against that of other runners, we can focus on performance goals. Here we look only at ourselves. We compare our performance to our own previous performances. When runners and other endurance athletes discuss their goals amongst each other, they make assertions like:

◆ I want to improve my 10K time to 38:40 minutes.

◆ I want to successfully finish ultra-marathon Y.

◆ Next year I want to complete the Ironman in less than 9 hours.

Those are performance goals we can control ourselves. They provide an answer to the question: What exactly do you want to achieve? Goal attainment is specific and measurable. We can control these goals much better, and tweak them when necessary, than we can the result goals, because here we are the masters of our destiny and we don't have to depend on others. Instead of just finishing an ultra-marathon, our excellent preparation allows us to spontaneously refine our goal during the course of the race (e.g., I can finish the 160 km ultra portion in less than 24 hours, regardless of how fast or slow other participants finish). Attractive performance goals can make excellent intermediate goals and thereby serve as a framework for a long-term performance development.

PROCESS GOALS

While result and performance goals (i.e., the question of what you want to achieve) are usually in the foreground, a third very significant kind of goal is surprisingly often disregarded, despite the fact that it can have such a critical impact. Performances and results don't come from nowhere. They are created, based on our actions. But how do we want to achieve our performances and which strategies are employed in what form? And what do we want to feel and experience when everything is going really well?

Since this type of goal deals with specific action-execution processes or performances, they are also referred to as *process* or *action goals*. They offer a detailed response to the question of "How?" in athletic performance. The advantage is that they very effectively make us focus on the here and now, help to avoid distractions and negative thinking, and steer us towards the positive aspects of an experience. The disadvantage is that they are not as good for building long-term motivation.

Example:

◆   Performance goal (i.e., What?): I want to finish the X run in a time of Y.

◆   Process goal (i.e., How?): My legs are loose and so is my head. I will run with small steps to spare my joints, am absolutely sure-footed, and can orient myself very well. At night, I feel fresh, alert, and in a good mood. I enjoy being out in nature and discovering new regions.

And what is the most important thing about running? Of course, it is supposed to be fun! We want to enjoy exercising and being outdoors, to find a flow. Regardless of whether we are training or competing, only when we are in the here and now, feeling good in the moment and letting things flow, can we achieve certain performance or result goals. When that's not the case, we are unable to really tap into our potential. And precisely how and what do you do so you feel good and in your flow while training or competing? (You can find detailed background information and advice on facilitating flow in my book *Flow Hunter: Motivation, Success, and Satisfaction in Running*.)

Research findings show that using a combination of the different types of goals produces better performances than the isolated use of just one type. However, timing is critical for optimal effectiveness. If we focus on a certain platform at the wrong time, it can hamper our self-motivation and self-leadership. It also makes sense to set the appropriate goals for training and competing, because we usually spend much more time training and preparing than we do competing. We can increase the quality of training with specific goal-setting processes while simultaneously boosting our motivation.

EVERYTHING HAS A PRICE: ATHLETIC GOALS WITHIN THE CONTEXT OF OVERALL LIFESTYLE

When we talked about SMART goals, we touched on the importance of always examining our goals to see if they are attractive and realistic. But even when that is the case, it is possible that they may not fit quite as perfectly into the context of our current lives. To put it more bluntly, the goal of becoming a national marathon champion is most likely not compatible with a demanding job in management that requires 60 or more hours a week of an athlete's time and includes lots of business travel. Most of us are probably aware of that. And yet there are always situations where there are conflicts or blocks because the athletic goals just don't fit well into the other areas of our lives.

It is therefore critical to the success of our goal-setting process to look at the goals we set within the context of our life as a whole, and uncover and eliminate possible obstacles. The following suggestions can help identify possible obstacles. If they are transparent and deliberate, that's half the battle, and you can once again work on fine tuning your goal, and, where appropriate, even bring third parties on board during this process.

◆ As the saying goes, everything has a price. What is the price of achieving a certain athletic goal?

◆ Let's assume the goal has been reached. How does that affect me and my surroundings? Am I okay with that?

◆ What might I possibly give up on my way to achieving my goal? Am I, and are others, ready to do so? Who might have objections?

◆ Is the goal really in line with my values, inner needs, and self-image?

◆ Is the goal in line with my goals outside of the sport, with my overall life plan, or with the demands in other areas of my life?

FROM EXPERIENCE: TRAINING MOTIVATION AT ROCK BOTTOM

A female runner from northern Germany contacted me because she wanted help with motivation and mental strength. Her running career was still in its infancy. She had made enormous leaps in her performance over a very short period of time, and now she was about to run the first marathon of her life. Moreover, she already had her eye on triathlons. Her training included a personal trainer. Although she really enjoyed running as an endurance sport, recently certain motivational problems had crept in. Surprisingly she found it increasingly difficult to make herself complete the training units. Even just the thought of training triggered negative emotions. The client wanted compact two-day coaching during which we would work on eliminating the motivational block and practice the ability to purposefully enter a pleasant state of flow to increase motivation.

Her initial response to my opening question (What brings you here?) consisted of lots of interesting information about her circumstances, including the fact that the runner worked in a very demanding leadership position. Instead of talking extensively about the problems, we then switched relatively quickly to the goal level. I asked her, "Assuming the coaching proceeds perfectly, we concentrate on exactly the right areas, and you return home satisfied and with the knowledge that you are on the right track and the changes you hope for are happening, what precisely would have changed, what would be different?" And what do you think happened next? Silence. While the problems were very much present, a specific goal for the coaching results wasn't.

So we started by working on that goal. The result: The runner simply wanted to enjoy running again. We incrementally fleshed out this goal, meaning the runner developed mental images of what it would be like, exactly what it would feel like in different parts of the body, and how it would manifest itself externally and be visible to others that she enjoyed running again. This created a very positive, effective image of the goal. It also became apparent in how shifting the focus from a problem to a goal caused the runner's facial expression and gestures to undergo a positive change in a very short period of time.

We also worked on resensitizing, which is actually the primary motivation for running, to the reasons for starting to run in the first place not all that long ago. The answer came swiftly and caused her to look thoughtful. Ultimately this runner was after primarily one thing and that was to create a relaxing balance to her extremely stressful, time-intensive, and demanding job. But her quick progress and improved endurance rapidly shifted her focus to performance goals, and that inevitably brought up the subject of the marathon and that the personal trainer told the runner that considering her fitness level, a time under four hours would be excellent and a great success. As we know, the runner had adopted this goal, at least on a conscious level. But her motivational problems or blocks indicated that her performance-oriented goal wasn't really in line with her actual needs. The 4-hour goal had imperceptibly built pressure. Once the runner became aware of this in conversation, she was able to make the conscious decision to let go of this less suitable performance goal and shift her focus back to her most important goal: simply enjoying running stress-free.

By implementing helpful self-talk strategies, focusing techniques, and linking thoughts and feelings to certain triggers, we then worked on the idea that just thinking about the next training session should generate pleasant anticipation, and that she would just allow her training to flow and enjoy running. Shortly after working with her, I received a message. The runner had not been this motivated and relaxed in a long time. And since she was once again running completely free of any performance pressure and without any particular times in her head, she felt like she was running faster and longer than she had in a long time. Bingo!

WHAT YOU SEE IS WHAT YOU GET: CAN YOU ALREADY SEE AND FEEL YOUR SUCCESS?

Discipline is simply a matter of purpose. Someone who has his goals in sight can hardly wait for the next opportunity to act.

—Arnold Schwarzenegger

While the goal-setting process is quite rational so far, we will now add an additional characteristic. Our goals really gain momentum when we don't just think about them and see them before our mind's eye, but when we actually physically feel them as though they had been realized. In a way, it is a kind of memory of the future. The more detailed and vivid your image of you achieving your goal is, the more likely you are to achieve that goal. The goals must effectively get under your skin or they tend to fizzle without any effect. The following questions will help you develop a detailed vision of your goal-attainment:

EXERCISE: GOAL-ATTAINMENT SAMPLE

This exercise provides the luxury of experiencing your goal attainment in advance. It makes psychological sense because intensive mental simulation isn't just fun, it boosts motivation and shifts our attention in the desired direction. The exercise also feeds our self-confidence. Take a little time and allow yourself the necessary quiet time to answer the following questions and to imagine them acutely, experiencing them:

◆ Where am I the moment I reach my goal? What do my surroundings look like? What could they look like?

◆ What exactly am I doing at that moment? What do I look like? What do I sound like?

◆ What am I experiencing and perceiving with all my senses?

◆ What am I thinking?

◆ What does it feel like to have reached my goal? Exactly what am I feeling and where in my body am I feeling it?

The repeated use or activation of this image triggers neural priming in the brain. Your impetus to act is activated and guided in the desired direction. It is like walking across a meadow. The first time you do so the path is unclear, so you choose a route and flatten some grass along the way. The more you travel this route the more visible the path becomes, until it is a beaten track showing you the way as you walk across the meadow. You can take your time and really savor this exercise, or periodically use it spontaneously for a quick refresher as you get more experienced.

WELL, DID YOU REACH YOUR GOAL? EVALUATION AND FEEDBACK

To ascertain whether or not a goal has been reached, checkable criteria must be formulated at the beginning of the goal-setting process. That is where the circle closes.

Regardless of whether it is a short-term intermediate goal or your main goal, you should properly reward yourself for your success. It doesn't have to be anything big, but we should be aware of the positive effect of small rewards and acknowledgements. And it goes without saying that reaching a goal sometimes requires a real celebration.

Regular feedback on the progress or achievement of intermediate goals is essential to directing personal development processes. It is the only way to systematically control processes over an extended period of time and make situationally necessary adjustments possible.

Goal-setting processes are always an approximation and, in a way, are subject to the trial-and-error principal. That also means that setbacks and failures are unavoidable, and if lots of successful celebrities are to be believed, they might be the most important ingredients on the path to success. As in other areas of life, it is about getting up when you fall down and handling failures constructively and learning from them.

CONCLUSION

When our goals are a good fit and are well entrenched, many things get much easier for us and we no longer have real motivation problems. And in the event it does happen, we can use that as a signal to reexamine our goals or paths to achieving our goals and adjust them to fit the changing framework conditions. This turns motivation problems into a kind of inner radar and an effective tool for self-improvement.

7-D HEAD CINEMA: LET THE MAGIC HAPPEN

The imagination is a man's power over nature.

—Wallace Stevens

5 7-D HEAD CINEMA: LET THE MAGIC HAPPEN

Who needs a television with 4K resolution when we can see the very best movies of all time anytime in 7D (and without electricity and a flat-screen TV)?! Movies we produce ourselves, whose screenplay we write, whose actions we determine, and in which we play the starring role will likely touch us deeply and move us like no other film ever could. A crazy idea? Yes, maybe so.

In our imagination, anything is possible. Our thoughts are free, virtually limitless. They don't seem to be bound to the laws of physics. Research also tells us that our perceptions and mental images can have a specific physical effect on every cell in our body. This body-mind connection is a miracle of nature. We may not yet truly understand the underlying effect mechanisms in their totality, but that does not keep us from already experimenting with the almost unbelievable possibilities that present themselves in the targeted use of internal imagery to boost our performance, health, and vitality, especially since research has provided lots of corroborating evidence of the positive effects of visualization on learning and athletic performance (Weinberg & Gould, 2015).

In this chapter you will find out how to achieve the following effects through *visualization*, the strategic use of internal imagery:

◆ Boost motivation and self-confidence

◆ Improve fitness level and the execution of movements

◆ Develop functional routines and prepare for eventualities

◆ Positively impact bodily processes

◆ Handle tricky situations more confidently

5.1 VISUALIZATION WITH VIRTUOSITY = 7-D EXPERIENCE PATTERNS

At first the term *visualization* seems misleading. One might think that it is only about visual aspects. Although most people perceive their surroundings primarily through their vision, visualization does not mean that internal images are limited to visual stimuli. On the contrary, it also involves our senses of touch, smell, hearing, and taste, as well as internal and external physical sensations. Visualizations generally become more effective the more sensory and perceptual channels are involved in the formation of internal images, or the more intensely and vividly they are experienced. In this sense, one could almost refer to them as *experience patterns*.

Visualization clearly differs from common visual thinking. Visual thinking tends to generate random internal images that can facilitate fear or anxiety, as well as a loss of focus when they have a negative tinge, which in turn has a negative effect on performance. By contrast, we consider visualization to be a conscious process during which positive perceptions are systematically and purposefully chosen and activated to affect our body-mind system. Chapter 2 already offered an insight into how visualization can affect many different body functions that impact our running performance and our well-being. The consistent focus on positive visualizations blocks out negative, self-limiting, or sabotaging thoughts. This increases the likelihood that we will truly give our best or meet our full potential.

Access to mental imagery can be different from person to person Emotions, colors, and sounds, etc. may be activated Instead of specific images. Of course, we can also use this to meet our objectives. Moreover, the ability to visualize is easily learned and is subject to the state we are in. Vivid images are more easily activated and often more intense when we are in a relaxed state or hypnotic trance.

5.2   VISUALIZATION GUIDE

We are able to play with our internal images in different ways, essentially adjusting them and changing them as needed. Their effect can change based on how they are adjusted. Let's imagine that we have access to internal controllers and switches much like on a stereo system. With these controllers and switches we can

◆ Play internal movies in real time, sped up or slowed down, or even overlaid with a still image;

◆ See things in color or black and white;

◆ Change the sharpness of images, from very crisp and detailed to blurry and downright grainy or washed out;

◆ Fade sounds, smells, and other perceptions and sensations in and out, and change their intensity;

◆ Perceive things with our own eyes from an internal perspective, or from an external perspective as an outside observer of ourselves;

◆ Zoom to an external perspective to be able to focus completely on ourselves or to consciously observe ourselves together with those around us;

◆ Zoom to an internal perspective and shift the focus to specific body parts or regions;

◆ Travel into the future or past and thereby change our handling of difficult, critical, and maybe even consciously blocked events;

◆ Stay very close to the perceived reality or imagine the wildest, most unrealistic things (which interestingly affect reality).

As we can see, the possibilities for designing our inner perceptions are practically limitless. With a little training, we can learn to control these design options and use them appropriately. Let's get started!

EXERCISE: BEGINNING VISUALIZATION: MY MOST RECENT RUN

Take a few minutes and focus completely on this exercise. Remember your most recent training run. Think about getting ready and then taking off. Let the entire training unit pass before your mind's eye like a movie. As you do so, change the perspective. Watch yourself from the outside as though you were flying alongside yourself in a tiny helicopter with a camera, filming yourself. Then switch to observing the running unit with your inner eye. Keep changing this movie's speed (from slow motion to fast forward) and try to let the movie play in your imagination at the same speed as reality. Let the movie play in color and black and white, at times grainy and other times very crisp. Add the sound and turn it off again. Repeat the same with smells, temperature sensation, the sensation of your clothes against your skin, your inner feelings.

And how was it? Easy? Excellent! You are probably a natural or a practiced visualizer. Congratulations! Or maybe it wasn't so easy? No worries, it's a matter of practice and as we know, practice makes perfect. The more you practice visualization, the easier it will become.

EXERCISE: DEFUSING AND SHUTTING DOWN STRESS AND NEGATIVE EMOTIONS WITHIN SECONDS

This next imagination exercise shows how we can influence accompanying emotions by purposefully changing a mental image. Burdensome, negative, or stressful memories or situations often lose some of their emotional dread when we can change our mental image or perception of them. This is helpful, for example, when a failure or disappointment nags at us, when we react emotionally during a conflict, or when we experience an upcoming challenge in advance as stressful.

◆ **Step 1:** Think of a negative or stressful event, in the past or future. Place yourself fully into that situation and start absorbing it from your internal perspective as intensely as possible in every detail. Now rate on a scale from 1 to 10 how strong the negative emotions are with 1 being very weak and 10 being very strong.

◆ **Step 2:** Now think about this event again, but with one major difference. This time you experience the situation from an external perspective as an observer. Imagine observing yourself in this situation from outside or above as though you were floating above yourself. Then rate once more on a scale from 1 to 10 how strong the accompanying negative or stressful emotions felt

◆ **Step 3:** You are watching yourself stand in some room looking at a television screen on which the negative event is playing in black and white. Afterwards, rate the strength of the negative or stressful emotions you experienced on a scale from 1 to 10.

In this exercise, the effect is usually felt immediately. The rating continues to go down from the first attempt to the second, and finally the third. If this has not yet happened with you, repeat the exercise several times and continue to change the mental image (e.g., you could add some happy, fun music). The more we distance ourselves from the mental image the less emotional we are. Instead of obsessing over something, we can consciously back away. Even if we only do it in our imagination, it already has an astounding effect on our emotions and thus on our body. Psychologists refer to this as *associating* or *disassociating*. While it is recommended to experience positive goal images as associated as possible, to completely immerse ourselves and be in the zone, we can learn to deliberately create a distance during negative experiences. This usually decreases negative feelings immediately and allows us to process those experiences in a more constructive way.

Since our thoughts are free we can get creative with the possibilities, but also with the impossible. And often it is the latter that has an astounding effect. Let's take a look at some other possible uses for visualization.

5.3　REMEMBERING A SUCCESSFUL FUTURE: IRRESISTIBLE WISH GOALS, PERFORMANCES, AND RESULTS

I prefer to remember the future.

—Salvador Dali

Let's stick with the television metaphor for a moment and imagine that one evening we have the agony of choice. We could watch a romance movie, an episode of *CSI*, an action comedy, a drama, a documentary, or whatever else we like. And what do all of these formats have in common? First of all, they are a matter of taste, and taste varies. Secondly, if we don't like a program we will most likely switch to a different channel. Maybe we don't change the channel right away, but it will no longer have our full attention. Our mind begins to wander; we start reading a magazine or looking at our phone.

Creating a mental image of reaching a goal is just like television. If we are not truly interested, we quickly change channels and shift our attention to other things. And if there is nothing worth watching we don't even turn the TV on at all. Our motivation works similarly. That's when we talk about *motivation problems.*

In the previous chapter we learned that remembering a successful future is an important element of the goal-setting process. For goals to become irresistible goals and be optimally effective, they must literally get under our skin. When we have internalized them and think about them, our bodies should tingle and we should break into a smile or display a facial expression or gesture that radiates determination. We may catch ourselves clenching our fists as our mind shouts "Yes!" Only when strong positive emotions are attached to our goal, will it generate an appropriate level of energy and motivation and maintain them long term. With respect to my personal activities and projects I would put it like this: The visualization and comprehensive internalization of a goal is successful when I feel an irrepressible desire and great anticipation to reach this goal, while simultaneously enjoying the path with all its individual steps to the fullest. This way I have perfectly combined result and process goals. The latter in particular is an important factor on the path to success: fun, joy, enjoying and being immersed in doing. The goal may be the objective, but so is the path.

SUGGESTIONS FOR VISUALIZATION OF WISH GOALS (ALSO WORKS WITH PROCESS GOALS)
When you imagine yourself reaching your goal, take the time to imagine the situation as vividly as possible. It is very well funded. You are the producer, director, and leading actor all in one. Here you will find a few more suggestions in addition to the detailed information in chapter 4 to help you produce attractive movies about achieving a wish goal.

◆ Imagine you just reached your goal: What do you see, hear, smell, and sense? What are you thinking and feeling?

◆ If this mental image isn't yet a film sequence, make it into a movie—the best movie of all time.

◆ Enlarge your mental images. Make them brighter and the colors more vivid. Give the movie more spatial depth. Put the image in focus!

◆ Add a suitable, stimulating soundtrack.

◆ Add sounds from people that are in the area, voices of people cheering you on, congratulating you.

◆ Increase the positive feelings until they are a perfect fit.

◆ Check to see how the changes to some of the film's aspects affect its appeal, and play around with the possibilities until you feel the performance is perfect for you

You should evoke your objectives again and again and enjoy them to the fullest. For instance, this is easily done at night before going to sleep, but also throughout the day. These visualizations can even be helpful during training and competitions as long as they are used appropriately. Doing so boosts motivation and self-confidence. Dream your goals and live your dreams day by day! Which takes us to the next topic.

5.4   MAGIC MOMENTS: PERFECT MOVEMENTS, PROCESSES, AND SEQUENCES

Imagination is more important than knowledge, because knowledge is limited.

—Albert Einstein

Every goal, every long-term path consists of many individual steps. As we have already seen, intermediate goals are essential for translating noble desires into specific everyday actions, monitoring progress, and making adjustments if necessary. Every athletic success is the result of the sum and quality of individual training units. Every training unit and every competition is the sum of a series of moments strung together. But what matters in the moment? What is important? How do we want to structure it?

Guiding questions for the visualization of processes:
◆ When is a moment a perfect moment, a magic moment?

◆ How would we recognize it?

◆ How would we recognize that everything is going great, that we're happy, and simply give ourselves over to running?

◆ What would it feel like if everything went smoothly and practically ran itself?

◆ Where in our body would we feel these feelings?

◆ What exactly would we do?

◆ What would we look like, how would other people perceive us?

◆ When we encounter unexpected challenges, what do we do to find smart solutions to difficulties and to turn them into a perfect moment?

These are precisely the questions we ask ourselves to define and visualize ideal process goals. By finding specific answers to these questions and translating them into mental images, we have created a perfect foundation: process goals that inspire action in the moment, in the present. By doing so, we greatly increase the quality and the fun factor of our training (and competitive activity) and are able to wholly prepare for impending challenges.

RUNNING WELL AND FEELING GOOD
Most runners probably only worry about two things: running well and feeling good. When we are doing well, we usually also feel good. Whether or not we do well also depends on how we feel and what goes on inside our head. So let's look at how we can influence both factors through visualization.

What determines whether or not we run well? Our fitness level—meaning our strength, speed, endurance, and mobility, but also our coordination, because the better and more easily we can control our locomotor system the less energy we need for the same performance. And it usually feels much different, namely, it feels good. As we saw in chapter 2, external, objectively identical loads can cause varying kinds of internal strain in different people. Even for one and the same person, the same load at different times can result in different amounts of effort. We see it all the time: The same route through the park can sometimes feel easy, while other times we struggle even though the basic external conditions and our fitness level are the same.

Could the cause be our psyche, the emotions and thoughts we carry with us? It is very likely. How can we reduce the strain through visualization and either increase our performance capacity or feel better while bringing the same performance?

The following sections show how we can reduce the strain by using visualization to

◆ improve our overall fitness level;

◆ improve energy efficiency, flow of movement, and running style; and

◆ activate positive, pleasant emotions and thoughts.

HOW CAN WE IMPROVE OUR FITNESS LEVEL?

FROM RESEARCH: THINK STRONG!

Dr. Dave Smith, a British sport psychologist at Metropolitan University, has done a series of studies on the effects of mental training or the use of visualization on physical performance capacity. Among other things, he conducted a test with 18 test subjects, in which their finger strength was measured with a gauge (Smith et al, 2007). Next, the group was divided into three randomly assigned subgroups. Group A then did special finger strength training with 20 repetitions twice a week for one month. During the same period of time, group B also trained twice a week with 20 repetitions, but their finger strength exercises were done only in their imagination (i.e., mentally). The control group did not train at all. After four weeks, the finger strength of all participants was measured again. What do you think the results of the study were? How did the groups progress?

While group A had clearly increased its strength performance as expected (by approximately 30%), the control group's values remained unchanged. But group B, which had completed only mental training, had also significantly increased its strength performance. While the increase was less than that of the physical training group, it still showed a definite increase of 16% as compared to the control group. In addition, electrodes attached to muscles measured that the intense visualization of the finger exercise activates the same muscles as the physical training.

Someone who trains intelligently doesn't always just develop or maintain his strength performance as part of stabilization training. Stabilization training, which targets core strength, has an effect on coordination abilities and thus running style. These muscles prevent premature fatigue as well as biomechanical stress, and therefore have a major impact on our running performance and internal strain. So visualizing strength training pays off. How to do it is quite simple.

EXERCISE: MENTAL STRENGTH TRAINING

Take the necessary time, relax and, as systematically and vividly as possible use all of your senses to imagine yourself completing exactly the same exercises you would normally do. Or maybe you would choose some new, other workouts. Regardless, place yourself in the movement sequence and feel the effort. Imagine what the training would feel like. This will allow you to increase your net training time and train even during times of athletic inactivity due to injury.

By the way, in another study, Smith pursued the question of how the frequency of mental training impacts performance development. Does it make a difference whether I mentally train once, twice, or three times a week? The more often you train the greater your performance increase. This means the use of visualization is the same as physical training. Three or four shorter units per week make more sense than one longer unit, but one unit is better than no mental training. Mental training is also an excellent way to supplement physical training as you build up your fitness level.

OPTIMIZNG ENERGY EFFICIENCY, FLOW OF MOVEMENT, AND RUNNING STYLE

EXERCISE: BOBBLEHEAD

A number of runners occasionally have a minor coordination problem before a run, when they stretch their quadriceps by pulling the heel of one foot towards the back of the thigh and then have to stand still for a little while on one leg. Some definitely start to sway or stagger. Here a simple visualization can immediately work magic and quiet down the system. It is also used in other sports (e.g., ballet) to maintain balance while executing difficult movements or to keep the body centered.

"An invisible cord gently pulls me upward."

Simply imagine that the center of your head is attached to a cord that goes straight up towards the ceiling, gently pulling your body upward and keeping it in an upright position. If this is too easy for you and you are already able to stand securely on one leg while you stretch, practice the exercise with and without visualization while standing on a balance board, ball, or balance beam with your eyes closed. The more advanced version of this exercise can help even accomplished, experienced runners fine tune their overall coordination. And finally, sport scientists recommend always integrating alternative load stimuli into your training. Trail runners in particular require surefootedness and good balance in rough terrain. During dynamic movements, very small rock ledges, pointy rocks, or roots must constantly offer adequate support. In your opinion, which visualization would be helpful in situations like these?

Apart from the esthetic aspects, our running style—meaning the type of intra- and inter-muscular coordination—has a critical impact on our performance and effort. A good running style is very effective because the energy expended is optimally converted into the desired forward movement. By contrast, a bad running style wastes energy unnecessarily, energy that we will likely lack in that critical moment on the way to our performance goal. Or it may keep us from smiling a little more or feeling a little better while we run, which in turn would have a positive effect on our performance or effort. I do not wish to start a debate about the right and wrong running style—that always depends on athletic demands, fitness- and coordination-related abilities, and biomechanical preconditions—but optimizing one's individual running style essentially requires one thing: an accurate motion perception (i.e., a mental image and feel for what this optimal running style should look like and most importantly, what it should feel like).

Do you already have a specific image of your ideal running style?

◆ Yes? Outstanding! Do you also implement this mental image? How did you arrive at this image and what can others learn from you? Share your knowledge while also being aware that others may be built a little differently and have different goals than you.

◆ No? You may think you're not that focused on performance; you're more concerned with enjoying running in a relaxed way. But let's assume you could relax even more mentally and emotionally and enjoy running even more with an easier, more enjoyable running style. Would that not be an interesting approach worth pursuing?

◆   No, but you would like to find out how you can work on your running style through visualization, among other things? Okay, thumbs up and eyes closed!

To make the effects of mental images of movements on actual movements more visible, I invite you to participate in the following experiment.

EXERCISE: MAGIC THUMB

Find a place where you can stand undisturbed and rotate around your body's axis with one arm extended. Plant your feet shoulder-width apart. They cannot move during the remainder of the exercise. Now extend your right arm forward and hold it in a horizontal position while holding your thumb in a thumbs-up position. Use the thumb as a kind of direction finder throughout the exercise, keeping your eyes focused on your thumb. During the first part of the exercise, rotate as far as possible to the right around your axis without twisting your legs or bending your knees. Take note of how far you got by memorizing the place behind your thumb, and then rotate back to the starting position.

The power of visualizing movement

You can now lower and relax your arm for a moment and close your eyes. While standing in the same spot, now with your eyes closed, imagine yourself performing the same movement with your extended arm and your thumb as a direction finder, except this time, imagine being able to rotate at least 8 to 12 inches farther than you did the first time. Repeat this simulation several times. Next, raise your arm once more into a horizontal position and with your thumb up, and, keeping your eyes closed, again rotate around your axis. Rotate as far as you can, and when you can go no further open your eyes. How far did you get during your second attempt? Compare the result with that of your first attempt.

The results are usually astounding. The result after the exercise was visualized is considerably better than during the first attempt. This shows how important the mental representation of the movement is to the actual execution, and what possibilities for improvement through the use of visualization lie dormant here.

USING METAPHORS AND IMAGES TO OPTIMIZE MOVEMENT

So-called *running style analyses* are a very common strategy for getting a visual image of one's actual running style. When a video recording is made of our movements and we are then able to receive immediate feedback, it is a way to provide valuable pointers and makes us aware of possible blind spots. However, we may still miss some critical information. What does my ideal running style look like? And what does it feel like?

The Internet and many books are full of detailed explanations of the optimal running style. This is, of course, helpful for orientation purposes. But from a psychological point of view, focusing on images and metaphors could be more effective for specific implementation because, unlike verbal information, movement metaphors generate right hemispheric mental images in our brain without conscious control. This promotes automatic and smooth movement sequences, which surely is every runner's goal. The bobblehead exercise allows you to experience this immediately. Even just thinking about a cord that gently pulls us upward by the head helps us to optimize body tension and balance on an unconscious level, without detailed verbal movement instructions of what precisely we should do when and how. Our movements are generally ideal when they happen intuitively without any control. The metaphor of the horse and rider expresses this perfectly: You consciously determine the direction while the horse, our subconscious, knows what to do.

Indigenous people on a hunt consciously imitate the creeping and focusing movements of a hunting mountain lion. If you ask athletes from various sports disciplines how to optimally execute a movement, you often get the reply in the form of a metaphor:

◆ Light-footed like a gazelle

◆ Kick it into turbo

◆ Confident like a rock against the waves

◆ As quick as an arrow

◆ As sleek as a cat

A study by Hanin and Stambulova (2002) confirms that athletes intensively use metaphors. They are particularly helpful for changing behaviors and improving performances when the athletes themselves generate them. For instance, the boxer Muhammad Ali thought about the following metaphors when he climbed into the ring for a fight: "I float like a butterfly and sting like a bee". And he lived up to this statement extremely well, much to the chagrin of his opponents.

EXERCISE: AS SLEEK AS A CAT

Let's assume you could see things from the perspective of a graceful cat. What would running feel like? How would you use your legs and plant your feet? What would you hear while running?

EXERCISE: RUNNING LIKE …

How would you describe your ideal running style? Which metaphor comes to mind? Imagine yourself as vividly as possible in that picture and pay particular attention to the way your body feels.

Are there any role models you can look to or runners you like to watch? Is their running style relaxed, smooth, and downright effortless? If the answer is yes, use them as models. Watch their style, then copy it. In your mind, fly alongside them as they run and observe them from the outside. Put yourself in their shoes. Run with their eyes and feel what they are experiencing as they run, what it must feel like to them. Completely immerse yourself in them and their movements. The more intensely and more often you do so, the better and stronger the neural pathways or imprinting become.

It is no longer possible to think of elite sports as working without mental imagery, metaphors, and role models to optimize movement sequences. They are systematical y integrated into physical training or are used as accompanying measures. Try it during your next training units, and as soon as you have found the metaphors and mental images that are right for you and are able to reliably activate the appropriate experienc2 patterns, they will also be helpful during competitions where you should be able to access them as automatically as possible.

ACTIVATING POSITIVE, PLEASANT THOUGHTS AND FEELINGS

There is another important factor that influences our movement flow: our *excitement level.* When we are nervous, stressed, or under pressure, our body is generally tense and our muscles may even tighten up. Of course that has a terrible effect on our fine motor skills, movement flow, performance, and effort. By using humor, relaxation techniques, and visualizations that are linked to fun, light, and pleasant experiences, we are able to counteract this purposefully and effectively. Which visualizations can you spontaneously think of to purposefully bring yourself to relax or laugh? In chapter 6.1, you will learn how to find an entire pool of possibilities for helpful visualizations. As the study by Smith on the effects of mental training on our fitness level has already shown us, visualizing strength training results in a strength increase. This means the mental simulation creates a certain effort that leads to muscle fatigue, which is followed by a *super-compensation effect.* After the effort, the fatigued system recovers beyond its original performance level, resulting in a training effect. But if muscular effort can be increased through visualization, the opposite must be possible as well, reducing effort through pleasant visualizations that counteract the feeling of effort. So let's play with visualizations. Let's .experiment, gather experience, and evaluate what is helpful to us personally.

EXERCISE: EXAMPLES OF SPONTANEOUS VISUALIZATIONS ON AND OFF THE RUN

Try out different visualizations during training and let yourself be surprised by what happens. Keep what you enjoy the most and what helps. Create something new according to your needs and tastes! Be humorous and open. Often the most funny things come spontaneously into our heads; they aren't really comprehensible to others, but that doesn't matter at all as long as they work for us. It is always important that we feel comfortable with them and that we have the feeling that they help us. Here are a few examples that you can try out yourself and use as a starting point for your own creations you could:

◆ Imagine a rubber band attached to your hips which pulls you relentlessly towards your goal (i.e., the finish line).

◆ If it is very windy, imagine yourself effortlessly piercing the wind like an arrow.

◆ When it rains, every drop that drips on your skin triggers even more energy and freshness.

◆ Glide up steep inclines with the ease of a magician.

◆ During long downhill stretches, look down from above and float to the bottom as majestically as a bird.

◆ During long lonely runs, imagine crowds of people who came just to see you, call out to you, smile at you, cheer you on, and run along with you.

◆ Draw energy from invisible channels like the trees you run past.

◆ Imagine there is an invisible power steadily pushing you from behind.

◆ Imagine carrying a backpack filled with helium. You touch the ground very gently and move with ease.

◆ You run as smoothly as this or that animal.

◆ You are as light as a feather.

◆ In addition to these running-related visualizations, you can also let your mind wander far away from running, to other places with other climates, to different times, different activities, etc.

EXERCISE: THE PERFECT TRAINING RUN

Take 10 minutes prior to the start of your next training run. Sit or lie down in a place where you will be undisturbed. Take a few deep breaths through the nose and exhale very slowly. Repeat this process for 3-5 minutes. You will gradually notice that simply focusing on deeply inhaling and slowly exhaling makes you increasingly calmer and more relaxed.

Close your eyes and imagine that your legs are completely loose and relaxed and that your entire body is filled with energy and drive. You are looking forward to the next unit because it brings you one step closer to your goal; it is another piece in the puzzle. You are privileged to be able to practice this sport or hobby, and for that you are grateful.

The closer you get to the moment you start your run, the stronger is your anticipation to enjoy this run. And then you're finally off. Whatever your goal for this unit may be, vividly imagine yourself on your way, strong, smooth, and in good shape, enjoying every step as you pass the different waypoints. With your mind's eye, see yourself cultivating a loose, relaxed, even effortless running style. Let the training unit pass before your mind's eye. Everything seems to work automatically. Keep encouraging yourself. The closer you get to the end of the run the more frequently you can hear yourself say: I feel really good! I could move mountains and keep running much farther. What a perfect training run. And then you take 2-3 quick breaths, open your eyes, go outside, and immediately start running.

This exercise is merely a rough guide to what visualization prior to training might look like. The content is completely up to you. What matters is that it fits you, and that your goals are integrated into the visualization. Will you try completing such a visualization prior to each upcoming training unit? With the right focus on the relevant process and goals, you will likely elevate your training's quality and fun factor.

Have fun at the movies!

THE ATACAMA EXPERIMENT: FUNCTIONAL THOUGHT CONTROL OR VISIONS OF A DEHYDRATED DESERT RUNNER?

When you run through the desert for a week at 113°F (45°C) with all your baggage, you might occasionally have some strange thoughts. It's good when you know how to focus on the important and helpful ones. What follows is a small sampling of strategic visualizations and metaphors that helped me to effectively access my performance while simultaneously enjoying the trip.

OXYGEN KICK VIA MENTAL CAPILLARIZATION

Our performance depends hugely on the energy supply in the working muscles, which in turn depend on the oxygen supply to the muscle cells. While only 3-5% of our capillaries in the muscles are open when we are at rest, during exertion that number increases 30-50 times over. And add to that an enlargement of the cross section; the entire surface area available for the provision of oxygen to the muscles can increase a hundredfold. This results in more blood flowing through the muscles, while at the same time the flow speed decreases. The result is that more nutrients or oxygen can be extracted from the blood in X amount of time. The more oxygen-deficient the blood that flows back to the lungs is the more oxygen can then be absorbed again (de Marées, 1992; Stegemann, 1991).

To optimize this process by appropriately focusing my attention, I vividly imagined how more and more capillary vessels in my body and muscles opened up. Before my mind's eye, an image appeared of a continuously bifurcating supply network that supplied the muscles better and more ideally with oxygen, and as a result I became more efficient and fresher.

SWISS CLOCKWORK, WELL-OILED MACHINE

I supported the aforementioned visual processes with appropriate self-talk by, for instance, telling myself over and over again that all of the cells in my body work together perfectly to bring me step-by-step closer to my wish goal. I occasionally also thought of an absolutely precise Swiss clockwork in which all of the parts, small or large, meshed perfectly and interacted virtually soundlessly, yet 100% reliably, in the background. Or of a well-oiled machine that does its job relentlessly.

EXERTION SIGNAL

To date, I run and train without a pulse monitor and purely by feel. When colleagues talk about pace, I usually have nothing to contribute because I am unable to connect that to my personal information or body sense. But I am aware that this strategy might also have disadvantages. When I start out too fast on a run because I feel euphoric about a major highlight in my life, I might not notice this or that signal my body sends, which can have dire consequences down the road.

I therefore worked out a kind of exertion signal as part of my preparation for the desert run. Trusting in the wisdom of my unconscious, I created a mental image of a traffic signal that automatically gives me feedback about my current effort. Green means everything is optimal, yellow means that I am going a little too fast and should slow down a bit, and red means that I should stop immediately. I can either consciously access this traffic signal in my mind or it can appear on its own as needed. Admittedly, it requires some practice, but I found it to be very helpful.

THOUGHT STOPPING AND 7-D SURPRISE CARLOS SANTANA LIVE CONCERT

I would like to close with a visualization that always generates lots of grins and laughter during my presentations. Why? Because it is pretty weird and has helped me in very difficult situations. You don't have to be able to fully relate to it, but the example illustrates two things:

1. How even unrealistic mental images can be extremely helpful

2. How different strategies and approaches can work extremely well together

After I had already been on my way for several days as a rookie runner in the desert, there was a moment when I felt really bad. I was running on a gravel track in the endless vastness of the desert. Of course I could feel the effects of the previous stages and kilometers. The midday sun was merciless. I could not see anyone in front of or behind me, and there was no aid station in sight. I was thirsty and I started to feel fatigued. I was actually pretty exhausted and sore. For a while I argued with myself, but eventually I was able to recollect myself and firmly said: *"Stop! You can do better! What can you think of that will help you feel better and make things go more smoothly?"* And that's when it came to me, my favorite visualization of the entire race. It linked aspects of my goal-setting process in a playful way with previously identified helpful resources that I used earlier in the course of the race and during preparation.

Carlos Santana, whose song "Try a Little Harder" from the 1970s had accompanied me through my entire preparation as well as the present competition as my number one motivational song, suddenly appeared next to me in person. And it got even better. He hadn't come alone, but had brought his entire band and a few friends. The core band was assembled on a carnival float and played "Try a Little Harder" live and exclusively for me. Since it was one of my key process goals to also view this desert run as a kind of exuberant party, the song was a perfect fit for my experiment. The lyrics really capture the goals and tribulations that many other runners most likely experienced here as well. At the same time the music exudes such a zest for life that you can't help but smile and bop along, even just in your head.

During my preparations, I always linked that song to my goal visualizations, so just hearing the music caused all the positive emotions that were related to reaching my goal to surface. It was incredibly motivating and energizing. So as I was running though the desert, this vehicle with my buddy Carlos Santana's band playing live music travels alongside me and creates a great vibe. It was an awesome show!

Then, while part of the group provided good music and entertainment, some of their colleagues rolled out fresh, moist, cool and fragrant sod right in front of my feet, just like they do in soccer stadiums. Since mentally I was no longer running in dusty, sandy shoes filled with small rocks, I was able to perfectly capture the feeling of my feet being cooled, able to breathe, and running on a pleasantly soft surface. Glorious! I indulged in this surreal mental image, very quickly regained my good humor and felt the fatigue and pain leave my body—or rather my consciousness. I was able to finish that stage with a very good ranking and in a great mood. Party on!

5.5 THE BIG PICTURE: VISUALIZING COMPETITIONS

Success in a competition is more than the sum of successful goal setting and optimal movement. The challenges are complex and multilayered:

◆ How can I rest before the race (if I need it)? How and where can I sleep well to be rested at the start?

◆ What is the best equipment choice? How, when, and what do I eat before and during the competition?

◆ What are the route conditions and orientation like along the way?

◆ What kind of climate should I expect?

◆ What are my biggest challenges? What do I do if ...? What is my plan B? Plan C?

◆ How do I structure my race? What strategy makes sense? What forms of togetherness and conflict should I be prepared for?

We are able to mentally prepare for competitions in different ways; we can go through the entire thing in detail, work with embedded visualizations, and work up solution strategies for potential problems in advance, but there isn't that one strategy that will make you happy and successful. That is why, for the sake of clarification, I would like to present you with two different opposing approaches to preparing for competitions. It's a little bit like a vacation, and many runners actually combine their vacations with running competitions. While some people plan all the details of a vacation well in advance, others book a spontaneous flight and allow themselves to drift from place to place. Both have advantages and disadvantages, and both are primarily a matter of type.

STRATEGY ONE: DETAILED COMPETITION SCRIPTS

My colleague and academic advisor, Dr. Oliver Stoll from the University Halle-Wittenberg, had a dream. That dream rattled around his brain for many years and in 2015, it was finally time. He registered for the 100K run in Biel, Switzerland. As part of his preparation, Oliver gathered as much information as he could, did research, studied experience reports, and built a very comprehensive profile of this competition. Based on all of this information, he developed a very detailed script, a type of meticulous mental time schedule. This script broke the run down into phases or stages, provided information on what precisely would happen when, where what difficulties might lurk, how to handle them, and so on. He memorized this script so the schedule was clear down to the last detail and existed before his mind's eye like a movie. The script helped him to develop routines prior to the race that lent him the necessary orientation and confidence during the competition, along with the motivation to stick with it in spite of some difficult moments (Stoll & Becker-Kopsch, 2015).

Athletes that need security and structure—and who find great pleasure in researching and analyzing detailed information about races—do very well with such competition scripts. Elite runners will also thoroughly plan their race strategy and the competition's progression. But of course the value of detailed scripts doesn't just depend on the individual type and his athletic goals, it also depends on the competition's specific challenges. The shorter and more standardized a competition is, the more sensible it is to create a script that covers every detail. However, a longer, more open-ended, and adventurous competition will make it more difficult to work with meticulous scripts; something else might be more helpful for a one-week run through the Kalahari Desert.

STRATEGY TWO: "GO OUT AND HAVE FUN" (JÜRGEN KLOPP, SOCCER COACH)

Since this chapter includes a lot of talk about images, movies, and scripts, it reminded me of the time I spontaneously produced a movie with my friend Tobias Meinken. This time I'm talking about an actual film you can watch at the movie theater. We had always planned on writing a script for our documentary film *Marathon at Mount Everest: The Highest 42,195 km in the World*. We planned to, but it never happened. To be honest, our unconventional approach to this project earned us lots of sneers. Nevertheless, we thought deeply about this project and let ourselves be guided by a strong vision;

regardless of what happened, whether or not we found a sponsor, we were determined to make an amazing film about the Everest marathon and have fun doing so! We were also aware that this adventure required us to react to the local conditions in Nepal with absolute flexibility. The result was an award-winning documentary that regularly earns us extremely positive feedback.

To some extent, this strategy might also be a reflection of my own current approach to competitions. I personally find the detailed work with meticulous competition scripts based on tons of information about a race too analytical. This kind of overanalyzing is not my cup of tea, and might also put one at risk of ruminating too much and falling victim to *paralysis by analysis*. I frequently encounter runners who nearly drive themselves crazy by absorbing all sorts of information before a race, and then feel conflicted about different opinions and end up spinning in circles.

Running is my hobby and I don't want an event to lose its magic because I mentally picked it to pieces. I set up a framework with goals based on what I want to achieve, and, most of all, what I want to experience on this path. With respect to competition challenges that are new to me, I also think about the key challenges and how I can overcome them. However, I focus on a few key elements I consider critical. The rest comes together on site, during the process.

I love adventure and always try to keep it light even as I tackle major challenges. It might sound crazy for someone to refer to a 250 km run through the Atacama Desert as a party. But it works for me and that is also what my performance and process visualizations look like; of course I want to finish, but I primarily want to have fun and enjoy the process. For me, by focusing on fun, pleasure, and lightheartedness, I don't feel any pressure. Of course that requires a certain amount of flexibility and spontaneity, and a relaxed approach to uncertainty, which is not everyone's thing. But it works for me.

What both approaches have in common is the fact that you cannot get in the right frame of mind for an event by seeing things through rose-colored glasses. You can't work with just wish goals that will then magically program you for success, as some mental trainers promote. *Mental contrasting* is also very helpful because it ascertains—sometimes more, sometimes less—which difficulties, negative situations, setbacks, and obstacles should be expected, and how to handle them. However, the results should then be converted to positive process goals and visualizations.

EXERCISE: VISUALIZING A COMPETITION

Before your mind's eye, visualize how you would spend the evening before an important competition. Everything is going according to plan. You are alone or with the people that really matter to you. The atmosphere is pleasant and you have one last meal that gives you the feeling of your body optimally fuelling up and drawing energy from it. You go to bed and have a very pleasant night, sleep well, and wake up the next morning completely rested. Maybe you already know exactly what you need to do before the start of the race. Everything seems to proceed almost on automatic pilot. But maybe you pay particular attention to preparations right before the race.

No matter what your approach might be, you are aware of a growing sense of anticipation; you can hardly wait to be at the start. You feel a pleasant tingling in your body and an overwhelming desire to take off running. Your final preparations are complete. You stand at the starting line and feel completely confident. Finally the time has come: The race begins.

The start has a liberating effect on you. Imagine yourself running the race of your life from the first to the last stride. You find your perfect rhythm. The energy just flows, and you run nearly effortlessly, enjoying being on the road. Stride for stride, mile for mile, every time you feel a hint of fatigue you think about your goal or imagine your muscles surrounded by a warm, bright light that supplies them with new, fresh energy. Nothing stops you. Your confidence increases as every step brings you closer to the finish line. You spur yourself on, believe in yourself, and really enjoy running.

Maybe you are intensely aware of your surroundings or maybe you are completely focused on yourself. Throughout the race, you keep our eyes focused on the correct route. And then you glimpse the finish line and everything happening around it. You take in this moment as you relentlessly approach your goal. It is within reach. 3 – 2 – 1. Yes, you made it! You reached the finish line, had a perfect race. You feel fantastic, feel your heart beating, feel your breath, your entire body. You enjoy the success, alone or with others. Your body soaks up the atmosphere at the finish line. It was a perfect run.

Of course this is just a rough example of what visualizing a competition could look like. Integrating your individual result, performance, and process-related goals as well as the metaphors you respond to and find helpful will make the visualization optimally effective. And what matters here, too, is that using this visualization regularly can be extremely helpful for putting yourself in the optimal frame of mind for a competition.

(POSSIBLY) FROM EXPERIENCE: SHARKS HAVE TEETH

As the story goes, a coach for a national swim team in Australia thought about how to get an even better performance out of his athletes. Convinced that visualization techniques can work magic, he came up with the following approach.

The waters around Australia are populated by a number of sharks, some of which, at least Great Whites, are considered dangerous. The coach suggested to his squad that during training they should vividly imagine a shark pursuing and gaining on them. It's actually a pretty clever idea. And if that isn't an incentive, I don't know what is. You could argue that this visualization might cause this or that athlete to freeze in terror, or at least make him unable to optimally perform his laps. But it might be worth a try. At least until one athlete raised his hand and asked, "Great, but what do I do after the turn?"

I hope you have lots of fun experimenting with visualizations that are right for you! Be creative and allow yourself to be surprised by what might work for you and the improvements that result in this or that area.

USING RESOURCES

6 USING RESOURCES

Once the goals are mentally and emotionally embedded through the use of visualizations, we focus on *implementation*. Ideally a first critical step has already been taken by visualizing processes and posing the question of how to reach a goal. Brain-appropriate goal management and the use of visualizations are already definite success-supporting strategies, but what else helps us on the path to our goal? What individual strengths and talents could assist us? Which skills are useful, maybe even essential? Are there other resources we can use to help us achieve our goal as effectively and intelligently as possible?

In this chapter you will establish an entire set of individual resources and receive suggestions on how to further develop additional important mental influencing factors pertaining to athletic performance and health. You practice your ability to quickly turn very different resources into powerful visualizations and, most importantly, the ability to optimally access critical skills precisely when you really need them.

6.1   RESOURCE RELOAD: THE SWISS ARMY KNIFE OF MENTAL TRAINING

SOUND FAMILIAR?

You're relaxing at a restaurant or sitting in the car, strolling through a store, not thinking about anything in particular, and suddenly you hear a certain song. A song that automatically, and like the flick of a switch, reminds you of a particularly pleasant experience. Maybe it was a great vacation, your first love, a successful party, an athletic or professional success, or whatever. Immediately your thoughts revel in those memories, bringing back images, situations, and emotions. Maybe you feel a tingling somewhere in your body. Maybe a smile appears on your face and you're aware of a sense of well-being. Whenever we think about the past, we activate areas of the brain where *experience-based knowledge*—knowledge about what we did in a certain situation and what consequences resulted—is stored. It would be smart to tap into this knowledge and use it more systematically for our goal attainment.

DETOUR INTO BRAIN RESEARCH

We perceive approximately 10-12 million pieces of information per second, but very few of them make it into our consciousness. Nevertheless, during every experience, multi-layered information is stored in different areas of the brain: perceptions of our sensory organs, physiological or physical sensations, thoughts, emotions, and behaviors. When we remember past experiences, in addition to these vivid sensory impressions and emotions, those areas of the brain that store information about what we did in those particular situations or how we behaved to achieve certain things are activated.

Experts refer to *tacit* or *experience-based knowledge*, which they differentiate from *factual knowledge*. This knowledge is partly conscious, but often unconscious and thus can only be verbalized to a point (Ufer, 2001).

For example, as I work on this book, I am typing on my keyboard fairly automatically, without thinking about it. My 2.5-finger system makes this process more or less fluid. My fingers find their target and hit the desired keys more or less accurately. But when I am not at the computer and someone asks me to quickly tell him where on the keyboard the letters K, W, F, and Y are located, I hesitate and have to think about it. It usually only works after I've created an image of the keyboard (i.e., by vividly imagining typing something specific). That is also why, as we saw in the previous chapter, using metaphors while learning movements is so valuable.

And what do typing and running have in common? Well, one common coaching goal is to run looser and more relaxed during a competition. If you have experience with fast, loose typing using the 10-finger system, it represents a resource you could use in running. We will come back to this.

Since emotions and bodies are an interactive unit, positive memories and thoughts create positive emotions and a positive energy level within the body. Unfortunately, this is also true for negative memories and thoughts. If you stood next to me right now, I could prove to you how your thoughts affect your performance, positively or negatively, within a millisecond, depending on your thought content. But since I am probably not standing next to you right now, you can do the following astounding experiment with someone else and experience this with your own body.

EXERCISE: THE POWER OF THOUGHT

Find a partner. Standing upright, laterally raise one arm and hold it in a horizontal position. Your task is to hold the arm in this position. Before your mind's eye, transport yourself to a negative experience. Once you have chosen the experience and have immersed yourself in it, let your partner know. He will then try to push your arm down by pressing down on it with his wrist. Please do not use brute force! It suffices to let your partner feel how much power is under the hood.

Afterwards, loosen up a little and take some deep breaths. Next, imagine yourself having a particularly positive experience as you again hold your arm in a horizontal position. Your partner will again try to push your arm down. What do you notice? What differences do you notice between the two attempts? The following usually happens: When visualizing a positive experience, the arm is very strong and can only be pushed down with lots of effort. By contrast, during a negative visualization, the arm often drops almost without any force or at least yields very quickly before the attention shifts away from the visualization to the arm. Below is another interesting variation on this exercise.

A good example of how our thoughts affect our physical strength.

Let's summarize:

1. When we remember successful situations from the past, we are able to reactivate the underlying experience-based knowledge and use it to meet other challenges.

2. Remembering positive experiences—as well as positive thoughts in general—has a positive effect on our mood and body sensations and affects our performance and our sense of well-being.

How can we use these insights to more confidently access our resources—meaning all of the strengths, sources of power, and talents that lie within us or are present in our environment—to meet future challenges? First, by creating reliable access to precisely these resources, and second, by learning to really activate the appropriate resources at the critical moment.

We have now used the word *resources* several times within a short period of time. But what exactly are resources? Simply put, *resources* are all of those things that have in some way helped, benefited, or somehow advanced us. We can find resources in many different areas of life: athletic activity, on the job, family, hobbies, and so on. Resources are always a matter of opinion; something one person may experience as a resource may not work for someone else. What matters is the individual perspective; if I experience something as resourceful or helpful, it is a resource to me. This is why developing suitable individual strategies is so important to the success of mental training or coaching processes.

Resources can be:

◆ Our knowledge, abilities, hobbies, and experience

◆ Our skills, talents, and habits

◆ Past successes, goals achieved, and challenges met

◆ Key experiences, lucky coincidences, and important events

◆ Our personal convictions, values, and attitudes

◆ Character and personality traits

◆ Animals, people, and role models

◆ Friends, colleagues, and family

◆ Job, financial situation, and safeguards

◆ Art, music, movies, images, and poems

◆ Our dreams, visions, and unfulfilled wishes

EXERCISE: THE ABCS OF RESOURCES

This is an excellent exercise for detecting and reactivating helpful abilities, thoughts, emotions, and other supportive sources of strength. Moreover, these resources have a positive effect on our self-confidence. During the first part of the exercise, you will detect helpful resources. Subsequently, you will practice the spontaneous visualization or activation of these resources.

PART ONE: DETECTING RESOURCES
Lay out a chart with four columns. Write the letters of the alphabet in the left column. Label the remaining columns "Resources," "Situations," and "Result or consequence."

For each letter, find one or more resources that begin with that letter. They can be adjectives, nouns, names, catchwords, or whatever pops into your head. These resources can come from very different areas of life. Write down in which specific situation or situations you have experienced each resource or where it has proven beneficial. Afterwards, ask yourself how this resource helped you. What did it lead to? What was the result? What makes it so valuable to you? You can proceed alphabetically or skip from letter to letter. Be creative.

Apropos: Creativity research suggests that when the obvious solutions or aspects have already been ascertained, valuable ideas will still follow. So take your time and keep trying, even when the initial euphoria has subsided.

Table 10 Example of the ABCs of resources.

Letter	Resource	Situation	Result or consequence
A	Adventurous	Difficult mountain climb done alone in 2009	Believe in one's own strength and improvisation skills. Attitude: What's important in life? Insight: Often less is more.
B	Berlin	Finished marathon in 2 h 29.07 min	Insight: Running hypnosis and strategy worked great and will be used in future.
C	Cecilia	Various conversations, my wife believes in me and has my back.	Self-confidence, trust, love, and life's happiness
	Cello concert	Recent Christmas concert. Went great, flowed without having to think about it.	I know what it's like when even difficult things run like clockwork.
(…)			
Z	Confident	In spite of difficulties preparing for race X, I always believed I would succeed and never lost focus.	Didn't allow pressure to build; stayed focused; celebrated intermediate steps and successes.

PART TWO: ACTIVATING RESOURCES

After you have created your ABCs of resources, spontaneously and randomly choose letters from the alphabet and then mentally place yourself in one of the resource situations. Try to feel this visualization as vividly as possible. After a while, switch to a different letter and again immerse yourself in a resource situation. Or have a partner call out a random letter and then mentally place yourself in an appropriate situation; tell your partner what you see, hear, smell, feel, and think. As you do this, take note of the changes in body language, facial expressions, and gestures.

This exercise is perfect for practicing the ability to quickly place oneself in *resource states*. Or in other words, we learn and practice to activate mental, emotional, and physical states, or to experience patterns that can have an immediate positive effect on our motivation, performance, stress, and sense of well-being. The more we practice this, the faster and more vividly we will be able to do so in the future. It's basically mental training! And the more resources we have at our disposal during difficult moments, the better. Moreover, these resources hugely increase self-confidence because they help us zero in on our strengths, talents, positive experiences, and all of our major and minor successes that have sometimes been forgotten in the course of our hectic everyday lives.

Furthermore, this exercise is an ideal source of material for the *resource reload*, which is focuses on making certain mental resources available on demand for specific future challenges. Let's take a look at how it works.

RESOURCE RELOAD: ACTIVATING UNCONSCIOUS STRENGTHS ON DEMAND

The goal of *resource reloads* (Ufer, 2013) is to create reliable access to motivational, performance-enhancing, or otherwise beneficial resources on demand so that the processes on the way to our goal will run as smoothly as possible.

A large part of our behavior is automatic, based on the idea that if situation X occurs, do Y. These connections are usually learned or result from systematic training processes during which many repetitions and growing experience turn conscious knowledge into unconscious skills. We know this from driving a car (e.g., for example, whenever we turn, we use our blinker or whenever the engine has reached a certain number of RPMs, we shift gears). While beginning drivers are still pretty overwhelmed during their first driving lesson and must pay lots of attention to confidently operate the car, after a certain amount of practice these processes take place virtually automatically and in the background without our having to focus much attention on them.

Of course we should also use such conditioning for our mental training by deliberately linking a resource—an experience pattern—with a situation during which we wish to access precisely that resource (e.g., whenever situation X arises during a competition, activate resource Y). The goal is to develop individualized routines and then let them proceed automatically at critical moments (Mischel, 2014). That allows us to better harness our strengths, abilities, and talents during future challenges.

EXERCISE: FUNCTIONAL AUTOMATISMS

Which three attractive if-then links would you like to put into practice more often or better in the future during your everyday life?

Table 11 Establishing functional automatisms via if-then conditioning.

If (Situation or experience)	Then (Resource)
If I feel pressure or anxiety building,	I immediately relax with this or that breathing technique.

In order for a resource reload to be successful, it is important that we determine specific key impulses whose presence will automatically activate the desired resource or link it to the challenge. There are various ways to do this.

KEY TO RESOURCE ACTIVATION
◆ Internal keys: catchwords or phrases, mental images, visualizations, symbols, thoughts, emotions, gestures, music, or something similar to remind ourselves of our strength and to activate it.

◆ External keys: external stimuli or situational circumstances such as the starting signal at a race, the presence of rain or darkness, an opponent's attack, etc.

◆ Sometimes what was originally an internal key (e.g., a catchword or image) can become an external one when we put it on a card that we hang in a prominent spot or place somewhere to fuel our motivation whenever we pass by.

The key is then used as a kind of switch based on the premise that whenever key X arises, resource Y is activated. For instance, I tell myself or I imagine that if I retie my running shoes just before the race (key) or when I hear the starting signal (key), then I will consciously or unconsciously remember the sublime feeling of confidence that I had after that fantastic presentation I gave last month in front of the company's biggest client where I managed my time perfectly (resource) or the day I finished a race with a surprise PR (resource). As always, it is very individualized, and as you can see, it is possible to link multiple resources and trigger stimuli, which can make the whole thing even more effective. But maybe we should begin with a slightly simpler resource reload.

EXERCISE: RESOURCES RELOAD IN PRACTICE

1. Set a suitable goal.
2. Determine helpful resources.
3. Detect resources.
4. Activate resources.
5. Link resources to triggers or future challenges.

The resources reload consists of five phases. Actively go through these, using a key resource. Following this, you can increase the complexity at your discretion.

GOAL SETTING

We already focused extensively on brain-appropriate goal management. It is important to first find consistent answers to the following questions: What do I want to achieve? How do I want to achieve it? What do I want to experience in the process?

DETERMINING HELPFUL RESOURCES

Exactly what are your key challenges? What are the defining factors and critical moments on the way to achieving your goal? Building on those, consider which abilities, strengths, emotions, behaviors, sources of external support—in short, which resources— are necessary or useful for a particular challenge in order to achieve that goal in the manner you wish.

DETECTING RELEVANT RESOURCES

In which situations inside and outside the sport have you already demonstrated the respective resource? Important: It should not come as a surprise to you that the context within which the resources have already been exhibited is insignificant since we can make them available for other areas. The practice examples illustrate this very well.

ACTIVATING RESOURCES

Mentally place yourself in the situations in which you have already exhibited the resources. Let the situation come to life before your mind's eye; use all of your senses to fully experience the situation. What do you see, hear, and smell? What do you feel where on your body? Which thoughts run through your head? As always, what matters is this: The more vivid and intensive, the better.

LINKING A RESOURCE TO FUTURE CHALLENGE

◆ **Version A:** Once the visualization of the resource has been optimally activated, listen for a catchword, sentence, image, or gesture to come to mind, and embed the resource within the future challenge with the following strategy. Tell yourself that whenever you tell yourself that word or gesture, you will remember that resource. Practice this again and again, and over time you will enter the respective resource state quicker and more vividly. To really fully embed the resource, first do this activity seated with your eyes closed, then with your eyes open; then while you are walking, and then while you are running.

◆ **Version B:** Prior to a challenge, visualize how the resource is activated while you master the challenge. Continue to repeat to yourself that when situation X arises, you will automatically remember that resource. Imagine yourself also working with your own internal keys during the challenge, and notice how they unfold or increase their desired effect.

We can have a very refined approach to perfectly fine tune the whole thing. We can develop an entire network of resources with the appropriate triggers that are available to us at critical moments and even amplify each other automatically. The use of self-hypnosis is particularly effective in detecting unconscious strengths and abilities, and to tune or support our internal autopilot so the necessary resources are available on demand in situations where we need them.

FROM EXPERIENCE: TESTING IN FLOW, RUNNING IN FLOW (OR, WHEN YOUR FINGERS BECOME YOUR ROLE MODEL)

At some point, a newspaper published an article about my work under the topic *World Champions of Training*. My research found that there are people who are definitely able to achieve certain things and who always demonstrate that ability during training, but in serious situations, like competitions, these people appear to experience a block and are unable to access their abilities they way they would like to. They never live up to their potential. One runner read this and contacted me with the following question: *"Hello Mr. Ufer, the topic World Champions of Training reminds me very much of my own problem, although it has nothing to do with sports. My job requires me to get a driver's license. According to my driving instructor I am a very good driver, but as soon as I take the driving test, I come unglued. Nothing works. It's been years. Can you help me? Oh, by the way, the next driving test is in four days!"*

When I asked him how he wanted to experience the test, what he wanted it to feel like if everything went perfectly, he replied that he would be focused, yet relaxed, would have everything under control, and would not begin to worry. To the question of where in his life he had previously experienced this, he replied, "While playing computer games."

As a result, I strongly encouraged him to mentally place himself in the experience pattern of playing computer games, to subsequently link this experience pattern to a series of key stimuli on the day of the driving test. There were so many key stimuli, which occasionally appeared simultaneously, that he could no longer avoid them. Of course, I cannot provide a transcript of the one-hour coaching session, but for clarification purposes, here are a few of the links we established:

◆ As soon as the alarm clock went off in the morning, he would look forward to the test as though it was going to be the best computer game session of his life.

◆ The moment he got in the car and felt his weight sink pleasantly into the seat, he would enter a focused but relaxed state in which he is mellow (like he would be while playing computer games) but still aware of anything important, and in which things seem to proceed automatically without you having to consciously think about it.

◆ When he turned the ignition key and the car started, then he would…

After years of suffering, the candidate passed the test. He claims the resources reload played an important role because he had never been so relaxed while still feeling focused and wide awake.

Here is another example. During her coaching session, a female runner had identified a job-related resource as helpful that at first glance did not have much to do with running: typing with the ten-finger system. She was an executive secretary and very adept at receiving lots of information while simultaneously processing it or converting it to nearly error-free text at lightning speed without having to think about it. To do so, many muscles and ten hard-working fingers use fine-motor skills and coordination to work together. As soon as you think about it too much, the process falters. Do you see parallels to trail running here? In any case, this woman successfully used this personal resource to overcome some challenges during training and competitive runs.

THE ATACAMA EXPERIMENT: MULTIPLE RESOURCE RELOADS

SMOKING FEET?

During my preparations for the Atacama Crossing I was able to identify one aspect as instrumental to the success of this venture: the feet. During a multi-day desert run, the heat makes them swell, the sweat macerates the skin, sand and rocks have a sandpaper effect, and the weight of the backpack adds pressure from above, for hours, for days. No wonder many runners suffer from giant blisters and deep wounds, which make progress more difficult or can seriously jeopardize a successful finish. My process goal was clear and I planned to stay very focused on it: to keep my feet as fresh as possible. But what exactly should that feel like?

Were there past situations I could refer to? That reminded me of a brief vacation during which I walked barefoot on the beach, right along the water's edge. I created a vivid mental image of this experience—the water rhythmically washes across my feet and a pleasant breeze amplifies the cooling effect. I am not strolling alone, but hand in hand with my wife Burcin. In addition to the vivid feeling of freshness. there is a feeling of deep love and gratitude, and the knowledge that both of us truly value the small things in life. It is refreshing, grounding, and relaxing.

I linked this resource to different triggers during the race, and for a little variety I also used a slightly modified form. Instead of strolling on the beach, I imagined myself walking barefoot in an alpine meadow with my wife. Again, I could virtually feel the soft grass and the dew. Here is what's important: While beautiful images appeared before my mind's eye, the feelings were what mattered most. I therefore periodically focused purposefully and intensely on my feet to generate the same sensations there, while still being aware of and enjoying the beautiful landscape.

THE LICANCABUR SYMBOL

The Licancabur is an approximately 6,000 m (19,685 feet) high volcano on the border between Chile and Bolivia. During my search for resources or situations in which I had already given an, in my opinion, exceptional endurance performance in a tough environment, I remembered my solo climb of this volcano a few years earlier. On the way to the top, I had caught up to a biathlete and his guide. We climbed the final meters together, during which the biathlete had to take regular breaks and did not look particularly happy about it, but commended me for my strength. The view from the summit across the Atacama Desert and the Bolivian Altiplano was incredible; the feeling at the top was sublime.

Whenever I imagine Licancabur, I activate that incredible feeling of pride and strength I felt back on that mountaintop. At the same time, my body is flooded with the certain knowledge that I am able to handle strenuous and exotic adventure projects quite well. And the following was the kicker in this whole thing: The Licancabur is a very prominent landmark and was quite frequently visible during the race. I did not have to imagine it (like I did during my preparations). Again and again I simply looked upon this beautiful mountain and practically brimmed with strength and self-confidence.

It is always very exciting to see the variety of personal material that surfaces when we engage with our own resources. In a way, every successful resource reload is also a wonderful expedition into one's self.

A volcano as a resource

6.2   FOCUSING ATTENTION: LEARNING FROM THE GRAND MASTERS

Once you have worked through the resource reload explanations, you might justifiably ask yourself the following question: If I have to permanently imagine certain things or if I am supposed to do this or that with my feelings, is there even any time left for running? Am I not already fully occupied with just my mental strategies? Or in other words: When should I focus on what?

If we ask around the scene when which strategy helped whom, the answer unfortunately won't be any easier. For instance, top runner Paula Radcliffe tells us that during marathons, counting to 100 three times (which is a mile) allows her to focus just on the moment instead of how many miles she still has to run. At the same time, she focuses on her breathing and steps (Kolata, 2006). Other athletes focus on their physical sensations, on the back of the runner in front of them, the spectators, the scenery, music, mental images, math problems, etc.

FOCUS! BUT HOW? ASSOCIATION VS. DISASSOCIATION

Sport scientists and psychologists have long tried to figure out which concentration strategies are more promising while running. In doing so, they differentiate two basic types of concentration: *association* and *dissociation*. We either concentrate on the act of running, the race, or managing the athletic task. We focus on our breathing, physical sensations, pace, pain, and motion sequences. This also includes monologues like "Keep going!" or "Relax your shoulders!" Here we refer to *association*. Or we distract ourselves and shift the focus away from the actual task at hand, away from running or the race. We might, for instance, look at the scenery, count trees, daydream, solve math problems, thing about problems at work, listen to music, etc.

These terms have already come up during the visualization topic, but here they have a slightly different meaning. And maybe the term *dissociation* isn't such a perfect choice because in psychology it also describes clinical, pathological phenomena or personality disorders. But this wording is generally accepted in running and endurance sports and is actively debated within the scene. Because runners and scientists are searching for the answer to the question: What is better, association or dissociation?

EXERCISE: WHAT I FOCUS ON WHILE RUNNING

When you think back to your most recent runs, which associative or dissociative strategies did you employ? Compile and weight them, with the most frequently used technique at the top, then the second-most frequent, etc. Next to each item, list the effects it had on you.

Table 12 Weighting association and dissociation.

Association > Effect		Dissociation > Effect	
1 ...		1 ...	
2 ...		2 ...	
3 ...		3 ...	
Etc ...		Etc ...	

So do you tend to use associative or dissociative techniques? In which situations do you use them and what determines their use? Are there differences between training and competing? Which ones do you find particularly effective and why?

Maybe you had some trouble with allocation? That would not be surprising since many strategies aren't necessarily an obvious fit for one of the two categories. For instance, when Paula Radcliffe counts to 100, on the one hand it has little to do with the task of running, meaning it is dissociation. But on the other hand, it helps her to stay focused on the moment, possibly even to synchronize her thoughts and running rhythm in the here and now. Isn't that also association? What other examples can you think of where allocation is difficult? Or maybe you can even think of additional subcategories to further differentiate associative and dissociative actions? The following illustration shows how we can further divide the original categories into an *internal* and *external*, as well as a *narrow* and *broad form of attention deployment* (Stevinson & Biddle, 1998).

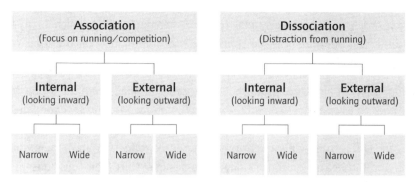

Figure 6 Focus of attention while running.

Masters and Ogles have compiled 20 years of research on this topic. Although the research results on the effects of the two different ways we focus attention are not consistent and there were a number of methodological problems, certain trends can still be seen.

Most runners prefer dissociative strategies, and that's good because deliberate distractions from the struggles, exertion, and pain of a long run reduce symptoms of fatigue and thus individual stress. The result is that dissociative techniques evidentially increase endurance performance. This was proven most impressively in a number of studies. It also sounds reasonable that one should be able to run longer when there is less awareness of the pain, and one feels better and is enjoying the scenery, etc. So much for the advantages of dissociation, which are also its disadvantages. Because we are less focused on running-relevant bodily processes, we risk ignoring important information that we should be using for our self-regulation. It happens again and again that less experienced runners go out too fast in those big city marathons because the atmosphere along the route and all the hustle and bustle make them feel so euphoric, or they still bristle with energy at the start. That often comes back to haunt them later in the race and causes unpleasant and even painful moments (e.g., hitting the wall), as well as worse performances or slower times.

By contrast, very experienced, performance-oriented, top athletes are more likely to use *associative strategies.* They consider the precise sensory feedback regarding their body as essential to their performance (Birrer & Morgan, 2010). Only when they have a differentiated view of their bodily processes such as breathing, pain, and tightness in the leg muscles and the shoulders can they make appropriate, race-related adjustments to their pace. Incidentally good, performance-oriented runners place their associative focus primarily on one thing: optimizing fine-motor coordination—and thus their running economy—by relaxing the locomotor system (Birrer & Morgan, 2010) which in turn has a positive effect on performance (see chapter 6.7 for information on the topic of movement flow and running style).

Strictly speaking, that would take us back to our process goals and the resource reload; exactly how do I want to do something and *what do I want to experience* when everything goes smoothly? The advantages of associative techniques are also their disadvantages, and this is true even for performance-oriented runners. Marathoners who focus too much and too heavily on their bodily processes may shift their consciousness too much towards negative perceptions such as fatigue and burning muscles. According to a study by Stevinson & Biddle (1998), they experience the phenomenon of hitting the wall sooner and should practice doing only brief body checks.

Of course, next to personal goals, the demands of the actual competition (e.g., the length of the race) is also an influencing factor. In summary you could say that the shorter and faster, meaning the more intense a workout or race is or the faster a runner wants to be, the more he will focus on associative techniques. Dreaming about taking a walk through a juicy meadow during a 5,000 m track race to keep your feet fresh certainly isn't situation appropriate and would probably diminish the performance. But it would almost certainly help someone who is running for 18 hours or longer in an ultra trail run while carrying a 17-pound backpack to occasionally take his mind off his aching muscles. You don't have to be a prophet, psychologist, or sport scientist to come to that conclusion.

Ultimately, both fast performance-oriented as well as slower (pleasure) runners use both strategies alternately and can benefit from them, albeit to different degrees. The U.S. sport psychologist Nideffer postulates that we are in a state of optimal performance capacity when we can switch back and forth at will between the different forms of attentiveness (Nideffer, 1976; Nideffer & Sagal, 2001).

Since it is often not possible to draw a definite distinction between association and dissociation (Summers et al., 1982) and we already possess powerful tools through the use of process goals and resource reloads, I would like to direct your attention to the world of chess- precisely those tools.

WHAT CAN RUNNERS LEARN FROM GOOD CHESS PLAYERS?

We have learned, from previous remarks regarding goals, visualization, and resources, that we are able to consciously direct our attention to aspects of the present, past, or future in order to activate optimal resources. Moreover, we are able to distinguish between *conscious* and *unconscious action control.* The previous model (*association/dissociation*) is based primarily on the assumption that attention is consciously directed to different aspects of our experience to optimize self-regulation. Of course that can be tricky since, on the one hand, the capacity of our brain for conscious perceptual and work processes is extremely limited as compared to unconsciously occurring processes, and on the other hand, the more intuitive or automated an athletic performance, the better it is.

For this reason, I would like to think outside the box and see what inspiration we might find outside of running and sport psychology, namely from chess players. Now you may think that chess isn't a sport, but I believe it is a sport, namely a mental sport. And since we are talking about developing mental strategies, this brief excursion is well worth it. So let's take a look at what distinguishes really good chess players from less good ones or amateurs, and transfer those findings to running.

FROM RESEARCH: HOW DO EXPERTS CONCENTRATE?
A very enlightening experiment on the development of expertise was conducted within the scope of scientific research that, in my opinion, can provide us with a solution, a simple key to the ability to optimally focus our attention.

Figure 7 The chess experiment.

What distinguishes amateurs from experts? Due to a vast amount of practice, the latter are able to complete complex tasks and handle challenges extremely fast without having to think about it. The perceptive ability and recall of experts in the area of special skills is clearly superior. De Groot (1965) proved this with his chess experiments. You can try the following experiment right now, if you like.

Expert chess players, average players, and novices or amateurs were given the following task: The participants were shown different chess positions on a chess board for five seconds each, and afterwards were asked to reconstruct the positions. How many chess pieces do you think the participants were able to place correctly? And once you have tried it yourself: How many chess pieces do you remember? The beginners averaged about four pieces, which approximates the channel capacity of our working memory, meaning the amount of information that can be consciously processed simultaneously. By contrast, the experts were able to reconstruct 20 pieces. That far exceeds the normal capacity of a working memory. They developed so-called *chunks* in which many important constellations of characteristics from a certain situation are condensed into a single unit of information (Simon & Gilmartin, 1973). What a layperson sees as 20 individual pieces of information (i.e., the positions of chess pieces) that have to be processed, the expert sees as a single piece of information (game position X).

Experienced experts are able to process multiple pieces of information simultaneously and can promptly adjust their essentially automated actions without having to think about it. And here, I believe, lies a key to optimally focusing and improving performance capacity in runners.

Instead of assuming that we must always consciously focus on this or that, we should learn, analogous to the chess experiment, to automatically access a network of helpful experience patterns and resources on demand and (this is the critical part) without consciously having to think about it. Of course we still have conscious control, but lots of things can run on their own in the background. It is precisely this ability that makes an expert and that helps runners to run masterfully or achieve personal goals faster, smarter, and more relaxed.

Let's take another look at the example of Paula Radcliffe. Most likely we would already feel overwhelmed by continuously counting to one hundred during a marathon when we are already at our limit, constantly starting over again while also trying to control our breathing and strides. For her, it is probably like child's play and completely automated while she also thinks about her strategy and keeps an eye on the field, etc.

The key to success is to develop unconscious mental routines or automatisms in which helpful, beneficial experience patterns are activated as much as possible without having to consciously direct our attention. This key generally doesn't just drop from the sky, but must be acquired or perfected through experience from practice. In view of that fact, I cannot help but invite you once more to regularly practice and refine. It is relatively easy, highly effective, and possibly also your key to a performance beyond what you previously imagined possible.

THE ATACAMA EXPERIMENT

As previously mentioned under resource reload, I had determined a number of key stimuli beforehand and linked them to the appropriate resources, meaning I created functional if-then links and rehearsed them (Mischel, 2014). Whenever a key stimulus occurs and I consciously or unconsciously perceive it, the respective resource is activated (i.e., the mental focus is directed to the corresponding experience pattern). But what happens when different triggers or key stimuli overlap or merge? Staying with the original example of a beginning driver: Often the beginner breaks a sweat upon approaching an intersection in a busy big city, has to use the turn signal, shift, check the mirrors, observe the traffic laws and all of the other more-or-less rule-abiding traffic participants, while simultaneously processing the driving instructor's directions. On the other hand, someone who has been driving for a few years recalls these complex focus attention patterns automatically without having to think about it.

And that is exactly what happened during the Atacama Desert experiment. While I activated pleasant sensations of freshness in my feet, I could simultaneously perceive the Licancabur volcano and remember the sublime situation on the summit. Most likely one of the songs on my internal playlist stored in my head was playing and allowed me to cheerfully skip through the hostile desert. And while I was having a conversation with a fellow competitor and had to give him my conscious attention, in the background my unconscious traffic signal did its job and alerted me with blinking red lights before my mind's eye, that I was going a tad too fast.

6.3   SELF-TALK: HOW WE CAN CONSTRUCTIVELY GUIDE THE VOICES IN OUR HEAD

Pay attention to your thoughts, for they will become words. Pay attention to your words, for they will become actions. Pay attention to your actions, for they will become habits. Pay attention to your habits, for they will become your character. Pay attention to your character, for it will become your fate.

—Talmud

Whenever we have a thought, we are basically talking to ourselves. Sometimes we do so silently and only in our mind, other times we say them out loud. Rarely are there moments when we aren't thinking of or about something, and the manner in which we do so has a significant effect on the way we feel, our self-confidence, our reactions to certain situations, and finally on our performance or goal attainment. In chapter 4, we covered the power of language, but due to its enormous importance, I would like to revisit this topic and add to the previous information. I think the best way to start is with a brief exercise.

PARTNER EXERCISE: THE POWER OF THOUGHT, PART 2

Stand upright again and laterally raise one arm. Your task is to hold the arm in a horizontal position. Then you say, loudly and clearly, "I hate stbility exercises." At the same time as you are speaking, your partner tries to push your arm down. Afteward, repeat this, only the second time, say, loudly and clearly, "I love stability exercises!" Your partner will again try to push your arm down and feel the strength in your arm. Compare the two versions. You will be astounded by how much your strength is improved when you use a positive experience pattern with the words "I love ...". You can also try out the exercise with tempo training, long runs, etc.

Speaking of love-hate, many recreational runners love the idea of a nice, healthy, robust, efficient body and a successful finish, but the process to get there also includes aspects we may not like so much, maybe even hate. We can often hear runners say, "I hate this!" or "I hate that!" Such self-talk has a negative effect and brings about mental stress, unconscious resistance, more or less noticeable but present muscle tension, etc. By speaking this way, we make the process, the path to our goal, unnecessarily difficult. It is better to try and find something positive in everything and put it into words inside our head.

"I enjoy or am looking forward to stability training. It is a way for me to spend important time on my core and with each training session I get stronger and improve my posture and endurance." Another example is "I don't like running uphill." What would be more helpful? May be I don't need to say, "I love running uphill" even though that could have an enormous effect (see practice example). But why not say, "I love running uphill and look forward to every yard. It makes me more efficient and tougher every time I do it"? Just try it with your next climb. Surely it will be more helpful than thinking, "Ugh, this is difficult and exhausting."

If you feel that the previous exercise is too far removed from running or you don't have a partner available, try the following exercise.

EXERCISE: SELF-TALK AND RUNNING PERFORMANCE

Find a nice track or a short circular course where you can repeat several intense runs of the same distance. After the warm-up, you will directly experience the effects of negative and positive self-talk on your running performance or speed. For instance, on a 400 m track you could run the first 100 m as fast as possible while constantly telling yourself, "I am slow, tired, and tense." Next run a 100 m recovery through the turn before running the straightaway as fast as you can while telling yourself, "I am fast, fresh, and relaxed." Repeat this combination several times. It is interesting to see how these small manipulations cause a change in speed and the physical and emotional state.

Let's take a more systematic look at the different versions of self-talk. We can differentiate the following types:

Positive self-talk
◆ Activation ("Stick with it").
◆ Self-confidence ("I feel good").
◆ Instruction ("Take small steps").
◆ Controlling fear and excitment ("Calm down").
◆ Resource trigger ("Key word for ...").

Negative self-talk
◆ Negatively worded instructions ("Don't hike up your shoulders").
◆ Worry ("I can't make it").
◆ Detachment ("I don't feel like it anymore").
◆ Physical fatigue ("My feet hurt").

Neutral self-talk
◆ Irrelevant thoughts ("Later I'm going to meet Kevin").

Positive self-talk helps control the focusing of attention, improves motivation and mood, increases self-confidence, and activates important resources (keys for if-then conditioning). It significantly contributes to our ability to meet our full potential, no matter what our goals may be. The longer the distance of a training run or competitive race, the more helpful neutral self-talk can be (dissociation).

Negative self-talk hinders us. It can downright sabotage our performance and goal attainment, as it neither directs our attention to important aspects of performance development, nor does it promote positive, helpful emotions. On the contrary, it makes it more likely that we experience fear, self-doubt, and tenseness.

Positive self-talk and self-directions that contain negative wording ("Don't be so tense") can also have a negative effect. In any case, they unnecessarily complicate things. For instance, golfers who receive very specific instructions to avoid making a certain error, when under pressure make precisely that mistake more often. Soccer players who have been given the instruction to place a penalty kick anywhere in the goal but the lower right corner, look at that corner much more often than any other place in the goal, which makes their focus and thus an optimal execution much more difficult (Janelle, 1999; Weinberg & Gould, 2015). While running, we have much more time to sabotage ourselves with negative self-talk, or at least make life more difficult than necessary. So let's pay close attention to the things we whisper and say to ourselves.

What exactly does our self-talk during everyday training and competitions look like? According to a study by Hardy and Colleagues (2009), athletes that keep a journal about their self-speech are much more aware of their negative self-speech and the resulting negative consequences. They use this awareness to make their internal monologues and thoughts more constructive, which can have a crucial effect on their personal goal-attainment.

EXERCISE: JOURNAL OF MY SELF-TALK

Make a list of typical thoughts, self-talk, and self-directions that go through your head during training or competitions. Under negative self-talk also list what was intended to be positive but had negative wording. In which situations does positive and negative self-talk occur and what effect does it have on you?

Table 13 Positive and negative self-talk.

Positive self-talk	Situation	Negative self-talk	Situation
Keep going!		Today I'm in a bad mood.	
Today I'm going to really go for it.		The rain gets on my nerves.	
Now take small steps!		Not so frantic!	
Etc.		Etc.	

FROM RESEARCH

In a summary of numerous studies, Hatzigeoriadis (2011) and colleagues were able to consistently see a positive link between self-talk and performance development. Interestingly, the coach's behavior also has an impact on the development of an athlete's self-talk. A democratic coaching style results more often in positive self-talk and less often in negative self-talk. A coaching style that is based on pressure and punishment causes athletes to develop fewer positive, and more often negative self-talk (Zourbanos et al., 2011). Hanin and Stambulova (2002) were able to provide empirical evidence that the use of metaphors is important and very helpful to athletes, particularly when the metaphors come from the athletes themselves (e.g., strong as a bull). We already mentioned the boxer Muhammad Ali and his metaphor of floating around the ring as light as a butterfly or a feather, and then stinging like a bee. Maybe you'll want to use "light as a feather" in the future, if you don't already. It works!

How can we create effective self-talk so they have an optimal effect? Below are three key approaches to improving our self-talk:

◆ Creating self-talk
◆ Using thought stop techniques
◆ Changing negative into positive self-talk

CREATING SELF-TALK

Self-talk is particularly effective when it is created based on the following criteria:

◆ **Short:** They should consist of short, succinct, and precise statements, individual words, phrases, or short sentences.

◆ **Positive:** Put into words what you want, not what you don't want.

◆ **First person present tense:** "I finish successfully" instead of "you will finish successfully."

◆ **Conscious and mindful:** Speak the self-talk out loud, consciously think them, and see them before your mind's eye, vividly feel them by using the appropriate visualizations. Also use your body language.

◆ **Repetition:** Regularly repeat your self-talk. Say them out loud again and again; use them to get in the mood for training, during training, and, with enough practice, while competing. Use scraps of paper or cue cards to keep important statements within sight, for instance on the fridge, the bathroom mirror, the dash of your car, etc.

◆ **Rhythm:** Catchy phrases work well, as do statements you can match to your breathing and stride frequency. As *mantras* they can have a downright hypnotic effect (e.g., "Fresh and free, that is me", "I'm running loose, I'm running loose, I'm running loose").

EXERCISE: TURNING GOALS INTO SELF-TALK

What important goals are you pursuing? How could you turn athletic wish goals, intermediate, or process goals into powerful positive self-talk statements to accompany you on your way and help you every second, so you can reach your goals in a smarter way while fully enjoying the journey? As usual, there is no golden rule. Just find what works for you. And as you practice, statements can certainly change so they are an even better fit. You just need to experiment.

Table 14 Goals and self-talk phrasing.

My important goals	Self-talk phrasing
2016 Olympics in Rio	I'm a winner!
Improve endurance	Step by step
Etc.	Etc.

Self-talk formulas can also become excellent triggers or keys for a powerful goal imagination.

THOUGHT STOP TECHNIQUES

Thought stop techniques are as simple as they are effective. Whenever we notice ourselves engaging in negative self-speech, we say out loud or tell ourselves mentally, "Stop!" You can supplement this with an appropriate gesture like, for example, clapping your hands, snapping your fingers, striking an object with your hand, etc. We can also intensify this process through visualization by imagining that we are hitting a big red button or sounding a kind of horn that has a flashing light and makes a silly sound. "Meeep!" Of course you can customize this to your liking, but it works very well to promptly interrupt a negative thought sequence. Next, we ideally offer our brain something else to focus on (i.e., we replace a negative with a positive form of self-talk). In addition, we can practice appropriate if-then conditions to make this process go as quickly as possible. But to do so we need to have an idea of what might be more helpful to us during a specific negative self-talk, or what we should focus our attention on as an alternative. The following strategy helps with that.

TURNING NEGATIVE SELF-TALK INTO POSITIVE SPEECH

Nearly everyone occasionally holds negative monologues. It's completely normal. But it is advisable to turn those into positive ones, particularly in performance-related situations, in order to direct attention to performance-enhancing and productive things instead of needlessly sabotaging or limiting ourselves.

EXERCISE: TURNING NEGATIVE SELF-TALK INTO POSITIVE SPEECH

◆ Begin by writing down typical self-talk that you know yourself to engage in and which can have a negative effect on performance, goal-attainment, well-being, and self-confidence, or get in their way. Think about the situations in which the various negative self-talk occur and why.

◆ Next, search for alternative, positive phrasing. As soon as you have completed a list, you can transfer the results to a table in which you replace the negative self-talk with positive speech.

Table 15 Turning negative self-talk into positive speech.

Replaced by	
Negative self-talk	Positive self-talk
I'm just not getting healthy.	Healing takes time. I keep working on it and do something for it every day.
This heat makes it hard for me to run.	Anyone can do easy. I adjust my intensity according to the temperature and practice, bit by bit, to also follow through in tough conditions.
Darn, I always trip.	Focus on the route and lift your feet a little higher.
I hate these long runs.	Every practice run is a gift and long runs are especially big gifts.

FROM EXPERIENCE: WE LOVE HILLS

The head coach of the cross-country team at Penn State University, Harry Groves, conducted an experiment. As part of preparations for a competition in difficult hilly terrain, the coach and the athletes changed the previously mostly negative self-talk, such as "Damn brutal hills" or "Man that's going to be damn hard" to "We love hills" or "I love hills." This turned the difficult conditions into a kind of partner or ally. When the race started, the suspense rose. The team in question engaged in a heated contest against the competition. For a long time, the leading runners were neck in neck. And then, after a few kilometers, there was a nasty hill. The head coach stood at the base of the hill and called to his approaching athletes, "We love hills, we love hills." Within a split second, his runners suddenly pulled away from the competition, gained a nice advantage on the hill, and in the end were able to win the race (Lynch & Scott, 1999).

ATACAMA EXPERIMENT: THE DESERT AS A DANCE PARTNER

Time and again I hear conversations or thoughts like "It's going to be a red-hot battle" or "I defeated the mountain," etc. With most people, thoughts that focus on fighting, toughness, and confrontation will lead—even imperceptibly—to higher, less helpful stress levels. It would be more relaxing, joyful, and productive to not turn challenges into adversaries that must be defeated, but rather into partners with whom you enjoy the moment. When I used to be more active in rock climbing, I always heard other climbers say that they were "fighting against a wall" or "defeating it." My own definition of the sport was a dance with the rock, the two of us as partners. Because without the rock, there is no climbing hobby; without tricky spots in the wall, there is no personal growth, no sense of achievement. By making the challenge my partner instead of my adversary, even just with respect to my language, I create a playful lightness.

And this also works with running. It is the attitude with which I started in the Atacama Desert. It was supposed to be a perfect dance at a fantastic party: the desert and myself on the dance floor of the ultra-marathon. Since I like to dance and also attend parties, this metaphor worked for me. Again and again, I reached the checkpoints and stage finishes with a huge smile on my face, grateful for the moment as though I was at a salsa party. Of course, in the heat of the moment, you sometimes step on your partner's toes, and that can hurt for a second, but I chose this hobby freely in order to enjoy it, not to fight it. Instead, I am interested to see what a run, no matter how challenging, has to offer in terms of experiences and opportunities for learning and growth.

SELF-DECEPTION?

It could be true when we tell ourselves, "I love running hills," "I'm a rocket," or "I'm a winner." But what if it is an exaggeration? Aren't those positive affirmations in particular counter-productive? No, not if they are a good fit overall. By using such positive images, we direct our brain—and thereby our attention—towards desired target states and resources. And lots of repetitions help us create and maintain neuronal canalization and as a result, reality. That is how advertising works and it is also how mass media works. And even if we don't love running hills all that much, in a competitive setting, this self-talk can make the difference for runners who struggle with running hills.

6.4   YOU'RE ALLOWED TO COPY: LEARNING FROM MORE OR LESS GLAM MODELS

A noble example makes difficult tasks easy.

—J.W. Goethe

If we didn't hit pay dirt in spite of the extensive ABCs of resources and we believe we don't have access to certain abilities, can we simply copy other people? Do we have to be ashamed if we do so? Does that even make sense?

Who isn't familiar with this scenario from school or other types of tests? Your neck gets longer and longer and you want to gain some inspiration by looking at your neighbor's paper. For those less hardened individuals, it may result in elevated blood pressure. Makes sense, because if you get caught you'll be in big trouble. And besides, it's pretty embarrassing. Copying is often not acceptable behavior and is penalized. On the other hand, learning through copying or observation is considered one of the most powerful human learning principles.

Humans acquire new abilities and knowledge largely through *imitation*. This is based on our ability to observe other people, to put ourselves in their shoes and relate to their experiences. Every person can do that. Children imagine they are Superman. Adults read books or watch movies and put themselves in the protagonists' place, see the world through their eyes, and root for them if the movie or book is good and touches them.

The strategy of putting yourself in other people's shoes is very well suited for sports to effectively change, improve, or acquire motion sequences, behaviors, and attitudes. That is when we choose the right role models.

EXERCISE: LEARNING FROM ROLE MODELS IN FOUR STEPS

COPYING ROLE MODELS
1.   Choosing a suitable role model.
2.   Creating a mental representation of the model.
3.   Identifying with the role model.
4.   Linking the role model to a challenge.

The following guide will show you the important steps towards making progress by copying role models.

Choosing a suitable role model

Choose someone who is good at what you would like to be able to do better (e.g., staying loose and relaxed before a race, demonstrating mental strength or composure, handling defeat well, having a great running style). As you can see, the number of topics we can copy from others is extensive, even downright inexhaustible.

Creating a mental representation of the role model

Imagine your role model before your mind's eye. Do this as vividly as possible, like an observer. What are all the things you notice? What does the role model look like? What are they wearing? Where are they right now? What exactly does the role model do and how does do they react in your mind to certain challenges? What do you like about them and why? Have you possibly exhibited such behaviors before, at least rudimentarily or maybe in a different context?

Identifying with the role model

Imagine you would be able to literally slip inside the role model, be in their skin, be completely in their shoes and see the world through their eyes, perceive things the same way. For instance, for movement role models, imagine as vividly as possible the physical sensations that occur during a certain movement. What do you sense? What does it feel like when your foot makes contact with the ground, the swing of your arm, your leg stride, the tension in your trunk or upper body, the position of your head? What does that feel like to you? Or with athletes that are effective yet always appear calm, relaxed and in a good mood: Precisely what do these runners do? What is their heart rate, their muscle tone or body tension? What might they be thinking? What does that smiling face feel like? The more detailed and differentiated your perception, the deeper and more present is the visualization experience and the better are you able to use it in the future. This identification alone can work wonders.

Linking the role model to a challenge

On this subject, also see the last step of the guide to resource reload. With self-talk and visualizations like "Whenever I experience situation X, I remember model Y or to be as loose as Y," you can establish access to these resources in the future.

With a little practice, this strategy will be enormously effective. The interesting part is that role models don't have to be real people. The media gives us access to many real and fictitious models we can use for our personal development. There should be something for everyone. It is also feasible to use two or more role models—the best of both worlds, you might say. You also don't have to find every aspect of your role models worth copying. Simply focus on the areas that are valuable and important to you.

FROM EXPERIENCE: MODEL LEARNING AT THE POLAR CIRCLE

During a wintery stage race at the Arctic Circle, I had to run 230 km primarily while wearing snowshoes. Due to unexpected amounts of fresh snow that again and again caused me to sink up to my knees and occasionally even up to my hips in the snow and due to the major elevation gain, running often slowed to an exhausting walk. The crux of the story is that I am a bad walker. The result was that other participants easily passed me during the walking sections while I tried desperately and with lots of effort to stay with them. It was frustrating and I told myself, "Stop! Something has to give. What do you want to take away from this race and what do you want to learn?" And I quickly realized that what I wanted to learn or do better was strategic walking. But how do you do that during a race? I focused intently on models in my surroundings.

During the race, I watched the Danish participant Allan more closely. He was able to walk very fast in difficult terrain. The most important insight for me was that he could maintain a high stride frequency at the same rhythm for long periods of time. I also remembered that a tall lanky person that can walk incredibly well and fast.

I once observed this person at the so-called "F*** the Kaiser" Marathon where we had to complete approximately 2 km laps, each with a 125 m rise, on a hill in Dortmund.

Michele Ufer at the 230 km ICE-ULTRA race.

The speed and composure of this person, who called himself, appropriately enough, *Strongwalker* and also writes a blog under the same name, made a lasting impression on me. In spite of walking, in the aforementioned marathon, this person left many runners in the dust. And so I continued to vividly put myself in the shoes of this tall, lanky person with the giant strides during the walking sections at the Swedish Arctic Circle, and imagined myself taking big or—for me—giant strides, but with a high frequency yet still loose and lanky.

Although you certainly won't find my wintery motion execution in the north of Lapland in any textbook, the effect was nevertheless astounding. By imitating two role models, I was able to improve my individual and situation-appropriate walking technique so rapidly that I could pass many athletes that were initially far ahead of me on the 90 km leg. And I felt better, looser. Maybe at the next race I will try what I did in my childhood: imagine I am Superman.

6.5 ACT AS IF: FAKE IT TILL YOU MAKE IT

We probably all know people we would describe as being fakers (i.e., someone who presents—or tries to present—himself differently, better, than he actually is). It is usually not intended as a compliment and we have our own thoughts on that matter. At least once we have seen through the deception. Of course, deception can be very functional and help us achieve goals.

For instance, in athletic competitions, it is beneficial to deceive our opponents about our actual state. We can pretend to be exhausted and demoralized while actually brimming with energy, thereby giving them a false sense of security. We can pretend to be full of energy and self-confidence, when in truth we may be experiencing a major physical low. Those kinds of games aren't just of tactical importance. We can also use them for our benefit.

In this book, we have frequently talked about the fact that our thoughts, emotions, and body are one unit and influence each other every second. We can use this in a positive way by employing mental techniques to affect our bodily processes and emotions. But we can also take the opposite approach and use our body to specifically affect our thoughts and emotions. Would you like an example?

EXERCISE: BODY LANGUAGE, EMOTIONS, AND THOUGHTS

Begin by sitting down like you just received some sad news that really depresses you. Your head is lowered, your shoulders slump, the chest is caved in, the corners of your mouth are turned down, and you have a stony expression on your face. Can you feel your mood turn more negative simply because of your posture? Now imagine a pleasant experience while maintaining this posture. Are you able to mentally put yourself in that place? Or can you feel optimistic? Most likely that's not possible.

Next, sit up and imagine being in a wonderful mood, downright euphoric and full of energy, optimism, and self-confidence. Maybe you just successfully finished a special race, found a new job, the love of your life, or whatever. Surely you notice an immediate change in your body. You straighten your upper body, probably take a deep breath, raise your chin, gaze into the distance, your facial expression changes, your face is radiant, maybe you smile. Try to place yourself in a negative experience while maintaining this posture. Do you feel frustrated? It will be difficult.

We smile when we are happy. But the opposite is possible, too; we are happier when we smile. There is a famous experiment on this subject that you are welcome to try out yourself (Lessmöllmann, 2006).

EXERCISE: (DON'T) LAUGH!

Figure 8 The pencil experiment: The effects of forced smiles.

For this exercise you will need a thick pencil or a toothbrush. Hold the pencil or toothbrush between your teeth without your lips touching the object. Can you do it? Very good! This exercise alone will improve your mood, not just because you look, well, interesting but because the facial muscles used for smiling are activated. Now hold the pencil with just one corner of your lips. The facial muscles are blocked and the brain no longer receives signals to be happy.

During social psychologist Fritz Stark's study at the University Würzburg, Germany, the test subjects were shown a number of cartoons after the lip exercises. Those who did the forced smile were happier afterwards and rated the cartoons as much more positive. So the activation of facial muscles alone changed the overall mood and perception—and probably more than that.

Here's the best bit: The smile strategy not only puts you in a good mood, but it also improves performance. Philippen and colleagues (2012) were able to prove that endurance athletes who smile perceive stress as less subjectively demanding. Brick, McElhinney, and Metcalf (2018) take up this point and show in their research that targeted smiles can indeed have positive effects on the performance of long-distance runners. The colleagues investigated the question of how different facial expressions affect the running economy (i.e., oxygen consumption for the same performance). Those tested completed four identical training sessions under four different conditions: without any instructions, frowning, relaxed, and smiling. The frowning unit found the training more strenuous. The smiling runners showed a significantly reduced oxygen consumption compared to the others (i.e., a better running economy). So smiling really is worth it! But we can influence ourselves beyond our facial expressions, as the following explanations impressively show.

In another experiment at Harvard University, test subjects were divided into two groups (Cuddy, 2012). Group 1 was told to assume a strong and self-confident posture and hold it for two minutes (e.g., stand tall, hands on hips). Group 2 was told to assume a less energetic or self-confident posture and also hold it for two minutes (e.g., seated, chin down, hand at the back of the neck).

A series of subsequent tests showed that after the experiment, the test subjects with the confident posture were significantly more adventurous and had 20% higher testosterone levels while the group with the low-energy posture was less adventurous and showed decreased testosterone levels. The experiment by Riskind and Gotay (1982) moves in a similar direction. The test subjects had to stand for several minutes in either an upright or a hunched position and afterwards had to complete a tricky task while moving freely. The upright test subjects showed significantly more endurance than the hunched subjects.

You already know why assuming a self-confident, winning posture can be extremely helpful, even if we're not really feeling it. Psychology also follows physiology. Outside of the running community, runners often have a reputation of being extremely tense and stubborn. This quote by Rilke may fit the bill here or there: *"What's on the outside is what I live on the inside."* But whatever the reasons for a tad too much stubbornness may be, the preceding information and exercises can not only help us improve our performance but also directly and simply bring a little more relaxation, joy, and lightness to our athletic activity.

6.6   TESTING AND CREATING SELF-CONFIDENCE

If there is a kind of faith that can move mountains, it is the faith in one's own strength.

—Marie Baroness of Eber-Eschenbach

In October 2015, the running world was mesmerized by events in Frankfurt, Germany. The German marathon runner Arne Gabius destroyed the 27-year-old previous German record at the Frankfurt Marathon with a time of 2:08:33. And he did so after running his first marathon just one year earlier. A few days before the marathon, he did a remarkable interview with the daily newspaper, *Welt*, from which other runners could certainty learn a thing or two. Full of self-confidence during his interview from October 24, 2015, Gabius told *Welt* about his thoughts and ambitions (Naher, 2015).

Die Welt: You made a major announcement that you plan to break the 27-year-old German marathon record by Jörg Peter, 2:08:47. Why do you put so much pressure on yourself?

Gabius: I don't feel any pressure. I know that I can run between 2:07 h and 2:09 h. All the Kenyans I tell about my first marathon immediately reply, "Then you'll run 2:06 in your next race."

Die Welt: Excuse me, but 2:06? That would be a new European record.

Gabius: Why not? I think that's the problem we have here. The German runners think about limits. Last year they told me that no German runner can run under 2:10 anymore; that's the sonic barrier. Now they say 2:06 is the limit. That's nonsense. I don't have limits in my head.

Die Welt: So do you think you might even be able to run below 2:05 in the coming years?

Gabius: Right now I'm only thinking about 2:07. But below 2:05? Why not, in the future? The American Ryan Hall ran a 2:04:48 in Boston in 2011. I look to runners like that.

Die Welt: You said, "German runners have limits in their head." What does that mean? What specifically are you criticizing?

Gabius: In recent years we have focused on the wrong target times for the marathon. The previous benchmark of all things was 2:12. It was some kind of limit. Another limit is the fact that we see African runners almost without exception as unbeatable miracle runners. We have thereby sharply scaled down our own standards for marathons.

My goodness, such self-confidence! Psychologists refer loosely to *perceived self-efficacy* or *perceived competence* and mean the personal expectation of being able to successfully handle desired challenges or access performances, whereby any success is credited to one's own skills. You could also call it the belief in one's own abilities.

Since they trust in their abilities, people with a high degree of perceived self-efficacy approach difficult tasks with more determination than people who doubt themselves and their abilities. They react less fearfully, lose hope less often, demonstrate more perseverance, and a higher frustration tolerance when dealing with setbacks. Of course, this does raise the likelihood for success, as confirmed by a summary analysis of 45 studies on the relationship between self-efficacy expectations and athletic performance (Moritz, Feltz, Fahrbach, & Mack, 2000). Success in turn raises their self-confidence, so that they tackle more difficult and more complex tasks. In short, they have more faith in themselves and therefore achieve more. People with a high degree of perceived self-efficacy are also happier and healthier.

Our perceived self-efficacy affects:
◆ our choice of goals or their degree of difficulty;

◆ the amount of effort we put into the goal-attainment process;

◆ our perseverance and tenacity in the face of difficulties and barriers; and

◆ the level of success in our actions.

EXERCISE: TEST YOUR GENERAL PERCEIVED SELF-EFFICACY

The following test has been used successfully for the past 20 years in 27 languages, and measures one's subjective belief of being able to successfully handle situations with critical requirements on our own (Schwarzer & Jerusalem, 1995, 1999).

On a scale from 1 (not true) to 4 (very true), please check the number or box that most closely applies to you.

Table 16 Perceived self-efficacy test.

Item	1 Not true	2 Barely true	3 True	4 Very true
I can always manage to solve difficult problems if I try hard enough.				
If someone opposes me, I can find the means and ways to get what I want.				
It is easy for me to stick to my aims and accomplish my goals.				
I am confident that I could deal efficiently with unexpected events.				
Thanks to my resourcefulness, I know how to handle unforeseen situations.				
I can solve most problems if I invest the necessary effort.				
I can remain calm when facing difficulties because I can rely on my coping abilities.				
When I am confronted with a problem, I can usually find several solutions.				
If I am in trouble, I can usually think of a solution.				
I can usually handle whatever comes my way.				

EVALUATION

To find your score, add up all 10 of your answers, resulting in a score between 10 and 40. Where should we set limits and thresholds? Maybe it would make sense to repeatedly use the questionnaire to ascertain your personal development process, ideally at the beginning of a mental training program, and then again every few months. It would be a way to evaluate the effectiveness of your psychological training if self-confidence is a major issue. But for anyone who would like to have at least a tiny point of reference, in a standardization study with 2,019 German subjects, the following median values were ascertained, whereby the focus was not exclusively on runners but a representative sample of the population (Hinz et al., 2006).

Table 17 Standard values for the perceived self-efficacy scale.

	Men			Women			Total
Age in years	16-40	41-60	61-95	16-40	41-60	61-95	16-95
Mean value	30.8	30.1	29.8	29.4	28.8	27.6	29.4

Time and again we hear things like "You have to show more self-confidence," "Enter the race with self-confidence," or "He just needs a little more self-confidence and he can be great." But how does self-confidence work, or rather, how can you specifically foster it? Five key approaches have emerged from research.

THE FIVE MOST IMPORTANT SOURCES OF SELF-CONFIDENCE

MASTERING DIFFICULT SITUATIONS: THE KEY TO SUCCESS IS SUCCESS

Our *experiences* are the primary source of our *perceived self-efficacy*. Mastering difficult situations and experiencing personal successes increases our self-confidence, at least when we recognize our abilities as the reason for these successes, instead of coincidence or external conditions. That is why it's so important to also do a little causal investigation and evaluate the process when we reach a goal, instead of doing so only when we fail (e.g., what worked well, not so well).

To create awareness of our successes we would do well to frequently remind ourselves of the things we accomplished or brought about in recent years in sports, our job, etc. A success journal of some sort, in which we briefly jot down our successes like a diary, can be very valuable. Retrospectively, it is extremely helpful for fueling your self-confidence, because the hustle and bustle of our daily lives causes memories of all the things we lifted and achieved over time to quickly evaporate. Often just one look at your journal can work wonders. For example, I print out my journal at the end of the year and really enjoy it. Many things that are no longer on my screen come back to me. I can also see progress. That feels good, and most of the time I end up telling myself, "Okay, you actually did a lot of stuff."

EXERCISE: SUCCESS JOURNAL

Simply create a table with two columns: Week and Highlights. Each week, spontaneously jot down some simple notes, such as highlights you experienced, all the stuff you've done, any good news, etc. One thing is important: No stress! You don't have to be a philosopher or writer. Brief reminders for yourself in your words are perfect. Sometimes there will be more to report and other times less. But, over time, a number of highlights will definitely accumulate (which, by the way, you can then use for your resources reload), and it may show some nice progress here or there. You might consider keeping separate journals for different areas, or you can keep one general one. Decide what works best for you while keeping it simple.

Table 18 Example of a simple but effective success journal.

Week	Highlights
1	◆ Formulated goals and monthly planning for January; awesome, I'm psyched. ◆ Super phone call with sponsor; yes, I will receive equipment and travel expenses for two years. ◆ First test run with new training group. Much more fun and more productive.
2	◆ PB 5000 m. Bam! Keep it going.
...	

OBSERVING SUCCESSFUL MODELS: IF HE CAN DO IT, I CAN DO IT, TOO!

And here it is again. Copying from the right role models also helps us here. We all learn by observing role models and are thereby able to vicariously create valuable experiences. When athletes with abilities that are similar to our own master a difficult challenge, we are more likely to also think ourselves capable of mastering that challenge. The more similarity we share with our role models, the greater the impact on our self-confidence.

Therefore, copying continues to be allowed, even desirable, but only from the right people!

VISUALIZING FUTURE SUCCESSES: REMEMBERING A SUCCESSFUL FUTURE

We have already talked quite a bit about this as well. By vividly imagining ourselves mastering difficult challenges, they lose their scariness. In our imagination we already see and experience that it is possible and that we can do it, but most of all we see how we use our abilities and resources to ultimately reach our goal. This fosters confidence, reduces the element of surprise, and makes us hungry for more. Here, too, it is important to break down distant goals into smaller intermediate goals. This way we don't just stand in front of a giant, intimidating mountain, but merely in front of a series of manageable hills.

SOCIAL SUPPORT: YOU CAN DO IT!

When other people give us encouragement we are more likely to believe in ourselves and feel more confident, at least as long as said support takes into account our actual capabilities and doesn't fuel unrealistic expectations. It is therefore always good to know who will stand by us during difficult situations. In light of this fact, it can be helpful to frequently communicate openly about our athletic goals and ambitions with the people around us and our community (at least as long as it doesn't put unnecessary pressure on us). This can lead to a pleasant surge of support among our friends and colleagues that we may well find extremely helpful.

Again and again athletes report that they feel like the people surrounding them carry them through their endeavors and athletic projects. Who is a helpful support to you already and what do you value in that person? Who might be able to do so (perhaps even more) in the future? To what extent do you even want support? Do you like for people to support you, or do you prefer doing things on your own?

These are questions for self-reflection that might give you some ideas. No matter what your answers may be, it is obvious that even individual athletes are generally not individual fighters—quite the opposite, in fact.

CONTROLLING EXCITEMENT: STAYING COOL

Our automatic physiological reactions to difficult situations are often the basis for our perceived self-efficacy. That can be tricky. A racing heartbeat, shallow breathing, shaky hands, and a queasy stomach are all interpreted as signs of fear and weakness, and quickly go hand in hand with self-doubt, regardless of whether or not the necessary abilities to handle a challenge objectively exist. When we are able to purposefully reduce such stress signals through relaxation techniques (see chapter 6.7), we are better able to analyze situations (after the initial fear reaction), directly resolve the idea that shaking equals self-doubt, approach challenges in a more relaxed state overall, and thereby increase the likelihood for success.

Let's just do it like Arne Gabius; we approach new, really challenging—and maybe even breathtakingly daring—yet realistic goals based on our previous performances. In doing so, we look to the right role models, remain relatively relaxed, and seek support from other people who are able to properly assess our abilities and other needs. They don't necessarily have to be Kenyans.

6.7   RELAXED EFFECTIVENESS AND EFFECTIVE RELAXATION

During an interview on the topic of "coaching for the head," I was once asked what would be the best thing one could do to combat nervousness and tension before a marathon that would also yield a good running performance. My expert answer was slightly mischievous, "Sex, sex, sex! But not too wild!" Okay, I did add more information, but I essentially hit the nail on the head. Sex is actually really good for chasing away the jittery nerves and fueling up on some self-confidence. But—and we will talk about this in more detail—does it even make sense to eliminate that feeling of nervousness, the restlessness and the tingling before a competition? What would the exact opposite be, and would that be better for our performance?

THE PURPOSE OF STRESS: INCREASING OUR PERFORMANCE CAPACITY

Whenever we perceive a situation as threatening, the *brainstem* (which, from an evolutionary standpoint, is the oldest part of our brain) automatically activates a number of physical changes that put us into a state of increased readiness. Hormones are released (e.g., adrenaline), resulting in an increased heart rate, higher blood pressure, faster and shallower breathing, dilated pupils, increased glucose release, perspiration, and increased alertness. Thousands of years ago, when we still roamed the land as hunters and gatherers, this reaction mechanism was frequently a matter of life and death. During dangerous situations, the body receives energy reserves within fractions of seconds and without conscious thought that facilitate the appropriate fight-or-flight responses.

Nowadays the threats are less physical and more mental in nature, but our brainstem doesn't care whether the danger is a dangerous predator or merely our thoughts. The stress reaction is the same and serves only one purpose: to increase our readiness via the appropriate activation mechanisms. In this sense, stress or nervousness aren't necessarily bad things. On the contrary, a certain amount of stress is helpful and productive.

And many athletes confirm they absolutely need the tingling, the pressure to enter a competition fully motivated and effective. However, other athletes appear to suffer from excessive activation and as a result cramp up, and seem to practically block themselves in critical moments. Of course it also happens that athletes come to a competition too relaxed, too loose. This can quickly give outsiders the impression that the athletes aren't taking a competition seriously enough. Too much isn't good, too little isn't good either. So what is the right amount to help us access an ideal performance?

IN THE ZONE: FINDING THE PERFECT AROUSAL LEVEL

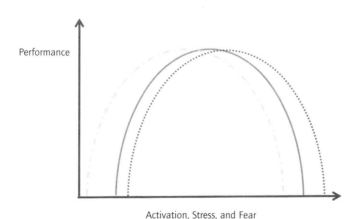

Performance

Activation, Stress, and Fear

Figure 9 Relationship between arousal level and performance.

Many things in life are a matter of the correct balance. It is no different in athletic competitions. Let's remember our inverse U-curve, because it illustrates very well the relationship between the extent of our arousal and our performance. The *Yerkes-Dodson law* implies that every specific performance requirement has an ideal activation level. This also means that every specific requirement must avoid too much or too little activation in order to be optimally efficient. When the activation is too low, we are tired and lethargic; when it is too high, we are tense and even panicky. We are optimally efficient when we can find a middle range. This range also differs from sport-specific challenges. The level that is helpful to a boxer or weightlifter is different from that of a golfer, while a 200 m sprinter requires a different level than a 24-hour distance runner. Moreover, the ideal level can also vary from athlete to athlete.

Two things are critical:

◆ Awareness of one's personal ideal activation level (i.e., the zone)

◆ The ability to properly increase or decrease the extent of arousal as needed in order to get into the zone.

With experience, we often develop a sense for where that range lies, but sometimes it can be helpful to look closer at this topic in order to do a little fine tuning. To find out where your ideal arousal level lies, you can do some forensic research and analyze your past—as well as future—competitions with the following exercise.

EXERCISE: TRACKING THE IDEAL PERFORMANCE STATE

◆ Begin by remembering your best competition or run. Take a few minutes to mentally place yourself vividly in that competition; really feel the situation. Then complete the following checklist (based on Weinberg & Gould, 2015).

◆ Next, repeat the process with your worst run or competition. Mentally place yourself in that situation as vividly as you can, and then complete the checklist.

◆ Now compare the two sets of answers. Usually the values pertaining to an ideal competition differ significantly from those of a bad competition. That certainly is a good first point of reference for the future. To further increase your awareness with respect to the relationships between feelings, thoughts, the degree of arousal, and the performance, and to identify underlying patterns, I recommend that you use this method to regularly analyze or evaluate future important training units and competitions. By doing so you will, over time, gain a highly differentiated picture and will develop a feel for what your ideal performance state looks like.

Table 19 Analysis of performance states.

It went extremely well.	1	2	3	4	5	6	It didn't go well at all.
I felt extremely relaxed.	1	2	3	4	5	6	I felt extremely anxious.
I felt extremely confident.	1	2	3	4	5	6	I felt extremely unconfident.
I felt in complete control.	1	2	3	4	5	6	I had no control at all.
My muscles were relaxed.	1	2	3	4	5	6	My muscles were tense.
I felt extremely energetic.	1	2	3	4	5	6	I felt extremely fatigued.
My self-talk was positive.	1	2	3	4	5	6	My self-talk was negative.
I felt extremely focused.	1	2	3	4	5	6	I felt extremely unfocused.
I felt effortless.	1	2	3	4	5	6	I felt great effort.
I had high energy.	1	2	3	4	5	6	I had low energy.

ADDITIONAL INFORMATION FOR FUTURE MONITORING OF PERFORMANCE STATES

It can also be very helpful to include the heart rates in this analysis. For instance, during sport psychology coaching, the ski jumper Simon Amman worked intensely on determining his ideal performance state and then reliably achieving it immediately prior to his jumps by using the relevant techniques. It turned out that he is most efficient when he gets his heart rate up to 180 BPM. Of course, he didn't just stumble across this insight; it was the result of intensive practice and reflection processes. Since he and many other athletes are validated by their success, I would like to encourage you to also invest a little time and brainpower in finding your ideal performance state, that fine line where you activate best, are focused and relaxed. On the one hand, this provides you with a specific, helpful process goal right before your eyes, and on the other hand, you gradually learn to make the necessary fine adjustment to put yourself in the zone.

During this next step, let's take a look at which strategies we can use to specifically affect the degree of our arousal. While mobilization measures help us to ramp up our activation, when we feel tired and weak, relaxation techniques help reduce excessive activation, nervousness, and fear.

GET PSYCHED!: ACTIVATION OR MOBILIZATION TECHNIQUES

Athletes generally find it easy to use activation techniques. However, it depends on the right timing and the right amount so we don't end up over-activated. Maybe we underestimated a race or an opponent, or we feel completely drained and weak. Maybe we don't care about our performance or the competition, or we are distracted. Maybe our body language isn't confident or we lack the right amount of body tension. We wish for the end of a run, or our coordination worsens. All of these things can be an indication that we have too little energy in our system and need to activate. The following techniques can help to promptly raise our activation level.

MOBILIZATION STRATEGIES

◆ **Power breathing:** Take several, relatively quick, deep breaths.

◆ **Body-based techniques:** Quickly tap hands against legs, arms, and chest; make fists and move the arms; tiptoe or hop in place; or perform a good warm-up.

◆ **Positive self-talk:** Aloud or to yourself, say things like "Step on the gas!", Go for it!", "Power!", or "Yeah!".

◆ **Music:** Make a motivational playlist you can listen to on an MP3 player before a competition or that you can play back in your head during a competition.

◆ **Visualizations:** Activate powerful mental images and perceptions.

Combining the various strategies to initiate differentiated experience patterns or activation states is particularly effective. I would like to elucidate this with two examples.

RESPIRATION + SELF-TALK + VISUALIZATION

When we take fast, deep breaths, we can say to ourselves, "Power in," as we inhale, and we can say, "Fatigue out," as we exhale. We may have also determined key words (e.g., "Power on") as part of our resources reload that, after the appropriate training, immediately put us in the desired activation state. As we intensify our breathing, we may also think about how we are reaching a fantastic wish goal, and what we are feeling at this moment.

MUSIC AND GOAL VISUALIZATIONS

We are able to link individual songs to very specific process and result goals. Because they are linked to powerful mental images and perceptions that in turn activate corresponding, energetic feelings (e.g., "This song has always gotten under my skin" or "Whenever I listen to this song, I imagine what it will be like when I have reached my goal"), they have an even stronger effect beyond their imminent intrinsic effect.

RELAX!: RELAXATION TECHNIQUES AND REDUCTION OF NERVOUSNESS, FEAR, AND EXCESS ACTIVATION

Successful athletes spend more time using relaxation techniques as part of their training than less successful athletes. Kudlackova and colleagues (2013) weren't the only ones to gain this insight during a recent scientific study. Many top runners also confirmed that the ability to relax and control arousal before a race is one of their most important qualities. A smooth, energy-efficient movement sequence is only possible with a focused and motivated yet relaxed body and mind. Only someone who is completely at ease even during the heat of the moment can shift his attention to the right things at the right time. And while the importance of relaxing the mind and body is well documented time and again, to date that insight is not sufficiently taken into consideration during training and competitions. Someone who wants to be good must be able to stay relaxed and loose. The following exercises illustrate that.

EXERCISE: MUSCLE GAMES

Begin by doing five push-ups during which you really tighten your entire upper body, arms, and hands. Afterwards, loosen up a little, and do another five push-ups, but this time maintain medium muscle tension, sufficiently activated but still nice and loose. You can definitely feel the difference. The second set is easier.

Here is another exercise. Sit at a table and rest your forearm and palm on the table. Tighten up your entire arm, wrist, hand, and fingers. Now rapidly tap your index and middle finger on the table for 30 seconds, moving them up and down. After a short break, repeat the exercise with relaxed arm, hand, and finger muscles. You will most likely immediately notice that the movement is faster and more fluid. When under tension, fine coordination is impeded and movements slow down.

USING RELAXATION TECHNIQUES HOLDS THE FOLLOWING BENEFITS FOR RUNNERS

◆ Relaxed muscles are more supple and less tense. This results in better coordination and less energy use. Improved circulation simultaneously optimizes the energy supply. The result is that we produce less lactate, are faster and stronger, and have more endurance.

◆ Our awareness is limited when we are stressed. Our thoughts often revolve around problems. Someone who is relaxed can react more quickly and better to new and changing situations in a race.

◆ Relaxed runners are better able to focus on important things. This increases our belief in our own abilities, which in turn increases the likelihood of a good performance.

◆ There is a strong link between general and situation-specific stress and the occurrence of injuries. People who are more stressed overall tend to have more injuries. Fear and stressful thoughts and feelings lead to carelessness, decreased control over the flow of movements, and a higher likelihood of injury. Here relaxation has a prophylactic and regulating effect (see chapter 7.4).

◆ More relaxed is usually more fun.

Below we will take a look at some strategies we can use to appropriately relax before or while running. Of course, there is a whole slew of techniques, but here we will focus on methods that are quick to learn and tried and proven for runners.

RELAXATION BREATHING

Relaxation breathing is highly effective, can be done easily almost anywhere, and is thus an ideal tool for regulating our degree of arousal. Our breathing has an immediate effect on our vegetative nervous system. When stressed, the following reflexive respiratory changes take place: more frequent breaths, fewer breaks between breaths, shallower breaths, and a shift from belly to chest breathing. This provides the body with more oxygen. Additionally the amount of carbon dioxide in the blood drops, which increases blood acidity. This in turn results in the increased excitability of nerve cells and thus the nervous system overall. Since there is usually no fight-or-flight reaction, we experience the very quickly supplied excessive energy as inner unrest. If this activation is too great and obstructive, we can counteract it very effectively by simply reversing the breathing pattern and thereby rebounding on our vegetative nervous system.

The fundamentals of relaxation breathing are:

◆ slowing down breathing,

◆ exhaling significantly longer than inhaling (2:1),

◆ lengthening the pauses between breaths, and

◆ using more belly breathing than chest breathing (while inhaling, the belly expands, not the chest).

We can intensify this process through self-instruction. Every time you exhale, simply say "Relax," "Calm," or something similar.

EXERCISE: RELAXATION BREATHING

Stand, sit, or lie down in a comfortable position and close your eyes, or fix them on a focal point. Place one hand on your belly at the navel. Begin by breathing consciously and effortlessly into the belly for 2 or 3 minutes. As you do so, imagine breathing into your hand and feel your belly rise as you inhale and return to its starting position as you exhale. Continuing your belly breathing, extend your exhaling phases so that every exhale takes approximately twice as long as your inhales. After a few minutes, allow your shoulders to drop lower with each exhale. Finally, take a few deep breaths and stretch your body.

EXERCISE: BREATHING VISUALIZATION

Sit relaxed and upright in a chair with your legs open. Close your eyes for better concentration. Inhale slowly through the nose while imagining a white cloud filling your lungs. First it collects in the lower third of your lungs, then in the middle, and finally the top third. Hold your breath for a moment and imagine fresh, clean air flowing through your entire body into every nook and cranny, absorbing all the metabolic waste and negative things. Now slowly exhale through the nose and feel pleasant relaxation as the now gray cloud that absorbed your internal stress, negative thoughts, and waste products leaves your body and dissipates into nothing. After exhaling, wait 1or 2 seconds and imagine your empty lungs before inhaling again. Repeat this process 10 to 15 times and imagine the cloud really reaching every corner of your body and spreading its healing effect (Lynch & Scott, 1999). Do this exercise regularly, before and during training, and, if that woks well, you can even use breathing visualization while you compete. You can also build your own exercise that might be a better fit for you. You already know the components.

PROGRESSIVE MUSCLE RELAXATION

No fearful mind can exist in a relaxed body.   —Jacobsen, 1964

Progressive muscle relaxation (PMR) is also very easy to learn and is considered an effective method based on scientific evidence. It has been tried and tested many times and is very popular among athletes because it takes little time and the positive effects are immediately apparent. Shorter practice sequences can be performed spontaneously nearly anywhere. PMR can also be used in the form of *flash relaxation* to achieve the desired relaxation reactions in just seconds.

It also helps athletes improve their body perception, which allows faster ascertainment of dysfunctional states of stress and their immediate dissolution.

PMR was originally developed for the effective reduction of fears. It is based on the following assumptions:

◆ Fear and mental tension lead to muscular tension.

◆ Relaxation and fear or tension cannot be experienced simultaneously.

◆ Decreasing muscle tension leads to decreased mental tension.

During PMR we move through a series of alternating tension and relaxation phases of individual muscle groups, whereby we focus intently on the sensation of contracting and relaxing. It is important that we only contract the relevant muscles. As a result, most muscle tension can be eliminated and a feeling of deep relaxation can be achieved. This again is irreconcilable with nervousness, fear, and tension (Eichhorn, 2002). Many studies have proven the effectiveness of PMR in reducing fear, nervousness, and feelings of restlessness.

EXERCISE: PROGRESSIVE MUSCLE RELAXATION (SHORT VERSION, 15 MINUTES)

Maybe you would like to save the following instructions as a recorded voice file so you can play them on your smartphone. It would allow you to focus even more closely on the execution.

Try to purposefully contract only the particular muscle region you want to contract. Make sure the adjacent muscles remain relaxed.

1. **Relaxing arms and hands**

   Sit comfortably in a chair and relax your muscles. Now close your dominant hand into a fist and contract your muscles tighter and tighter and pay attention to the tension in your fist and forearm. Hold that tension for five to seven seconds, and then relax. Pay attention to the relaxed state of your hand and forearm. Try to relax your fingers more and more. Squeeze your hand shut again and contract your muscles more and more, as you did before. Hold that tension and observe it. Then relax and notice the transition from tension to relaxation. It is important that you closely monitor the various sensations that take place during tension and relaxation. Repeat this exercise with your other hand.

   Now contract both hands and forearms, and then relax them. Again, pay attention to the transition from contraction to relaxation.

   Next contract the upper arm of your dominant side. Bend the elbow and tightly contract your upper arm muscles. Notice the tension, and then relax. You again feel the transition from contraction to relaxation. Relax the upper arm completely and notice the relaxation sensation. Then repeat the contraction of the upper arm, hold the tension, and then lower the arm. Relax and again notice the difference. Now straighten the arm so you can really feel the developing tension at the back of the arm. Pay attention to the tension, and then relax. Now allow your arm to rest comfortably. Continue to relax. You can feel the entire weight of your forearm and hand resting on the arm of the chair or on your thigh.

2. **Relaxing the facial region including neck, shoulders, and upper back**

   Sit comfortably in a chair. Pay attention to your forehead and firmly pull your forehead muscles upward so you have horizontal wrinkles on your forehead. Hold the tension and notice the sensation of tension on your forehead. Now relax and allow your forehead to smooth out. You can feel your forehead relax more and more. You can feel your entire scalp relax along with your forehead.

   Repeat the contraction and gradual relaxation of the forehead.

   Now contract your eyebrows so vertical wrinkles appear on your forehead above your eyes. Notice the tension and then relax. You can again feel the transition from contraction to relaxation.

   Now try to simultaneously create horizontal and vertical wrinkles on your forehead. Your forehead is now completely contracted. Hold that tension, then relax. Once again notice the transition from tension to pleasant relaxation. Allow your forehead muscles to relax completely.

Now squeeze your eyes shut and feel the tension in the eye region, then relax.

Keep your eyes lightly shut and notice the relaxation.

Next wrinkle your nose so you can clearly feel the tension on your nose, then relax again. You can now feel that your nose and nasal wings are relaxed.

Now clench your jaw and feel your teeth clench. Notice the tension in the entire jaw area. Relax. As you do so, allow your lips and cheeks to relax completely.

Now press your tongue against the roof of your mouth, notice the tension, and then let the tongue return to a relaxed position.

Press your lips together, hold that contraction, and notice the tension in your lips and cheeks. Relax and notice the difference between tension and relaxation. Now relax your entire face, the forehead and the scalp, eyes, nose, lips, cheeks, lower jaw, and chin. Allow the lower jaw and chin to hang down.

Now push your head back until you can feel tension in the back of the neck, turn your head to the right and notice how the tension changes. Roll the head to the left. Notice the tension and then raise your head. As you do so, notice how the tension in the back of the neck disappears.

Now drop your head forward so that the chin presses against the sternum. Pay attention to the tension in your neck and throat and then bring your head up. You will begin to feel more relaxed. Move your head to the front, then back, then to the left, and then to the right, moving in such a way that the tension in the neck and throat disappears.

Now raise your shoulders and notice the tension that is created. Let the shoulders drop and notice the pleasant relaxation. Tighten the shoulders again. As you do so, notice the sensation of tension. The entire back is taut. Now relax. Notice the relaxation as you get looser and looser. You can feel the relaxation radiate into your back muscles.

Now allow the back of your neck, your neck, jaw, and face to relax completely.

3. Relaxing chest and back

Allow your body to relax completely. Notice your breath as you inhale and exhale. After you inhale, briefly hold your breath and notice the tightness in your chest. Exhale and, as you do so, notice how your chest relaxes pleasantly. Inhale again and notice the tightness in the chest, then enjoy the relaxed feeling again as you exhale.

Now turn your attention to your stomach area. Tighten your stomach muscles and notice the tension in your belly. Relax the stomach muscles and notice the transition from tension to relaxation. Repeat tightening and relaxing your stomach.

Now suck in your stomach as far as you can, and notice the muscle tension. Now relax. Again notice the sensation of relaxation in the stomach.

Turn your attention back to your breath and feel the chest and stomach tighten slightly with each breath you take, and then relax each time you exhale.

Now turn your attention to your lower back. Round your back and notice the tension along the spine. Relax your back by allowing yourself to fall back into your chair. As you do so, relax your back. Allow the relaxation of your back muscles to radiate to the front of the body, to the chest, belly, shoulders, arms, and face.

Repeat the tightening and relaxing of the back.

4. Relaxing gluteal muscles, legs, feet, and toes

Tighten your entire body and then relax it. Notice your gluteal muscles, thighs, and calves. Now press your heels into the floor with your toes pointing up towards your face. As you do so, firmly tighten your calves, thighs, and gluteal muscles. Hold that tension, then relax. Again, notice the difference between tension and relaxation.

Press your heels into the floor again, but with your toes pointed away from your face this time. Notice the tension in your calves, thighs, and gluteal muscles. You can feel the tension travel from your feet, up your calves, thighs, and gluteal muscles. Now relax once more. Allow the muscles to get really loose and feel the relaxation radiate from your feet up through your legs and into your back, chest, stomach, shoulders, arms, and hands. Relax the back of your neck and face. Let your entire body loosen up and relax. Now you can feel yourself resting in the chair with all your weight (Kogler, 2006, pg. 248-251).

With practice, you will be able to combine several muscle groups. With enough experience, you will be able to forgo the contraction phase and immediately focus on relaxation. PMR can very easily be combined with other strategies. As you practice PMR, link the phases of deep relaxation to a key word or phrase (e.g., relax, let go). Eventually the key word will lead directly to a conditioned relaxation reaction.

BIOFEEDBACK

During *biofeedback* physical processes and properties that are usually not accessible to our sensory organs are ascertained, amplified, and visually or acoustically reported back to the system. This gives our conscious mind access to unconsciously occurring biological processes. We are then able to perceive even minute changes that usually remain below our perceptional threshold. The capturing and reporting of conditions and changes in heart rate, heart rate variability, brainwaves, muscle tone, skin conductance, skin temperature, breathing pattern, blood pressure, and blood oxygen level provides us with a very differentiated view of the processes inside our central nervous system. This knowledge allows us to far better control ourselves or rather our reactions in stressful situations.

Advantages of biofeedback methods

We can

◆ significantly increase our consciousness with respect to our physical processes;

◆ purposefully influence regulative processes of our central nervous system that are usually unconscious;

◆ make the immediate effects of our thoughts, breathing, and actions on our activation level visible and therefore easier to control; and

◆ immediately verify the effectiveness of relaxation exercises.

In addition to the expensive devices used in research, small equipment for end users is now available and is extremely well suited for providing the aforementioned advantages. Of particular interest is the possibility of performing biofeedback anywhere, flexibly and practically, with the use of smartphones. In my opinion, two biological parameters are of particular interest: *heart rate variability (HRV)* and *skin conductance level.*

The HRV describes the ability to continuously change the amount of time between heartbeats as needed within fractions of a second. What do you think? Is it a sign of good health and fitness when the amount of time between two heartbeats is very consistent or when it is variable? The HRV is considered a measure of an organism's overall adaptability to internal and external stimuli. Breathing already has an immediate effect on HRV. Our thoughts, too. When we are under extreme or chronic stress, our HRV is considerably lower. Due to the increased tension, the heart cannot react as precisely to changes. The HRV is thus an excellent biomarker for stress or health and performance capacity. Since many runners already use HRV measurements—obtained through wearable heart rate monitors—to better control their training load, I don't want to go into any more detail on the subject here, but I do recommend the use of HRV as a way to easily implement biofeedback training for better stress control. There are a number of inexpensive apps, which, combined with a suitable heart rate monitor, can help you get started with simple HRV biofeedback. Please keep in mind that to date, wrist devices do not offer reliable HRV data, so you have to go with a chest strap.

The second parameter we can use for biofeedback is the *skin conductance level*.

The term *skin conductance level* refers to measurable changes in the skin's bioelectrical properties. A very small, completely safe, and imperceptible amount of electric tension is applied to the skin via electrodes with a very slight current. The higher the level of activity of the sweat glands, the moister the skin is and the better it conducts electricity; this increases the skin's conductance response. The activity of the skin's sweat glands is determined by the vegetative nervous system (i.e., sympathetic and parasympathetic nervous system). When the *sympathetic* nervous system receives stress stimuli, it activates all of the organism's emergency functions and throws it into a heightened state of action readiness.

Of critical importance for biofeedback based on skin conductance values is that our hands also get moister. One theory on this phenomenon says that it gave our ancestors a better grip while, for instance, fleeing across the terrain. Once the threatening situation has passed, the *parasympathetic* nervous system gains the upper hand. Pulse and blood pressure drop and the blood glucose level goes back down. The organism is switched to calm in order to ensure recovery. The hands dry. We don't necessarily perceive these tiny changes through moist hands. The skin's sweat glands are thus a good indicator of internal tension (i.e., the increased activity of the sweat glands) and the rise in skin conductance values under the effects of stress stimuli is clearly visible. However, I have to point out once more that the changes often happen so quickly and are so minute, that we are unable to consciously perceive them without implements. For example, a stress stimulus can consist of mental activity, emotional upset, deep inhalations, or being startled by, for instance, sudden clapping.

The goal of skin conductance biofeedback is to reduce both the overall stress level (i.e., long-lasting tension), and a specific stress reaction to acute stimuli, seeking a lowering of the skin conductance value.

FROM EXPERIENCE: SKIN CONDUCTANCE BIOFEEDBACK

I would like to give an example on how to use a consumer device to change our arousal level. The easy-to-use device *eSense Skin Response* by Mindfield Biosystems works with a free analysis and training app on a smartphone or tablet.

To take measurements, two electrodes are placed on the tips of the index and middle finger. These conduct a very small, imperceptible amount of electricity, which provides information about the skin's current conductivity. The eSense device provides the user with an accurate report on the current stress level in the form of graphs, video, and audio displays, as well as a series of training programs.

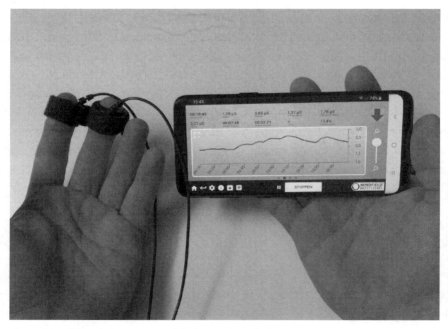

Figure 10 Taking measurements with the "eSense" device.

The following illustration shows how power breathing and relaxation breathing very quickly affect my body during a self-experiment. During deep accentuated breathing, the skin conductance value goes up right away, a definite sign that the vegetative nervous system is activated. By contrast, during relaxation breathing, the value goes down. Activation is reduced. Moreover, it clearly shows the effect progressive muscle relaxation can have on our activation level. It's also interesting to incorporate your own videos or MP3 files (e.g., relaxing music, recorded PMR routine). You can easily experiment with different techniques and thought content and test their effectiveness.

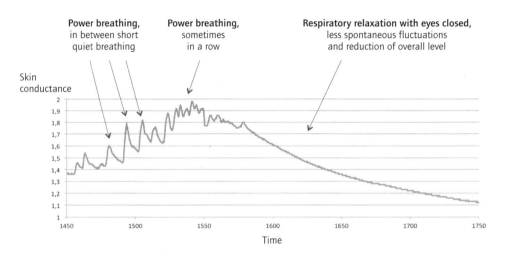

Figure 11a eSense measurement: the effects of breathing.

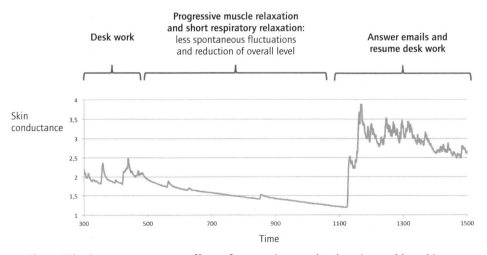

Figure 11b eSense measurement: effects of progressive muscle relaxation and breathing.

ERASING STRESSFUL THOUGHTS

We can play some clever games with stress-provoking thoughts and quickly erase negative emotions. Stressful thoughts are then no longer stressful. We already tried a corresponding exercise in the chapter on visualization. Let's take a look at some other options.

EXERCISE: THOUGHT MODULATION

Think of a stressful thought that is relevant to you personally (e.g., "I'm afraid I can't do it"). Take a few minutes to focus completely on this thought with your eyes open or closed and change your inner perception by saying this sentence to yourself in different ways, while observing the physical changes that take place.

◆ Repeat for two minutes like a skipping record.

◆ Change the gender and pitch of the voice.

◆ Change the direction of the sentence (e.g., from the front, the back, the side, close, far away).

◆ Change the volume, speed, and dialect (e.g., English accent, Southern drawl).

◆ Sing it or speak it like your favorite comedian or cartoon character.

During which version did you feel the biggest change? Which version changed the emotional impact the most? Repeat the sentence a few more times in that version. By changing thoughts via these creative games, formerly stressful thoughts are often experienced as unreal, less threatening, not part of oneself, or even funny and laughable. As a result, they become ineffective or at least significantly weakened.

EXERCISE: TONE

Focus again on a stressful thought (e.g., "I haven't trained well enough"). Now repeat the sentence several times, and each time change the tone by heavily emphasizing a different word:

◆ "**I** haven't trained well enough."

◆ "I **haven't** trained well enough."

◆ "I haven't **trained** well enough."

◆ "I haven't trained **well** enough."

◆ "I haven't trained well **enough**."

This exercise often has a similar effect as the thought modulation exercise.

FROM EXPERIENCE: SLEEPLESS NIGHTS

The night I finished writing this chapter, I woke up because an extremely unpleasant thought occurred to me. For weeks we had been waiting for permission from a forest ranger to hold our weekend running event TRAILDORADO, including the German Championship in 24-hour trail running. While two other forestry authorities had issued a permit just days after our application, one particular person gave us trouble. So that night I had to think about how one forester has been making our life unnecessarily difficult for about eight weeks now.

Now one might say, "Relax, you can't change anything." But that doesn't work because I had poured lots of blood, sweat, and tears into organizing this event, and we needed a decision to finally open up registration and organize lots of other things. I lay in bed totally frustrated, furious, and with a pounding heart, and was just about to get up even though it wasn't near time to get up. Then I thought: *Michele, you fool, you preach about wine and drink water. Forget that! Do the exercises you just wrote about.*

Half asleep, I completed the first two exercises to erase negative thoughts, and lo and behold, after what seemed like an eternity of tossing and turning I was able to calm down, get some distance from the stress, and go back to sleep for a while longer. Of course that still didn't solve the problem, but I was no longer so frustrated, and I got some sleep.

EXERCISE: QUESTIONS AND MORE QUESTIONS

Again think of a stressful thought, and then add the following thoughts:

◆ Think about a person who doesn't get stressed in a similar situation. How would he or she behave?

◆ What advice would you give someone else in the same situation?

◆ What will you think about this situation in another year?

◆ Have there been similar situations you've already dealt with?

◆ How do you plan to handle this situation?

◆ What positive things can you gain from this situation?

◆ What is the worst thing that could happen? Consider this if you can. What comes to mind? It can even be exaggerated and laughable.

These exercises help you sever the automatic link between a thought and a negative stress reaction by intensely focusing on a certain thought. The relevance can be changed so that the original thought no longer generates stress (Hoffmann, 2001).

Moreover, the following approaches can help reduce excessive activation or tension on and off the run:

◆ **Pre-start routines:** If we know exactly what needs to be done when, and our processes have been planned in advance of a competition, it gives us orientation. Such routines provide certainty. Certainty relaxes us and increases self-confidence.

◆ **Music:** A playlist of calm music with less than 60 BPM (beats per minute) is particularly effective. Our body gradually matches our heart rhythm to the music rhythm.

◆ **95% rule:** Someone who wants to give it all tends to tighten up. It's better to focus on giving 95%. Most of the time we remain looser and still achieve more.

◆ **Focus and process goals:** By not thinking about future results during a competition, but instead focusing on the process to get there, on the moment, on our body and its supple movements, on the loose swing of our arms, and the way our feet connect with the ground, we are able to reduce stress and fear. ("What do I want to experience or feel right now?")

◆ **Self-talk:** We should banish sentences like "I must ...," whenever they enter our mind, and we can stay calm by issuing self-instructions like "Relax," Stay calm," or "Keep your arms loose," and shift our focus to relaxation, especially when we use key words that are already linked to the relevant resources. We can also turn negative fear-born thoughts into positive ones. Instead of, "Oh boy, I am really nervous!" it would be better to say something like, "Awesome, my body is getting tuned up so I can really put the pedal to the metal."

◆ **Visualizations:** We can access relaxing images (e.g., sunset with my wife on a lonely beach) or use visualizations of a loose and relaxed running style to shift our focus to the process level.

◆ **Face check:** When we visit a popular nightclub, we often encounter a kind of face check at the entrance. If our face passes the test, we can enter the interesting area, the amusement zone. We can imagine ourselves doing something similar when we run. Our inner bouncer is most likely to let us enter the desired zone if he likes our facial expression. Our facial muscles have a major impact on the rest of our body tension.

When our face is tense, the body usually follows. When we relax our facial muscles, it also has a relaxing effect on the rest of the body. With a relaxed smile we can positively influence our mood and our body and reduce emotional peaks during stressful situations. Because when we smile or activate our laughing muscles, the brain receives the message that we are happy or joyful—and it might also help us calmly pass some dogged runners.

◆ **Sports hypnosis:** The use of trance or hypnosis techniques can be a very valuable addition to mental training and may generate more intense relaxation reactions more quickly.

As always, different techniques can be combined. There are no limits to the imagination.

With respect to personal goal management, you can of course also mentally go through phases of excessive and insufficient arousal as possible obstacles on your way to achieving your goal (i.e., mental contrasting). Someone who, in advance of a competition, vividly imagines being outside of the personal zone and goes through the unexpected or undesirable can then work out the appropriate process goals and action strategies and practice functional if-then links to bring to bear in an emergency (e.g., "Whenever I start to feel tired, I vividly remember the intoxicating feeling of crossing the finish line, and I mentally fill my muscles with new energy," "Whenever I feel myself tightening up just before the start, I tell myself my key word and activate a flash relaxation," or "Whenever I have gotten lost in the mountains due to poor visibility, I remain calm and carefully retrace my steps"). Athletes who plan for the unexpected are more relaxed in an emergency situation, and therefore also more successful.

FROM EXPERIENCE: JOY AND FUN VS. PERFORMANCE PRESSURE AND THE WEIGHT OF EXPECTATION

WHAT DO YOU THINK WE CAN TAKE AWAY FROM THE FOLLOWING STORIES?

Thomas feels good and has trained fantastically well. According to his training plan, he is due for a longer run. He spontaneously signs up for a local marathon and shows up at the start. A 3:30 h time would be great. He feels good and just lets things take their course without ambition and without checking his pulse or his watch. He forgets the time, enjoys being outside, and is surprised to see that he finished in 2:59 h. A new personal best!

Torsten has registered for an Ironman competition. Due to injuries and work, his training didn't work out as planned. He was going to cancel, but then a 60-year-old friend called and said he would like to do an Ironman. Torsten's cancellation email went into the trash. The night before the race they celebrated their reunion at a bar. Things got out of hand with respect to the amount of alcohol consumed. They didn't care; they just wanted to have fun. The effects of the night's revelry are very obvious the next day as they make their way to the start, still slightly woozy, but they successfully make it across the finish line, much to the surprise of the other participants and support staff. Their first Ironman is in the bag.

Another athlete starts a racing series. The goals are big. Preparations went perfectly, and his form was great. However, in spite of being in peak form, the first races didn't go well at all, and his chance of finishing in the top rankings overall disappeared. Then came the surprise: When the athlete finally had nothing to lose and just focused on having fun, he achieved his personal best.

What do these stories have in common, and what can we learn from their commonalities? Success and personal bests happened when there was no undue pressure and the focus was on enjoying the race. Pressure, regardless of whether it is external or self-imposed, is generally a bad companion that keeps us from achieving a top performance or from feeling good. Of course an adequate activation is required, but when we want something so desperately, or at least think we do, it has a negative effect: we tense up. Our fine coordination, energy efficiency, and lightness are lost. Things don't go as smoothly as they could. This results in increased negative thinking, which in turn has an immediate negative effect on physiological processes. It's a vicious circle.

The good news is that we always put pressure on ourselves. That means we could also stop putting pressure on ourselves, or at least minimize it. We control whether or not we allow our goalsself-talk, thoughts, and attitudes to build up internal pressure or not. That is also how we decide how to handle expectations that may come at us from the outside, what we want to accept, and what we don't. And since this topic often comes up during coaching, I want to expand on the question of how to minimize pressure or increase the likelihood that we will put less pressure on ourselves in the future.

FOUR QUICK WAYS TO REDUCE PRESSURE

◆ A helpful attitude would be to remember that we don't *have* to do anything! Goals and thoughts like, "I must ..." lead to unconscious reactance, meaning resistance and pressure. In the future, replace these with, "I will ..." or "I do ...".

◆ Think about which goals are truly important to YOU. Often performance-related goals or results that push to the fore (e.g., run marathon under X hours) may not be in line with your most important, very personal reasons for running (e.g., balancing work-related stress, health, spending time outdoors). It's not always about performance and doesn't always make you happy. And frequently ask yourself what you want to experience and how you can make sure that happens.

◆ Pressure, stress, and fear of failure cannot be experienced in a relaxed state. Someone who uses the aforementioned relaxation techniques (e.g., breathing techniques, progressive muscle relaxation, biofeedback, relaxing images and words) is able to effectively reduce pressure, stress, and fear within seconds during difficult situations, or prevent them from occurring in the first place.

◆ Smile! By purposefully using happy, joyous, confident facial expressions and gestures (e.g., laughing, upright posture, clenched fists), we have a positive effect on our experiences and are able to minimize the feeling of pressure. And many things in life are easier when we keep our sense of humor and don't take everything too seriously.

EXERCISE: STRESS TEST

If you would like to reliably test your stress level in just one minute, this exercise is for you. The test was developed by internationally renowned stress researchers, and is based on the knowledge that when presented with a test image, stressed people perceive the image very differently than less stressed people. The test image shows two identical dolphins jumping out of the water. The researchers learned that the more stressed a person is, the greater are the subjectively perceived differences between the dolphins. Please take a look at the test image (figure 16) before reading further.

What was your result? Maybe you belong to the large group of readers that might benefit from a little more rest and relaxation. The relaxation techniques introduced in this chapter are not just effective for short-term preparation to important events. They are also very well suited to lowering the overall stress level, creating more inner peace and tranquility in everyday life, and promoting regeneration after intense physical or mental demands and reducing risk of injury overall. Remember that only people who are able to balance phases of activation and smart recuperation will stay healthy and productive long term. Relaxation techniques can provide added value here. Regular use will result in a series of long-term positive effects on body and mind. And of course this has an effect on our ability to quickly deal with challenges that come our way.

And may be this not-so-serious test brought a smile to your face. That's good, because with all these methods to optimize motivation, performance, and heath in running, we should not always take things too seriously and should instead allow ourselves some fun and silliness.

PROFESSIONAL REGENERATION MANAGEMENT

In our performance-oriented society, recovery often has a negative connotation. In a world in which time is money and only performance seems to count, those who take time to recover are regarded as weak, lazy, demotivated, and unproductive. However, this is a dangerous way of thinking because sufficient and sensible recovery is an indispensable basis for physical and mental training processes and for increasing performance maintaining it in the long run.

From training science we know that it is ultimately during the recovery phases in which we improve our performance, known as supercompensation. At the end of a load, regeneration begins. To be better prepared for future performance demands, we recover a little beyond the original performance level. Ideally, the next stimulus will be the maximum of this "recovery over time." If we repeat this process, we will improve progressively. If we wait too long with the new stimulus, the supercompensation ebbs again and has no effect. If we wait too briefly, we do not have enough time for recovery. The efficiency decreases. In the long run, this can lead to physical overtraining or mental exhaustion.

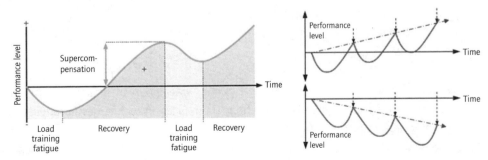

Figure 12 Supercompensation and overtraining.

We should, therefore, pay particular attention to the timing of recovery and stress. Many sports scientists are of the opinion that in a world in which the physical stress limits in top-class sport are already reached, professional recovery management in additional to psychological factors is becoming increasingly important. But how can we optimally control this process and, above all, avoid overtraining?

In the context of recovery management, it is crucial to have a sense of how strenuous certain stresses are for us. If an athlete feels that the same training or competition stress is suddenly more strenuous, regardless of the typical symptoms of fatigue, there may be deficits in recovery, illnesses, or psychological imbalances. Using a rating scale to measure the level of exertion can help to evaluate the issue.

EXERCISE: MEASURING EXERTION LEVEL

A rate of perceived exertion scale measures the subjectively perceived degree of effort of an activity within a few seconds. Simply evaluate the perceived effort of a past activity on the present scale. With regular use, you can recognize patterns and changes quickly. The scale begins at 6 because we want to measure effort, not relaxation.

6	
7	Extremely light
8	
9	Very light
10	
11	Light
12	
13	Somewhat hard
14	
15	Hard
16	
17	Very hard
18	
19	Extremely hard
20	Maximum exertion

Note: The scale was based on the assumption that the feeling of stress is related to heart rate. Since resting heart rate is usually around 60 beats per minute, the scale only starts at 6, which corresponds to 60 beats per minute. The maximum heart rate in healthy people is usually around 200 beats per minute, which is why the scale ends at 20. However, we all know that these values can vary greatly, especially for endurance athletes. It is, therefore, important to remember that the scale is only a subjective assessment of the load (= strain).

Another parameter used to control recovery and stress is physical and mental well-being. It is regarded as an excellent indicator of how well stress is managed. If health deteriorates over a longer period, there may be problems coping with everyday stress or physical or mental illnesses. The *Short Scale Recovery & Stress* (Meyer et al., 2016) is a tried and tested instrument and easy to use. It is also suitable for repeated measurements and long-term monitoring.

EXERCISE: SHORT SCALE RECOVERY & EXERCISE

The following chart lists eight components, each with four recreational and stress components. For each dimension there are keyword descriptions, whereby only the superordinate dimension is evaluated. The process takes only 30-40 seconds and enables direct and fast feedback.

	Does not apply				Completely true		
Physical performance strong, efficient, energetic, full of power	0	1	2	3	4	5	6
Mental performance attentive, receptive, focused, mentally alert							
Emotional balance content, balanced, in a good mood, everything under control							
General recovery Recovered, rested, muscular relaxed, physically relaxed							
Muscular stress Overstrained, tired, acidified, stiff muscles							
Lack of activation unmotivated, lethargic, listless, no energy							

	Does not apply	Completely true
Emotional imbalance depressed, stressed, annoyed, easily irritable		
General stress condition Done, weakened, overburdened, physically flat		

Note: This questionnaire is a translated but not yet validated version of the original German version of Meyer et al. (2016).

While a simple rate of perceived exertion scale is only useful for repeated use to determine any differences over time, the "short scale recovery & stress" can, in my opinion, already provide revealing information after the first use. Suppose you have tried the latter scale directly, what are the results? Are you satisfied? If so, how would you like to maintain or possibly improve the positive results? If not, what could be the reason that the results may not be as desired and how would you like to deal with them? But above all, because we want to be solution-oriented: how would you like to improve them?

Many people use heart rate belts and sports watches to keep regular logs of their running and performance data. How about running one of these scales? This can be done with relatively little effort using a spreadsheet or existing training software and is a great investment: little effort, great benefit. At least that's what many professionals and experts say. Why not learn from them?

THE DARK SIDE OF RUNNING AND HOW TO TURN IT INTO OPPORTUNITIES

It wasn't planned that way.
You can also build beautiful things with the stones placed in your path.

—J.W. Goethe

7 THE DARK SIDE OF RUNNING AND HOW TO TURN IT INTO OPPORTUNITIES

In life things don't always go according to plan. Quite the contrary! Where there is light there is also shadow. And yet we frequently hear particularly successful people from very different spheres of life say that personal defeats and failures have been a very important elixir on their road to success and growth. No matter how unpleasant and disappointing it is when things don't go as planned, when we fail in one way or another, don't get the results we are looking for, maybe even run into a wall, or have to struggle with other negative experiences and events, one thing always applies: Crises also present opportunities. Or more simply put: Where one door closes another door opens. To seize these opportunities we must keep our eyes open.

7.1 A THREAT TO BODY AND SOUL: THE NEGATIVE EFFECTS OF POSITIVE THINKING

We are all familiar with this: Whenever we are in a difficult situation, are not doing well, or are dealing with a failure, the following well-intended piece of advice is never far away: "Hey, think positive!" In the previous chapters we focused a lot on positive attitudes and perspectives. Those are, of course, very valuable and can be very functional. But—and I hope that message came through loud and clear—you don't have to think positive all the time. In fact, I expressly advise against it, and for good reason. Of course feeling confident, being goal oriented instead of failure oriented, and having a *realistic dose of optimism* have a positive effect on our health and life satisfaction, physical and emotional well-being, professional and athletic success. Many studies verify this. We also know that intelligent activation of positive images, thoughts, and feelings has a motivating effect during training, enhances performance during competitions, and can have a healing effect to injuries. But the dogmatic use of what is touted all over the land as *positive thinking* is less promising and possibly even dangerous.

MAKING A CULT OUT OF POSITIVE THINKING

Many people find the concept of positive thinking appealing, and it is a commercial success on the coaching and motivational scene. Countless books and CDs with unbelievable sales promote the easy way to happiness, wealth, and success. According to the credo, all you have to do is think positive. Many lecturers and motivational coaches jump on the bandwagon and preach that we can achieve anything if we just want to. But practical experience shows that this is usually short-sighted and simply untrue.

FROM EXPERIENCE: THE FAILED FIREWALKER

A running buddy and entrepreneur is very interested in the subject of motivation. Years ago, he participated in a *firewalk* with a famous motivational trainer. After a day of mental preparation, the participants were supposed to walk on glowing embers without burning their feet. In spite of the fact that cheap tricks are employed at some of these firewalks, such as burning down the coal until the top layer provides sufficient insulation, this curious runner's path led directly to the hospital instead of self-motivational nirvana. The soles of his feet were burned and for weeks he was unable to walk normally without crutches.

There are three bad things about this personal story: First, this is not an isolated incident. Second, it can result in instant physical damage. And third, this often has negative psychological consequences like increased self-doubt and shame, even guilt and the feeling of not being good enough, not being able to think positive. In July 2012, 21 participants at a motivational seminar held by the famous motivational guru Tony Robbins had to be taken to hospital with burns after an unsuccessful firewalk. One of the participants was quoted in a newspaper as saying that he had been unable to enter an optimal state (Burkeman, 2012).

FOOL ME ONCE...
A number of studies now show that those who should benefit most from positive thinking methods are most likely to experience negative effects. People who are plagued by illness, depression, or self-doubt; are unhappy with a current life situation; or don't possess the measure of success and recognition they wish for are often pushed further into disaster by positive thinking. Instead of dealing with challenges and negative things in a constructive manner, positive self-affirmation is imposed on them that has little to do with reality, let alone that takes into account individual or socio-structural circumstances (Scheich, 2001; Ehrenreich, 2011).

Do you really think you can run a marathon in 2:00 h just because you really want to and regularly expose yourself to a constant stream of positive messages like "I am strong," "I am a rocket," "I can achieve anything I want," or "I'm going to run a marathon in 2:00 h"? Admittedly, maybe you are an undiscovered talent with perfect biomechanical and physiological abilities, but in case you're not, these strategies from the school of positive thinking can quickly create frustration and self-doubt. Besides, it is important for your personal development to be aware of negative experiences like defeats and disappointments, to process them and grow with them instead of covering them up with positive thinking ("I'm fine, I'm super!"). This can lead to performance blocks or even loss of reality and psychosis. So let's keep our optimism and attitudes realistic without denying real difficulties. Let's also deal with the negative things that come our way, because that gives us some important material to find consistent answers to the question of precisely how we want achieve our goals, what we want to experience along the way, and how we want to handle sticking points (Oettingen & Gollwitzer, 2010).

FROM EXPERIENCE: FLIRTING WITH PAIN DURING A MARATHON
Several months after a sport psychology lecture, I was contacted by a marathon runner who thanked me for my suggestions. After several attempts, he had finally reached an important goal: running a marathon in under 3 hours. The following was something

he found particularly helpful: No rose-colored glasses that only see the positive based on the motto "You can do anything" and "Everything will be fine." Next to staying consistently focused on a goal and accessing performance-enhancing positive mental images and feelings, there was primarily one thing that heled him to succeed: mentally running through difficult situations during the race, particularly during the second half of the race, when your legs are running on fumes and burning. Not only did he achieve his goal, he even did a half-marathon best time in the second half of the race.

7.2 SHIT HAPPENS: HOW TO HANDLE FAILURE

You've prepared for weeks and months, sometimes even years, for an event that is very important to you. You've sacrificed lots of time for this athletic success and in the process may have occasionally neglected your family. You have worked painstakingly to achieve specific performance or result goals in the XYZ race, be it a new PR or simply just finishing. You are confident at the start, and for good reason, because the overall preparations and the training went perfectly well and you have the right gear. All signs point to success and goal attainment. And then you missed the goal. Sometimes you already know during the race, sometimes it's a close call, and sometimes it's just brutal (e.g., you completely falter or have to drop out). The failure happened and the disappointment grips you to the marrow. All of the assurances to see things in a positive way don't seem to help. Now what?

THE QUESTION OF WHY AND ITS POTENTIAL EFFECTS

Almost every athlete experiences failures, athletic slumps, and setbacks during his career. There are many different reasons for this (e.g., physical deficiencies, wrong attitudes, unsuitable equipment, underestimating the task, personal problems, bad luck). Athletes usually search for explanations to action results. In doing so, the results are attributed to a possible cause. Researchers also refer to this as *causal attribution*. We differentiate between two types of causal attribution. When a person blames himself for the cause of an event, it is *internal causal attribution*. When someone views other people, environmental influences, or other external factors as the cause of an event, it is called *external causal attribution*.

People tend to use an internal causal attribution when they are successful, meaning they see themselves, their abilities and actions as the cause for success. For instance, a runner thinks he has reached his competitive goal because he trained a lot and chose the right running strategy. If he fails, he will most likely use the external causal attribution, meaning he will attribute the cause for his failure to another person or environmental influences. For example, a runner may think he missed his goal because he had bad luck, the weather was bad, or the orientation wasn't clear.

This type of attribution protects one's sense of self-worth because we don't have to see or portray ourselves as the cause of negative events. We call this causal attribution *success oriented*. It has a positive effect on self-confidence and can be seen in people with lots of achievement motivation. People who ascribe success to themselves and failure to circumstances primarily look for tasks with a medium degree of difficulty, set realistic goals, and are more likely to achieve them, which leads to a realistic, positive self-image. However, they run the risk of ascribing failures to very external causes, letting a little healthy self-criticism fall by the wayside.

Failure-oriented causal attribution attributes success to external causes (e.g., luck) and failure to internal causes (e.g., one's own incompetence). Such a pattern damages self-confidence and is commonly linked to mindsets that are typical in people with depression. Failure-oriented people look for very easy or very difficult tasks, thereby avoiding realistic feedback on their abilities.

HOW DO WE HANDLE FAILURES?

The manner in which we process and deal with failure is extremely individual and always depends on the situation. When we actually see something as a failure is also an important factor. Blanket advice that doesn't take into account individual everyday reality can therefore make things much worse. Below are some suggestions based on the previous statements that have proven helpful in one way or another in dealing with temporary failures as well as veritable lows. It may not come as a surprise to you that I begin before a failure even occurs, then take a look at the moment a failure becomes apparent and how we, should it become a reality, can deal with it.

◆ It makes sense to regularly ask yourself: Why am I running? Why and when do I enjoy running the most? When does running make me feel particularly good and what goals am I pursuing apart from possible performance goals? Someone who can answer these questions will be considerably more relaxed in dealing with potential failures.

◆ Set realistic performance goals with a medium degree of difficulty. This will increase the likelihood of success, and a 50/50 probability of success motivates the most.

◆ Avoid overemphasizing result goals and always formulate process goals. The latter are just as important. Answers to the question "How do I want to reach my goal, and what do I want to experience?" may be used for specific action regulation and can have a positive effect on performance. And in the event you don't reach a performance goal, focusing on process goals is a powerful anchor that offers support, direction, and a potential reset into the next challenge.

◆ Positive ideas may be extremely helpful, but instead of picturing your positive goal attainment strictly through rose-colored glasses based on the school of positive thinking, also set flexible alternative goals and go through them in your mind for the worst-case scenario. What would be the best goal when everything goes really well? And what would be a minimum goal when things aren't going so well? What does failure even mean to you? In a competition, in training, or in some other area? And what would you do during training or a competition, or afterwards, when such a failure becomes apparent? What would be the worst that can happen? And how would that affect the rest of your life? Doing this removes some of the dread of failure beforehand, and, if worse comes to worst, you can take timely countermeasures, or at least prepare a softer landing. It is usually more helpful than strictly programming yourself for success, as some mental coaches advocate.

◆ Remember that you cannot force yourself to run well. The more internal pressure you build up, the more tense and inefficiently you will run, and the more negative your thoughts will be. Focus on your process goals!

◆ Admittedly, this next tip might sound glib, but it is powerful, and it is always an issue for people who largely define themselves by their achievements. Cultivate the attitude you are a good person and are fine the way you are! No matter what you achieve (in a competition or elsewhere)!

◆ Use helpful self-talk strategies and turn problems into challenges and learning opportunities (e.g., "If I can't make progress the way I want to, then I'll practice being patient," "What's done is done and can't be changed," or "Failure is a chance to work on my inner attitude or rethink my training system").

◆ Being disappointed every once in a while is totally okay and the most normal thing in the world. Disappointments and sadness, particularly when they are bitter disappointments, should be allowed to play out and be processed instead of being pushed away with positive thinking. That can backfire, just like when you try to push a ball under water and it pops up on the other side (e.g., inexplicable motivational problems, shaken self-confidence, recurring failures because you have made the same mistakes again). But the athletic failure should always be put into perspective: How serious is this really? What else is important in life? How much does this athletic failure affect the rest of your life? Your job? Your family, friends, other hobbies, etc.?

◆ To get out of a failure phase and not remain in a negative spiral, it helps to work with new wish goal visualizations (e.g., What will it feel like when I have gotten over this loss of form or this failure phase? What do I do? What has helped me come out of it and improve?

◆ From which role models could you learn to handle failure with confidence? What do they do? What could you borrow?

◆ And once the initial frustration has subsided, the most important part happens: The chance to view failure as an opportunity and seizing this opportunity to learn and improve. What can we learn from this failure? Failure is an excellent source of feedback, offering the most valuable advice on what you could do differently and improve in the future. And maybe it is a kind of starting signal for making some adjustments or changes? The first step could be to begin with the first item on this list.

◆ Or maybe you will write a book from which others can learn. How about the title *"Shit happens, and it is the fertilizer for personal growth"?*

A very nice example of how to use failures constructively is presented in the next chapter by Florian Reus, the 2015 World and European Champion in the 24-hour race, as well as the winner of the legendary Spartathlon race and thereby the double in the same year. He would most likely not have accomplished this lifelong dream without a few major failures that initially really wore him down.

7.3   CRISES, OPPORTUNITIES, TWISTS, AND TURNS: HOW DOES A WORLD CHAMPION THINK?

When I was planning this book, I initially wrote down dealing with crises as a possible topic because it is always hotly debated and generates an active exchange within the running and endurance community. But I quickly discarded the idea of addressing this topic, or at least this terminology. Because what does *crisis* actually mean? Do we talk about a crisis when things get physically or mentally difficult during training or a competition as we come up against our limits, or think we do? Or does crisis mean events are so extreme that it is a matter of life and death?

According to the dictionary, a *crisis* is a difficult situation or time that represents the apex and turning point of a dangerous development. When this development takes a permanently negative course, we call it a *catastrophe*. If we want to go with this definition, we will come to the conclusion that we very rarely, if ever, enter a crisis situation during our recreational runs, regardless of how performance oriented we are or how subjectively important something may be to us. The same should be true for professional athletes. I therefore suggest we disown the strategy we are all too familiar with from the media, namely immediately blowing everything up into an alleged crisis, and instead talk about *challenges* that need to be mastered.

While organizing the running event TRAILDORADO, which, along with a 24-hour trail race, features a supporting program with numerous lectures and workshops, I was able to recruit Florian Reus, winner of multiple German national championships and World and European Champion in the 24-hour race, for an exciting lecture. The topic was his path to becoming a World Champion. I talked to Florian beforehand and asked him for an honest lecture without clumsy, superficial, pretentious motivational babble, that instead focused particularly on the failures and obstacles on the way to his world championship title. Unfortunately I was so busy with organizing the event that I did not have time to attend the lecture myself. I merely managed to occasionally listen in to make sure the technology was working properly. During one of those moments, I heard Florian talk about how, after winning several German national titles, he experienced a series of bitter failures and had to repeatedly drop out of races. At that moment I realized that I also wanted Florian to be a contributor to this book to exchange views on strategy, attitude, dealing with failures, and maybe also on dealing with crises. During our conversations, it quickly became apparent that Florian is also careful with his use of the word *crisis*. Let's see what Florian had to say about his path to becoming a World Champion.

MICHELE: FLORIAN, HOW DID YOU COME TO RUNNING AND WHAT ARE YOUR PREVIOUS
ATHLETIC SUCCESSES?

Florian Reus: Inspired by a newspaper article I had seen by chance, I ran my first ultra-marathon in 2003, namely the 100 km race in Biel, Switzerland. I started doing 24-hour races soon after and have stuck with them. They are my main discipline still today. After several second- and third-place finishes, both at the World Championships and at Spartathlon, 2015 was supposed to be the most successful year of my running career to date. During that running season, I was supposed to win the World Championships and the Spartathlon. Another important success was winning the European Championships in the 24-hour race three times, since no other runner had previously been able to win this title that many times. My current personal best is 263.9 km.

MICHELE: FOR MANY READERS, 24-HOUR RACES—IN WHICH TOP RUNNERS LIKE YOU
COMPLETE UP TO 260 KM AND MORE—ARE UNFATHOMABLE. WHAT DOES AN AVERAGE
TRAINING WEEK LOOK LIKE FOR YOU?

Florian Reus: When I am not preparing for a competition, an average training week generally means running between 140 and 170 km. During the week, I usually train twice a day (i.e., morning and afternoon). On the weekends, I generally do a longer training unit of more than 35 km. When I prepare for a 24-hour race, meaning during the final eight weeks of the training process, my weekly volume goes up to 200 km, and in some exceptional cases it can be more than 250 km in one week. During this phase, the individual training units are also considerably longer (up to 80 km).

MICHELE: HOW DO YOU MOTIVATE YOURSELF TO BE ABLE TO COMPLETE SO MANY
LONG AND, TO SOME EXTENT, LONELY TRAINING UNITS?

Florian Reus: In my current situation, motivation isn't a huge challenge. In the past few years, my performance has reached a level that allows me to win important races, or to at least place near the top. By now, I can also rely on my vast ultra-marathon

experience and I am now able to run these races with lots of patience. Based on this knowledge, I am convinced that I have a chance in any of these 24-hour races when I start in good form. This thought also motivates me to complete my training units even when I don't feel like it, when the weather is bad, or when training isn't going as well as planned. But motivation was much more of a challenge back when my performance level was still much lower, the anticipated short-term successes didn't compare to those of today, and of course there was no guarantee that all of the effort would ever pay off in the form of great successes. Back then having a clear, long-term goal really helped me.

MICHELE: DURING A COMPETITION, HOW DO YOU MOTIVATE YOURSELF TO ACHIEVE TOP PERFORMANCES? WHERE DO YOU GET YOUR STRENGTH AND THE NECESSARY ENERGY TO PUSH YOURSELF TO YOUR LIMIT?

Florian Reus: What drives me are my specific goals, which I don't just set a few months before a competition, but that have been with me for many years. These long-term goals in particular really motivate me during a competition because I am aware of how much work and sacrifice I have already invested in that goal. Of course I am also driven by the social recognition, but honestly, in a fringe sport like mine it is completely out of proportion to the effort. Instead I very much want to achieve my personal goal, if only because I know the magical moments that are the reward for a successful race, and that stay with you forever.

MICHELE: HOW DO YOU GET IN THE RIGHT MINDSET FOR IMPORTANT COMPETITIONS? DO YOU HAVE CERTAIN ROUTINES OR PROCESSES JUST BEFORE THE START?

Florian Reus: Everything that happens before the start is pure routine, especially when it comes to practical things like, for instance, what to eat for breakfast. Everything that happens on race day is standardized because that is not the time to experiment. During the final hour before the race, I find it important to have a little private time. That's when I usually mentally go through the impending race, but only superficially because at that point I'm already a little tense due to the upcoming strenuous task. This time of reflection isn't a planned action—I primarily want to enjoy a few quiet minutes before the start—but thoughts about the race automatically penetrate just before the starting signal.

Overall, it is very important to me to start the race with a certain amount of humility and respect for the task ahead, because when you take a long ultra-marathon too lightly you've already lost the race before it even started. But those are things you can't learn right before a race. They are ultimately a matter of attitude towards the sport.

MICHELE: DO YOU HAVE ROLE MODELS? IF YES, WHO ARE THEY? WHAT DO YOU LEARN FROM THEM AND HOW DO YOU USE THEM?

Florian Reus: I don't have *one* great role model, but I am very inspired by the Japanese ultra-marathoners. I love how they run their races with such stoic calm and exude such humility outside of the race. I believe that the qualities these runners radiate, such as humility, modesty, discipline, and internal equilibrium, are very important factors for real success in the 24-hour race.

MICHELE: THINGS DON'T ALWAYS GO SMOOTHLY IN LIFE, YET IN GERMANY WE DON'T LIKE TO TALK ABOUT MISTAKES AND FAILURES BECAUSE THEY ARE INTERPRETED AS A SIGN OF WEAKNESS. WHAT ARE SOME OF THE LOWS, FAILURES, SETBACKS, OR LONG-TERM INJURIES YOU HAVE EXPERIENCED IN YOUR CAREER? HOW DID YOU FEEL AND HOW DID YOU COPE? LOOKING BACK, WHAT WOULD YOU SAY YOU LEARNED FROM YOUR MISTAKES AND DIFFICULT MOMENTS? HOW DID THEY HELP YOU PROGRESS AND HOW WOULD YOU HANDLE THEM TODAY?

Florian Reus: The low point of my career so far was definitely the 24-hour run at the 2010 World Championships. Back then, I already had the long-term goal of collecting international wins, and at this race I wanted to get at least a little closer to that goal, meaning I was aiming for a place in the top 20. After successfully qualifying for the World Championships, it was even more important to me to continue the upward trend after having had two so-so years, and to finally bring back some consistency to my results. But the race turned out to be a complete fiasco, so much so that I dropped out, completely unnerved, about four hours before the end of the race. That was the first time I completely lost my belief in my long-term goal, and the disappointment was huge because it meant that I had dropped out of four of the last five 24-hour runs. Back then, I even seriously considered ending my competitive career.

During my lectures, I always tell people that without those failures I would most likely not be standing in front of them, lecturing as a World Champion. I am absolutely convinced of this because in many ways these failures made me stronger. After a long break from competing, a greatly reduced training volume, and temporarily letting go of my personal goals after the aforementioned low point, I radically changed course. I took a critical look at my training, improved my parameters, and most importantly, I completely changed my attitude. These were all important factors that made the great successes in subsequent years possible.

MICHELE: WHAT CHANGES DID YOU MAKE WITH RESPECT TO TRAINING, PARAMETERS, YOUR ATTITUDE? WHEN WAS THE CRITICAL MOMENT, WHAT WAS GOING THROUGH YOUR HEAD, AND WHAT GAVE YOU DIRECTION?

Florian Reus: The training error was relatively easy to fix by paying more attention to a gentle buildup and avoiding the abrupt acceleration of my training volume. Back then, I worked full-time in my profession as a wine cooper. During those weeks of critical reflections, I also realized that such a physically demanding job that included seasonal peaks and which prevented training for several weeks could not be reconciled with the major demands of my performance sport. These factors gave me the courage to pursue a long-lost dream of starting a sports-related course of study. With respect to my attitude, there wasn't *that one day* when everything changed, but during that time I gradually became much more humble again. After first cracking the 230 km mark in 2007, I started subsequent races with the mindset of also having to crack the 250 km sonic barrier. Back then I did not see any alternative, and I had no plan B if, during a race, it should became apparent that I would not be able to achieve that goal. When I started over, I swore to myself that what was most important in these long races was finishing, and that should never be taken for granted. With that attitude, I staged my comeback 15 months after my low point, and was able to improve my previous best performance by 10 km. I still embrace these tenets today because since then I have not prematurely dropped out of a single race.

MICHELE: WHICH TEMPORARY, SHORT-TERM DIFFICULTIES AND CRISES DO YOU STRUGGLE WITH DURING YOUR COMPETITIONS AND HOW DO YOU DEAL WITH THEM? WHAT ARE YOUR THOUGHTS AND FEELINGS WHEN THINGS GET TOUGH?

Florian Reus: Patience is a very important factor, particularly during these phases. In such situations, I am able to stay very calm and patient by thinking about my experience. I have seen many times how one can regain one's rhythm after a major crisis and how the page can gradually turn with respect to rankings as well. It's not like I visualize a specific example, but it's worth a lot to me to have this experience-based knowledge in the back of my head during such phases. Moreover, during such crises, I think it's important not to start walking, but to keep running. That means you sometimes have to grit your teeth, but at least I know beforehand what I have gotten myself into, because these types of situations are inevitable during a long ultra-marathon. That is why it is extremely important to prepare for these phases.

MICHELE: DO YOU HAVE ANY MOTIVATIONAL LOWS? AND IF YES, WHAT DO YOU DO IN THOSE SITUATIONS?

Florian Reus: Actually, during competitions, I rarely experience crises caused by a lack of motivation. The inevitable lows during such a long race generally have other causes. During training, I of course have phases when I could use a little more motivation. For me, dealing with those phases largely depends on the respective phase within the season. During the time following a competition, I allow myself a lack of motivation without feeling guilty, even if that phase lasts two or three weeks longer than planned. I believe that's important to be ready to really fight again. During the training phases in which I cannot afford a motivational low, I use short-term, purely quantitative intermediate goals. For instance, I am motivated by achieving an intended weekly running volume or by completing my self-imposed daily working hours, which also includes my training.

MICHELE: DO YOU CONSCIOUSLY CONTROL YOUR THOUGHTS DURING RACES, AND IF SO, HOW? WHAT HELPS YOU? DO YOU HAVE SPECIFIC PSYCHOLOGICAL PROGRAMS THAT YOU REEL OFF AND THAT HELP YOU?

Florian Reus: During a race, I just try to do my thing with as much stoic calm and patience as possible. Consequently, I don't even really tolerate baseless euphoria that often arises after running a few kilometers, because over the course of such a long race that high is most often followed by an even greater low. Sure, if, for instance, the race seems to progress in my favor, I might permit the euphoria because then there is actually a reason that might also lend me wings for the long haul. But during a competition I basically try to focus exclusively on running, meaning I am constantly busy checking my speed, thinking about my nutritional situation, or questioning my strategy for the following hours. In the beginning years of my ultra-marathon career, I often purposefully kept myself occupied with thoughts that had nothing to do with the competition, or I used my MP3 player. But over time I learned that this wasn't really ideal for me personally, because I quickly fell into a state of lethargy.

MICHELE: IN OUR SOCIETY, PERFORMANCE PRESSURE AND THE WEIGHT OF EXPECTATION ARE VERY HIGH. WHAT DOES THAT MEAN FOR YOU? WHEN DO YOU FEEL THE PRESSURE AND HOW DO YOU HANDLE IT?

Florian Reus: When it comes to competitions, I am actually pretty blasé now about the expectations others have of me, which usually surprises me the most. But that is probably only due to the successes or primarily my consistent performance in recent years, and the associated faith in my own performance. I feel like I don't have anything to prove anymore, and my perceived self-efficacy before competitions like a 24-hour race is most likely very highly developed. The last few days before a race, I usually worry about catching a cold. But when I am at the start feeling healthy, I feel like I am calling the shots. As a competitive athlete, I of course put pressure on myself, but I don't feel great pressure from others.

MICHELE: SOME EXPERTS SAY THAT EXPERIENCING FLOW—MEANING IMMERSING YOURSELF IN AN ACTIVITY WITHOUT REFLECTION, WHERE EVERYTHING PROCEEDS EFFORTLESSLY AND VIRTUALLY AUTOMATICALLY—HAS A POSITIVE EFFECT ON MOTIVATION AND PERFORMANCE IN SPORTS. HOW ABOUT YOU? WHEN ARE YOU IN A STATE OF FLOW? DO YOU CONSIDER IT HELPFUL? CAN YOU CONSCIOUSLY ACTIVATE IT?

Florian Reus: In my estimation, the state of flow with respect to ultra-marathons is often greatly exaggerated, especially by the popular science media. When I think back to past competitions, I can remember one or two running phases, during which I experienced a state of flow. But it was ultimately just a temporary phase that presented a very small portion of the 24-hour race. To date, it has therefore never been a race-defining factor for me. Due to that fact, I don't even try to consciously achieve a state of flow. To do so, I would probably also have to back away from my tried-and-proven recipe of complete focus on the competition.

MICHELE: GIVING GENERAL ADVICE OR SUGGESTIONS TO OTHERS IN ABBREVIATED FORM IS NOT EASY, BUT ASSUMING YOU COULD SPONTANEOUSLY THINK OF ONE OR TWO OTHER TIPS THAT HAVE BEEN, AND MAY STILL BE, VERY HELPFUL TO YOU PERSONALLY, WHAT WOULD THEY BE?

Florian Reus: I think what's most important in ultra-marathon is an ability we have often forgotten in the age of limitless acceleration, and that is patience. Of course this ability doesn't just happen, but by learning from running and by consistently envisioning its immensely important impact, I am able to increase my patience. I have personally benefited greatly from these experiences in other areas of my life as well. In that regard, we may be able to learn something from the ultra-marathoners.

MICHELE: TO SUMMARIZE, IN YOUR OPINION, HOW IMPORTANT IS THE HEAD, THE MENTAL PART, OR THE MIND IN SPORTS OVERALL, AND IN RUNNING IN PARTICULAR? HOW HAVE YOU DEVELOPED THAT ASPECT OVER TIME?

Florian Reus: Generally speaking, you could say the longer the race, the more important the head. Thus the mental aspect is very significant in my races. Over the past 13 years, during which I have been an active ultra-marathoner, I have learned a lot on that front from my competitions, and in retrospect the failures in particular have been very important. But I don't do regular and methodical mental training in the classic sense. However, preparing for a competition is a regular part of my repertoire. For instance, during the final week before an important competition, I try to steer clear as best I can of other obligations. I use that time to focus on the run as much as possible. I do my best to mentally place myself in the phases that will be very difficult and to imagine what the pain in those phases of the race will feel like. That helps me to stay calm and patient during the race when these situations occur, because I mentally prepared for them.

THANK YOU VERY MUCH FOR THE INTERVIEW, FLORIAN, AND BEST OF LUCK IN THE FUTURE!

7.4   FROM RESEARCH & PRACTICE: MENTAL RESILIENCE AS MEANS FOR SUCCESS

Every person experiences crises. But why is it that some athletes stumble in times of crisis, while others navigate relatively quickly and confidently through difficult times and even emerge stronger? How can we promote mental resilience in order to cope better with crises and stressful situations in the future?

A magic word that has been quite en vogue for some years now is *resilience*. Resilience, or psychological resilience, is generally understood as the ability to cope with crises and to use them for personal and social development (Schumacher et al., 2005). It is regarded as a central success factor on the path to mental health and performance, particularly in sport (Hosseini & Besharat, 2010). There is a lot of advice on how to deal with crises. The crux: What is perceived as a crisis for some does not necessarily have to be a crisis for others. We all tick differently, have different goals, expectations, needs, and a different experience background.

A workshop I held with a national team makes this very clear. When asked how best to deal with crises in competition, instead of prescribing the desired "miracle pill," I first asked the athletes present what a crisis actually is for them; exactly how they or others recognize that they are in a crisis; how they experience a crisis; what emotions, feelings, thoughts are buzzing along with it. At first the athletes were irritated because I didn't give a generally valid answer, but instead invited people to self-reflect. It quickly became apparent, and not surprisingly, that the ways of seeing and experiencing things were different. They also differed regarding previous strategies for action in the supposed case of crisis. And against this background, new solutions and strategies are likely to yield different results and must be tried and individually adjusted.

After a stimulating, though brief, discussion I recommended that the athletes ideally acquire the appropriate psychological tools in advance and deal with potential crisis situations, or rather, challenges. You have already heard some relevant catchwords in this book, and they were also used in the workshop: process goals, mental contrasts, resources, etc. Those who are then mentally strengthened and prepared for tricky situations will most likely handle them better.

A study I conducted on the relationship between mental resistance and the use of mental strategies in endurance sports reinforces this view (Ufer, 2018). It was found that using seven mental strategies is positively related to mental resistance (see TOPS, chapter 3.7). However, it is surprising that the use of relaxation in the athletes interviewed is not related to resilience. This may be because the benefits of relaxation in general have thus far been underestimated and not as targeted.

Overall, we can say that the more often these strategies are used, the more resilient the athletes are. They seem to get through difficult times better and recover faster from stress. Thus, it's best that mental and sport psychological training start before the crisis.

Figure 13 Connection between psychological strategies and resiliance

Using the psychological strategies mentioned seems to be a promising start for the targeted promotion of general stress resistance or resilience. However, don't forget that environment, such as family, friends, team, trainer, caregiver, etc., can also have a decisive influence on an athlete's psychological resistance.

7.5   SPORTS INJURIES: THE ROLE OUR MIND PLAYS IN THE OCCURRENCE AND HEALING OF INJURIES

What is the best strategy for dealing with injuries? Not to get any, of course. But what if it happens anyway? Then you have to use your brain to make the healing process the best it can be and accelerate it. At first glance that might sound banal, and many would probably agree. But what does it look like in practice?

Running is healthy. That's what everyone says. And it's true if it is done with good judgment. Nevertheless, each year approximately 30-60% of runners complain about some unfortunate injury (Keller, 2009). And that in spite of the fact that running is neither a risky nor a contact sport as is the case with many combat and game sports. Yet barely a minute goes by without someone in some forum asking for advice. Sports injuries (i.e., physical trauma) that result in temporary or permanent physical impairments or a hiatus from athletic activity seem to be the order of the day. What are the causes?

Of course we initially get the obvious answers to that question, for instance, stress and strain from rolling the ankle or a poor running technique, overloading or overtraining, fatigue, and (rarely) collisions. What causes stress and strain or overtraining? It doesn't come from nowhere.

A number of studies show that in addition to the above reasons, psychological factors have a massive impact on the probability of injury occurrence and the duration and quality of rehabilitation after injuries.

STRESS, MENTAL SKILLS, AND THE OCCURRENCE OF INJURIES

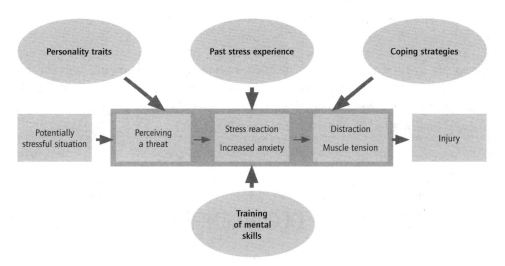

Figure 14 Stress and sports injuries (Weinberg & Gould 2015).

Stress plays a key role in the occurrence of injuries. Many studies confirm that athletes who experience general or situational stress also have more injuries than less stressed athletes (Johnson, 2007; Williams & Andersen, 1998).

Stress *only* occurs whenever we perceive a situation as threatening, thus it depends on our individual perception and personality. A mountain run can trigger stress in some, pleasure in others. Some panic just thinking about hitting the wall and have a stress reaction, while others could not care less. Some are able to calm themselves when they get overly anxious, while others are plunged into a negative cycle and nearly drive themselves crazy. That is why the results from Smith and colleagues (1990) are no surprise. They found that the less developed an athlete's mental coping strategies are, the higher the overall risk of injury.

Additional research results show that athletes engaging in sports with a very high injury risk had significantly fewer injuries after psychological training (e.g., progressive muscle relaxation, self-talk, visualizations) than the comparison group that did not receive such training (Johnson et al.; Madisson & Prapavessis, 2005).

But why does stress result in increased injuries? Attentiveness is interrupted. There are more distractions and our peripheral cognitive ability narrows. During critical moments, we may see important things or obstacles at the edge of our field of vision too late or not at all. Our reaction ability is also lessened. Simultaneously, our muscle tension increases. This stress state disrupts fine coordination and flexibility. There is probably no further need to explain what might happen. Surely you can find a few nice, injury-laden examples.

This means people who have less stress in their lives and athletic endeavors overall (e.g., competition, imminent failure) get injured less often.

NO PAIN, NO GAIN: DANGEROUS VALUES?

Pushing your limits in order to progress is a regular part of training. It can be quite unpleasant and really tough, and it has to be to set the necessary load stimulus. But it is something entirely different when we regularly ignore or downplay signs of stress and overtraining in the spirit of "more is better." Sports physicians think that many runners return to running too much, too fast, too often, and too hard after injuries, and caution that injuries due to overload are on the rise. Why is that?

"No pain, no gain." "Go hard or go home." All of these sayings speak to a certain performance culture. Suffering through pain and downplaying injuries is hip because

"only the hardened get into the garden." But let's not forget that everything in life comes at a price. The price for embracing this macho culture where it seems sexy to endure or understate pain and where all too often short-term gain is placed ahead of long-term health is a significantly increased risk of injury (Heil & Podlok, 2012).

Growing social media networking and activity may also fuel this trend. It is very fast. Nearly every second, new status updates and videos of heroic highlights appear that quickly relativize one's own achievements and performance, at least in those with a slightly less robust sense of self-worth, and may induce some athletes to go too fast too far in order to garner recognition and be "on the inside."

It is not uncommon for runners and athletes who overdid it to limp around on crutches a few years later, or take an hour to get out of bed, or no longer run due to other health problems.

A cynic may draw parallels here to everyday working life and the growing burnout phenomenon. Ultimately everyone must decide for themselves how they want to live, how far they want to go, and what priorities they wish to set in life. We are in charge and can control the likelihood and frequency of injuries by managing our stress and strain. In chapter 6.7 I presented helpful instruments for the intelligent control of recovery and stress; these have been tried and tested in practice. It's good to remember them from time to time—or to actually use them—as the following example nicely shows.

FROM EXPERIENCE: TRAIN HARD AND SMART
The U.S. sport psychologist Keith Bell (1980) worked on this topic with a well-known swim team. Since athletes frequently suffered from symptoms of overloading, a program was created whose primary goal was to help athletes recognize the fine difference between functional but possibly extremely unpleasant training stimulus, and signs of pain from overloading. Moreover, and that was probably the hardest part, they worked on acquiring a different attitude or mindset. With the first signs of overloading, athletes were supposed to, in good conscience and after consulting with their coach, immediately reduce their training load. Of course that is not an easy exercise and requires a sensitive balancing act as well as increasing body awareness. But the one-year project paid off. During the process, the team changed its original slogan of "No pain, no gain" to "Train hard and smart." The result was that the athletes stayed healthy and performed better. Nice slogan, right?

REACTION PATTERN DURING INJURIES

You tried to avoid it, but unfortunately it happened anyway. The injury took place. Now what? How do we react? Usually pretty emotionally. Often the psychological consequences of an injury are more severe than the physical impairments. According to Hardy and Crace (1990), we can differentiate five different emotional stages or reactions, particularly after severe injuries:

◆ *Denial:* "It's not that bad."

◆ *Frustration:* "Darn, why me?" or "My stupid knee!"

◆ *Bargaining:* "Okay, when this is over, it will never happen to me again" or "It'll get better fast."

◆ *Depression:* "Poor me, I won't be able to run for a while!"

◆ *Acceptance:* "It can't be changed. I'm injured, but life goes on."

Of course not all athletes progress through all five of these steps in succession. Instead we can jump back and forth between the different patterns, but there is consensus that a positive effect on the healing process generally only takes place after the appropriate level of acceptance.

OUR RELATIONSHIP WITH OUR OWN BODY

Many athletes and runners see their body as something that simply needs to function and as merely a means to an end (e.g., performance increases, increased sense of self-worth), and they often exploit their body accordingly. They get angry and frustrated with their body when it doesn't perform the way they want. Often self-talk ensues along the lines of "That stupid Achilles tendon" or "My knee is acting up." Those are the typical dysfunctional patterns that Ievlana and Orlick (1991) encountered during a study in athletes whose injuries take a particularly long time to heal. By generating frustration and stress, they not only hinder the healing process, but can also facilitate additional injuries. Since our attitude towards our body is critical to the healing process, Meiss (2009) suggests the following strategy to examine one's relationship with their own body.

EXERCISE: EXAMINING OUR ATTITUDE TOWARDS OUR BODY

Imagine your body as an independent person, a good partner that you must treat with care, maybe even a child or a good friend you're concerned about. Surprise yourself with the mental image that is conjured up. What does that partner look like? How does he affect you? What kind of relationship do you have with him? Now put yourself in his place and look at yourself from his perspective. What does he think of you? How is he doing? How does he feel? What does he want or expect of you?

When injuries occur more frequently, it could also be helpful to examine your personal approach to your sport as well as your inner attitudes.

FASTER RECOVERY AND RETURN TO THE SPORT WITH MENTAL STRATEGIES

FROM RESEARCH: FASTER REHAB

When runners get injuries, it is usually to the lower extremities. So let's look at a study that examined the rehabilitation process or the course of recovery for athletes with injuries to those areas. Ievlana and Orlick (1991) compared two extreme groups of athletes with similar knee and ankle injuries. Group 1 consisted of athletes that were able to recover from their injuries in less than five weeks. Group 2 consisted of athletes whose recovery process was very slow at more than 16 weeks. What was the reason for this enormous difference in spite of identical or similar injuries? What did the athletes in Group 1 do differently than those in Group 2? What do you think?

Here is the answer. The faster recovering group used significantly more mental strategies, such as setting specific goals and using positive self-talk, visualizations, and relaxation techniques.

Larson and colleagues (1996) conducted a similar study. They asked hundreds of coaches how their athletes that handle injuries very well differed from those that did so less well. Here, too, it became evident that primarily mental factors make the difference: a more positive attitude towards life in general, but also towards the body and the injury, more motivation, and more goal orientation.

Stress doesn't just play a key role in injury prevention, but also in healing after an injury. Heart rate, blood pressure, and overall energy demand are higher when stressed. *Muscle tension*, too, which can result in increased pain and decreased blood supply to the injured area. Stress causes an increase in the release of catecholamines and glucocorticoids. This prevents our immune cells from reaching the injured areas to remove damaged tissue. Moreover, in addition to interfering with healthy sleep, stress seems to impede the production of growth hormones that are critical to the building of new, healthy tissue (Perna et al., 2003). Frustration and other stresses slow down and impede the healing process.

USE IT OR LOSE IT: MENTAL TRAINING IN REHAB

We have already thoroughly addressed the use and effects of movement visualizations. If you skipped over that chapter and landed here, or wish to briefly refresh your memory on that topic with regard to rehabilitation processes, I recommend the content of this passage.

What happens when we no longer use well-trained muscles? They atrophy. And when we have a cast on a leg after an operation or a leg brace or crutches that greatly restrict our movement and weight-bearing ability temporarily, the lack of stimuli—or rather lack of use—causes our muscles to sometimes atrophy extremely quickly. A formerly shapely thigh is now as thin as a rake. With mental training, we can prevent—or at least mitigate—this process. We visualize ourselves completing certain athletic movements without actually doing them.

NEUROPHYSIOLOGICAL PROCESSES

By intensely visualizing ourselves running or cycling, we activate the exact same areas of the brain as the actual movement. The execution of real movements may be inhibited, but the excitation spreads to the muscles involved in the actual movement and can be measured there in the muscle tone. Experts refer to *neuronal canalization*. This means that, by merely imagining movements, we enervate the same muscles as the actual movement. The more intense the visualization, the more intense the canalization. While they are weaker overall than if we were actually jogging on the beach or cycling across the Alps, these impulses are nevertheless sufficient to significantly reduce muscular atrophy during phases of restricted movement. And this also decreases our muscular imbalances as well as the amount of time needed to rebuild later.

Sports injuries quickly result in impaired inter- and intramuscular fine coordination. Top athletes notice this within a day or two, even after just slight injuries. Longer absences result in intensive rehabilitation. Fine coordination must be relearned together with systematic muscle building. The aforementioned mechanism is effective here, too. The use of mental training sequences makes it possible to relearn and establish movement patterns and routines significantly faster. Studies have repeatedly verified the positive effects of mental training on movement coordination (Roland & Zilles, 1996)

And ultimately the use of movement visualizations known to have a positive emotional effect also makes psychological sense and can benefit physical therapy and rehabilitation. Vividly reliving past successful runs or anticipating a particularly nice future run or event generates positive emotions and a more confident basic mood. Brain research tells us that positive feelings are, in a way, lubricants for learning. Let's also make use of this for rehabilitation after sports injuries.

In summary: Muscular atrophy and the length of time needed for laborious rebuilding can be reduced with mental training in the form of intensive movement visualization.

Furthermore, we already mentioned that intense mental imagery can also influence supposed autonomic bodily processes. You may be familiar with this old trick: When your hands are cold, vividly imagine more blood flowing to your hands. Also imagine a warm color, like a dark orange, flowing through your hands. Some people also imagine what their hands would feel like if they held them over a pleasantly warm fire. Try it some time. And if it doesn't work right away and your hands don't get warmer, you already know that practice makes perfect!

One thing's for sure: Focusing attention on a specific body region, in this case the hands, can bring about desired physiological changes in precisely that area. Freedivers and fakirs, that are able to shift large amounts of blood to the desired areas via intense focus or mediation, have reported the same. It can be assumed that every person possesses the ability to bolster healing processes via intense mental imagery and focus (Schmid, 2010).

SUGGESTIONS

If our performance doesn't consist of running as fast, as far, or as enjoyably as possible, but rather to recover as quickly and as smoothly as possible, the optimal interplay between body and mind is of critical importance. Body-focused measures as well as physiotherapy should be supplemented with mental strategies to facilitate the perfect healing success. This would take a person's totality into consideration and can have a huge positive effect on recovery. The following suggestions are based on empirical studies and working with injured athletes. They have a positive effect on post-injury rehabilitation.

◆ **Appreciating one's own body:** Someone who treats his body generously and appreciatively, and speaks to it or the affected body regions in a positive manner, does well by himself. The opposite (i.e., confrontation and conflict) leads to frustration, stress, and unhelpful emotions.

◆ **Goal management:** Specific goals help us increase our motivation and commitment. What would be a realistic date to start competing again? How many times a week should I do rehabilitation exercises? What are my specific goals for each week? Do I have a tendency to do more than is sensible on a day when I feel a little better? If so, it is all the more important to follow a consistent schedule to avoid the risk of torpedoing the recovery by overloading.

◆ **Positive self-talk:** Instead of "Shoot, it takes so long," "Darn tendon," or "I'm just not getting back in shape," it would be better to say, "My body is taking the time it needs," "Be patient; it is time well spent because you will come out of this phase reinvigorated," "Whatever happens, and whatever I feel, I am getting better each day," or "My injury is mine, right now it is a part of me. By taking good care of it I am also taking good care of myself and will recover (more) quickly."

◆ **Relaxation techniques:** Injuries initially result in frustration and anger. But the ingredients for recovery are relaxation, rest, and hope. So use the described techniques to reduce stress and frustration and to generate positive emotions. The effects are varied and lead to relief from pain and muscle tension as well as improved circulation and additional positive hormonal changes.

◆ **Visualization:** Regular movement visualizations help us work on our fitness and coordination. As a result, we experience less deterioration and increase our net training time in spite of our limited mobility. Moreover, we are able to certifiably intensify our physical healing processes through intense visualizations (Schmid, 2010). Regularly shift your focused attention to the injured or ill parts of the body. Talk to your body out loud or in your mind. Imagine healing taking place before your mind's eye. Imagine metabolic processes being stimulated (or suppressed), and what that feels like and how it affects the relevant part of the body. Imagine healing colors flowing through the affected parts of the body. Vividly remembering past runs that went perfectly also helps to keep your movement memory fresh.

Imagining that you have overcome the injury and your form is even better than before can be incredibly motivating.

◆ **Setbacks:** Sometimes it happens that rehab hits a plateau, or we experience the occasional setback. That's when it is important to stick with it and keep our eyes on our goals and continue to pursue them. Positive goal visualizations, self-talk, and support from friends and family are helpful.

◆ **Thought control:** Injury phases can be exhausting. Makes sense. And even with the best intentions, negative images and thoughts can sometimes crop up. It is human, but not helpful. We should acknowledge them and then insert a neat thought-stopping technique and refocus our attention on positive, constructive things. Due to two operations in 2015, I have personally had to rearrange or cancel not only athletic goals, but also many professional and private commitments on a very large scale. That can be pretty frustrating. But is frustration productive at that moment? Not usually. Accepting, rethinking, and rearranging are better for our emotional equilibrium and thus for healing.

◆ **Injury as an opportunity (part 1):** When we are on a forced break for a while, we are able to enjoy other important things in life that otherwise might fall by the wayside. We can get reorganized and review our priorities. We have more time to learn new things, for instance about medicine, psychology, or other topics unrelated to running.

◆ **Smiling:** Smiling has always been the best medicine. It has been known for ages and now has also been proven scientifically. Whenever we are in pleasant company, watch a fun comedy, or attend a party (Easy now!), positive feelings trigger the release of endorphins which reduce pain and muscle tension and counteract stress and its ramifications.

◆ **Relativization:** We often take our sport and ourselves too seriously and as too important. A slightly more relaxed attitude and the realization that a sports injury isn't a life-threatening crisis, but rather a temporary inconvenience from which we will most likely recover quickly and from which we may learn a few things, feels much better and makes it a lot easier to deal with. So let's not get carried away, and let's use the injury as a resource that helps us get a little smarter and learn more about ourselves.

◆ **Injury as an opportunity (part 2):** Maybe you could also ask yourself why the injury happened now. What message might it hold? Is it a wake-up call? If so, what does it mean? If I am unable to immediately understand and relate to it, assuming the injury is an action from the depths of my subconscious and is actually well intended, what could that intention be?

EXERCISE: BASIC APPROACHES TO HEALING MENTAL IMAGERY

You can use the following imagery to support healing processes. You will most likely think of other images as soon as you get into the process and begin the visualization in a relaxed state.

◆ Focus intensely on the location of your injury. Think about warmth or other pleasant relaxing feelings flooding the area.

◆ Imagine more and more white blood cells traveling to the injured area.

◆ Imagine injured tissue and other metabolic substances being removed, and muscles mending.

◆ You might even envision a type of magician or healer pointing a magic wand at the injured area or touching it, causing healing energy to affect your body from the outside. You might imagine feeling a tingling sensation inside the injury.

◆ Frequently retrieve the image of what it will be like when the injury is completely healed.

◆ And remember: "Imagination is more important than knowledge, because knowledge is limited." —A. Einstein

EXERCISE: HEALING MENTAL IMAGERY IN MORE DETAIL

I find a comfortable, relaxed position. My body relaxes. I take deep breaths. With each breath I take, I feel the energy streaming into my body. As I exhale, all of the tension leaves my body through my nose. I feel the soles of my feet relax. I let the relaxation travel from my feet to my ankles. I feel the relaxation spread from my calves and knees to my thighs. I allow the relaxation to gradually spread throughout my body until it reaches my fingertips and the top of my head. I feel pleasantly warm and soft. My eyelids are heavy. I again notice the relaxation flooding my entire body. I inhale, briefly hold my breath, and allow my muscles to relax even deeper as I slowly exhale my remaining tension. I enjoy the feeling of relaxation for a few moments. Now I shift my attention to my injury. I create a mental image of my injury. I focus intensely on the affected area. I can see the relaxation activate my immune system. Strength streams to my injury. Healthy tissue begins to grow. Dead and injured tissue is removed. Toxins, bacteria, and anything unhealthy is removed. My body is cleansed. Healing spreads like light inside the injury. It touches every nook and cranny and forces the pain to retreat. I exhale the pain and inflammation. I inhale health and tranquility. The injured area gets smaller. It is completely surrounded by relaxation. New, healthy cells form. My immune system gets stronger and stronger. My body works for me. It heals. I inhale and exhale. I am completely relaxed and think about the healing process taking place inside my body. I feel pleasantly warm and peaceful. I breathe. Now I decide if I want to slowly wake up or drift off to sleep... (Ullrich, 2013).

Ultimately we all wish to get back in shape as quickly as possible after a sports injury and get back on our feet. And it is nice when you are able to structure this process in the best possible way by using cutting-edge strategies. But even with all that motivation during rehab, the main premise is and remains this: *Patience* is a tiger's sharpest tooth.

FROM EXPERIENCE: BEWARE OF BLANKET ADVICE ON THE INTERNET

In late May 2015, I was at a sports clinic for outpatient surgery when right after the procedure, while making small talk, I learned from the nurse that the boyfriend of a runner who had won a 230 km race just a week ago was waiting two cubicles over for his surgery. I briefly thought out loud that it could be Kristina, who had just won the JUNUT ultra-marathon, when I heard a cheerful, "Hey, is that you, Michele? No, it couldn't be. You're here, too?" from next door. A crazy coincidence and a great source of material for this practical digression.

Of course, we can get lots of good and helpful tips from the Internet. And so I immediately began to search for suggestions for my upcoming rehab. As is so often the case, opinions vary widely and in the end things can get confusing pretty fast, because not all knee operations are created equal. One meniscus operation is not like another meniscus operation, and one meniscus suture is not like another meniscus suture. The devil is in the details and significantly impacts rehab requirements. While my running buddy, who was operated on by the same doctor at practically the same time, was able to resume normal loadbearing after just one week, I was faced with wearing a knee brace for six weeks, crutches, and decreased bending and loading, as well as several months of exercise hiatus and very gradual moderate build-up. Both of us were there for an outpatient knee, or Meniscus, repair, but the specific knee structure, the endogenous tissue, were completely different. And even with the same procedures, healing processes can vary greatly.

When we search for tips and recipes we should always remember that every body and every procedure, but also every genesis, is very individual. Sensible suggestions should take this into account, but rarely do so in forums or on community sites, and can therefore do more harm than good.

7.6   EXERCISE ADDICTION: WHAT EXACTLY IS IT AND AM I AFFECTED?

Maybe you are one of those runners who run relatively far, often, and long. If that's the case, people you know may have called you an exercise addict, more or less in jest. But maybe you are also part of a group of average runners, who previously have not stood out with their running performance, but who, by implementing the mental strategies in this book, have gotten such a motivational thrill and performance boost that you have trouble keeping your feet still and are drawn almost magically out onto the course. So at some point you may ask yourself (if the people around you don't do so first) if you have become addicted to running.

Those who train very often and a lot compared to other athletes are quickly pigeonholed as exercise addicts. The media also frequently covers exercise addiction as a topic, often rather superficially. Many runners react to such coverage with a chuckle. Some, it seems, feel that they or their sport are being targeted and also react with less reflective comments. And while the topic of exercise addiction may not be one of the core topics of this book, I nevertheless find it important and beneficial to take a valid look at this issue. It will allow us to be better informed and able to participate in the next discussion about exercise addiction while also knowing whether or not this attribute applies to us. And we will be able to provide some guidance to others.

I had a long conversation with Melanie Schipfer, who did scientific research on the *exercise addiction* phenomenon as part of her dissertation, and in the process developed a diagnostic tool we would like to present for the purpose of self-testing, after this interview.

MICHELE: MELANIE, WHAT IS YOUR EXERCISE BACKGROUND?

Melanie Schipfer: I started running in late 2008, and ran my first marathon in April 2009, more or less after training for a half marathon planned in mid-June of that year. Since then I cannot imagine my life without running. In 2010, I switched to triathlons, participated in every distance class, and ended the season with a long distance event (3.8 – 180 – 42.2 km) that wasn't really planned. Ever since then I am in love with this distance. My biggest athletic accomplishments are:

◆ winning first place as part of the German National long-distance team title in 2014 (Challenge Roth, Team Erdinger, alcohol-free, together with Julia Gayer and Daniela Sämmler) and

◆ winning fourth place, AK Ostsee Man Glücksburg (2015).

MICHELE: THE SUBJECT OF YOUR DISSERTATION WAS EXERCISE ADDICTION. HOW DID YOU CHOOSE THIS TOPIC? WHAT INTERESTS YOU OR FASCINATES YOU ABOUT THIS SUBJECT?

Melanie Schipfer: Back in 2009, my father labeled me as an exercise addict. Of course that led me to do some self-reflection and soul searching. But whenever I was out with my club mates or training partners, it seemed to me that I was rather inexperienced and completely normal. In 2010, at the start of my Master's program in applied psychology, I asked Dr. Oliver Stoll when someone can be considered an exercise addict. In a sense, the answer to my question was the starting signal for my subsequent doctoral thesis. It was: "I can't answer that. Because according to ICD-10 and DSM-IV (*Diagnostic and Statistical Manual of Mental Disorders*), there is no such thing as exercise addiction." And there I was. There are reports in the media all the time about alleged exercise addicts, but the diagnostic manuals DSM-IV and ICD-10 do not categorize exercise addiction. My curiosity was aroused.

What fascinates me about exercise addiction? Everything! But among other things, the conversations with endurance athletes I conducted as part of my dissertation, and the conversations and discussions with their family members. The realization of how important it is to also consider the position and perspective from which the athlete's behavior with respect to exercise is viewed. Are you yourself a part of the scene and active? Or are you more of the opposite? At some point you ask yourself, "What is normal?" For some, it is normal to train ten hours a week in addition to juggling a job and family. Others cannot even fathom that and consider it anything but normal. Is an athlete who works towards an important personal goal with vigor, an edge, passion, determination, sacrifice, blood, sweat, and tears an exercise addict? If that is the case, does that mean all of our professional athletes and Olympic athletes are exercise addicts—or more accurately workaholics—or simply passionate athletes? What motivates the athlete? Do all those many hours of athletic activity help athletes to

◆ complete the necessary training to achieve personal goals?

◆ run away from, suppress, or compensate for a problem they don't want to deal with?

◆ have a reliable method (or even the only method) to achieve a sense of well-being or inner equilibrium?

MICHELE: WHAT EXACTLY IS EXERCISE ADDICTION AND WHAT EFFECTS CAN IT HAVE ON EVERYDAY LIFE?

Melanie Schipfer: Currently there still is no generally accepted definition of exercise addiction. The scientific community differentiates between *primary* and *secondary exercise addiction*. Primary exercise addiction occurs as an independent phenomenon, whereby the focus is strictly on athletic activity. The sport serves as an end in itself, and the addictive behavior is often linked to feelings of anxiety, depression, or even psychoses.

Tomlinson (2010) describes exercise addiction as a psychological dependency on activity that must be performed at least once a day. If the athletic activity cannot be performed, those affected suffer from anxiety and feelings of guilt. They engage in athletic activity in spite of injury or illness, and even manipulate social and family engagements to ensure their daily athletic activity. The sport can be practiced independently of others, is not competition oriented, and is easy to execute.

In my dissertation, I proceeded on the assumption that primary exercise addiction can be viewed as a behavior that provides a sense of control, and the restoration of mental equilibrium that is threatened by, for instance, the occurrence of a critical life event or problem. Those affected view the sport as the only effective means to compensate, as well as experience and restore well-being (by decreasing alternatives). Since the problem is not solved but suppressed, the cause becomes hidden. During exercise deprivation the hidden problem resurfaces and leads to a perceived loss of situational control and wellbeing. Withdrawal symptoms and psychological strain follow, which must be countered with more exercise.

Secondary exercise addiction is a behavior pattern found particularly in patients with eating disorders (Anorexia nervosa, Bulimia nervosa) with obsessive-compulsive and perfectionist tendencies. Among the most frequently stated reasons for exercising are calorie consumption and weight management, affecting figure and attractiveness, and regulating negative mood or negative body image, as well as anxiety and tension.

MICHELE: HOW COMMOM IS THIS PHENOMENON? IN YOUR EXPERIENCE, TO HOW MANY ATHLETES DOES THE LABEL *EXERCISE ADDICTION* ACTUALLY APPLY? AND HOW GREAT IS THE PSYCHOLOGICAL STRAIN?

Melanie Schipfer: In national and international professional literature, specific numbers on the prevalence* of exercise addition are low. Publications list a primary exercise addiction morbidity rate in Germany of 3.5% to approximately 4.5% of polled athletes, while international studies show between 3% and 45.9% of polled athletes. In our sedentary society, we can assume the morbidity rate to be extremely low. By contrast, the prevalence* of secondary exercise addiction is estimated to be much higher than primary exercise addiction, since the frequency of excessive athletic activity among people with eating disorders lies between 40% and 70%.

I have no hard and fast answer as to the level of psychological strain in those affected. But it is difficult to achieve problem awareness without psychological strain. And without problem awareness, it is difficult to help those affected since people are generally only prepared to change their behavior when the amount of psychological strain has become unbearable. And let's be honest: Why would we want to give up something that is good for us and that we have no problem with?

MICHELE: WHAT CLUES MIGHT THERE BE TO DETERMINE IF WE, OR MAYBE OUR FRIENDS OR TEAMMATES, ARE ADDICED TO EXERCISE OR AT LEAST AT RISK?

Melanie Schipfer: The following characteristics can be indicators of primary exercise addiction:

◆ The athlete has no control over his or her behavior.

◆ The affected individuals experience psychological strain caused by the latent problem as well as the exercise addiction.

◆ The athlete experiences withdrawal symptoms (e.g., restlessness, aggressiveness, tension, irritability) on days without athletic activity.

◆ The motivation to exercise is not the desire to improve performance, but the desire to satisfy the addiction.

◆ Engaging in the sport primarily serves the compensation of one or more latent problems (e.g., the gaining of control or restoration of the mental equilibrium).

Prevalence is the rate of people afflicted with a particular illness at a particular time or during a particular period of time (compared to the number of those examined).

◆ The sport's health benefits are irrelevant; those affected exercise even during illness, infections, and overloading.

◆ Competitions tend to be meaningless to exercise addicts; upcoming competitions serve as a justification to exercise.

The indicators of secondary exercise addiction are similar to those of primary exercise addiction, but an eating disorder must chiefly be present.

MICHELE: WHAT CAN WE DO WHEN THERE IS AN EXERCISE ADDICTION DIAGNOSIS? WHAT MIGHT THE SUPPORT LOOK LIKE?

Melanie Schipfer: To date, there are no guidelines for the treatment of exercise addiction. During my dissertation research, I came across few suggestions for the treatment of exercise addiction. A suggested first step was a reduction in the amount of exercise under a doctor's supervision to allow the body to adapt. During the second step, the affected individual's dysfunctional beliefs could be identified and alternatives created and cultivated via motivational interviewing or cognitive behavioral therapy. But as long as no research-based guidelines for the treatment of exercise addiction have been published, sports addiction will likely be treated in the same manner as other behavioral addictions.

MICHELE: AWESOME, THANK YOU SO MUCH FOR YOUR COMMENTS, MELANIE!

EXERCISE: AM I AN EXERCISE ADDICT?

Please consider as exercise any regular activity you do to raise your heart rate, such as swimming, cycling, running, aerobics, free weight training, etc. There are no right or wrong answers in this questionnaire. Everyone will answer these questions differently, depending on the way it fits him or her personally. Please decide spontaneously on a scale from 1 (does not apply at all) to 7 (always applies) to what extent the following statements regarding your athletic activity apply to you over the past three months.

Table 20 Am I an exercise addict?

		Does not apply at all						Always applies
1	After exercising I am excited about life.	1	2	3	4	5	6	7
2	I'm irritable when I can't exercise.	1	2	3	4	5	6	7
3	I feel more carefree after exercising.	1	2	3	4	5	6	7
4	After exercising I feel better about myself.	1	2	3	4	5	6	7
5	I get restless when I can't exercise.	1	2	3	4	5	6	7
6	I hate it when I'm unable to exercise.	1	2	3	4	5	6	7
7	I exercise to avoid being bored.	1	2	3	4	5	6	7
8	When I can't exercise I feel like I can't deal with life.	1	2	3	4	5	6	7
9	I exercise to get rid of onco-ming tension or irritability	1	2	3	4	5	6	7
10	I feel guilty towards my family for exercising so much.	1	2	3	4	5	6	7
11	I exercise to be healthier.	1	2	3	4	5	6	7
12	The amount of exercise I get has become a problem.	1	2	3	4	5	6	7

		Does not apply at all						Always applies
13	After I exercise I am okay with myself and the world.	1	2	3	4	5	6	7
14	My exercise volume interferes with my social life.	1	2	3	4	5	6	7
15	I exercise to feel fit.	1	2	3	4	5	6	7
16	I exercise to prevent heart disease and other illnesses.	1	2	3	4	5	6	7

EVALUATION

The questionnaire* to record the exercise habits of endurance athletes is a screening tool that allows athletes to be classified as *exercise committed*, *exercise focused*, and *at risk of exercise addiction*. The classification is based on guidelines that were developed with the help of approximately 2,000 endurance athletes. However, an informed diagnosis can only be made during a personal psychological consultation.

* The presented questionnaire is a translated but not yet final validated version of the original German version from Melanie Schipfer's book on sports addiction in endurance sports (Schipfer, 2015).

1. **Expectation of positive consequences:** Scale value = (item value 1 + 3 + 4 + 13) / 4
   Represents pleasant feelings and inner satisfaction after physical activity. The knowledge that positive consequences (e.g., well-being) occur during or after exercise is the stimulus to achieve these consequences again through athletic activity. Here exercise serves as a positive amplifier for the development, form, and preservation of well-being (i.e., expectation of positive consequences). When the affected person is unable to exercise, achieving a sense of well-being is denied. We can go on the assumption that exercise is generally associated with a pleasant feeling and inner satisfaction, a state that addicts as well as non-addicts experience.

2. **Problems with social environment:** Scale value = (item value 10 + 12 + 14) / 3
   Shows a clash between exercise volume, job, family, and other social obligations. Constant exercise consumption can lead to neglect of the social environment and associated obligations. With its outside view of the athlete's behavior, the social environment can be seen as both a supportive and a moderating supervisory body.

If exercise is the cause of increasing conflict with the social environment, it can be expected that this characteristic is present to a greater degree in exercise addicts and those at risk of exercise addiction than unaffected athletes.

3. **Health reasons:** Scale value = (item no. 11 + 15 + 16) / 3
    Represents the health-promoting aspect of exercise and sport. High values would speak against exercise addiction (or the risk of exercise addiction) and for commitment to exercise since the sport's health-related aspect is a priority. For people with exercise addiction (or who are at risk of exercise addiction), health is not the primary motivation, rather they engage in the sport or exercise at the expense of their health. This dimension is therefore inverted to reflect the cumulative value of the overall score.

4. **Withdrawal symptoms:** Scale value = (item no. 2 + 5 + 6) / 3
    Stands for occurring symptoms of exercise addiction and represent a key aspect in the diagnosis of exercise addiction. They are considered difficult to diagnose since exercise addicts generally barely accept or tolerate phases of no exercise. A high value in this subscale makes it possible to classify respondents as *symptomatic but not addicted* or *at risk*. To be able to call it exercise addiction, the values from *Expectation of positive consequences, Problems with social environment,* and *Exercise as a compensation method* must be included in the result analysis.

5. **Exercise as a compensation method:** Scale value = (item no. 7 + 8 + 9) / 3
    Stands for the use of exercise or sport to compensate for one or more latent problems (e.g., critical life events such as the loss of a family member, separation, unemployment, or serious illness) and to offset a concomitant psychological imbalance, thereby generating a subjectively perceived gain in control. If the affected person is unable to exercise or engage in the sport, they lack the critical means for compensation. This brings out the latent problem, followed by a subjectively perceived loss of control. The sport or exercise and the associated *positive consequences* (e.g., well-being) restore the subjective feeling of being in control and the mental equilibrium. This can lead to compulsive behavior with respect to sports. This dimension is one of the main criteria for exercise addiction. It was therefore double-weighted when the overall score was created.

6. **Overall score:**
    Scale values: (Expectation of positive consequences + Problems with social environment + (8 - Health reasons) + Withdrawal symptoms + (Compensation method x 2))

Table 21 Classification of your results.

	Sport or exercise-committed	Sport or exercise-focused	At risk for exercise addiction
Expectation of positive consequences	<5.4	>5.4-6.7	>6.7
Problems with social environment	<1.6	>1.6-3.6	>3.6
Health reasons	>6.6	>4.9-6.6	>4.9
Withdrawal symptoms	<4.6	>4.6-6.6	>6.6
Sport or exercise as a compensation method	<2.6	>2.6-4.6	>4.6
Overall score	<20.4	>20.4-26	>26.2

So, are you an exercise addict? Most likely not, and that's good to know, right? In the future, when people make stupid exercise addict comments, you now can confidently reply, "Nope, I'm not! I tested negative! Everything is fine the way it is." But maybe the test gave you food for thought. That would also be a valuable outcome. That means we have achieved your goal.

Disturbed Personalities: Are frequent and extreme runners actually crazy?

In the previous chapter, we demystified the subject of sports addiction some and certainly relativized the actual significance for many athletes. But there is another cliché that many passionate sportsmen and women, at least in German-speaking countries, are confronted with again and again: "Don't you have to be a little crazy to do such things?" Crazy, crazy, somehow disturbed, at least unlike others. These are the pigeonholes into which many outside of extreme running place runners. Though the comments are not really meant to be mean, often they are perceived as disparaging, or at the very least, annoying. But what is it about these comments? Are runners who are on the move relatively often and for a long time, or who like to look for extreme adventures in unusual places, perhaps actually a little disturbed, or at least tick differently than the others?

Messed-Up Personalities?

What does crazy really mean? Our everyday understanding of crazy and disturbed always implies "being different from the others," but otherwise remains rather vague, which is why we first want to take a look at science. According to DSM (diagnostic and statistical manual of mental disorders, American Psychiatric Association, 2013), mental disorders are "a persistent pattern of inner experience and behavior that deviates markedly from the expectations of the socio-cultural environment." The magic word here is "enduring." We can (and should) all do something extraordinary from time to time. We speak of disturbances, however, only in deeper, inflexible patterns of thinking, feeling, and acting that affect life and cause suffering. However, one might wonder if the term *disorder* is even correct since 14% of the total population can be diagnosed with it, says British psychology professor Dutton in his book on psychopaths (Dutton, 2012). And look at what's going on every day in politics, in the kitchens and offices of companies, in the stock exchange, in football stadiums... So it might make sense to talk only about personalities. This approach is confirmed by a study that shows that all personality disorders listed in the DSM can be mapped using the characteristics of five central personality traits, the "Big Five" (Saulsman & Page, 2004).

Personality Coordinates

The Big Five model is the most widely used model to describe human personality (McCrae & Costa, 1999). The model includes five relatively stable parameters, each with contrasting character traits, and it can be used to make very accurate predictions about health, performance, occupational preferences/strengths, and personal development (table 22).

Table 22 Big Five personality model

Big Five factors	Weakly developed	Strongly pronounced
Open to experience	Conservative, cautious, practical, adjusted, loves routine	Innovative, curious, imaginative, independent, loves variety
Conscientiousness	Messy, careless, impulsive	Organized, careful, self-disciplined
Extroversion	Cautious, serious, reserved	Sociable, cordial, fun-loving
Tolerability	Unscrupulous, suspicious, uncooperative	Compassionate, trusting, helpful
Neuroticism	Calm, secure, self-satisfied	Vulnerable, anxious, worried, insecure, self-pitying

Let's get back to my initial question. There have already been several studies on the personality of long-distance runners. There were no significant differences between (ultra-) marathon runners and the normal population (Janouch, 2016, Stoll & Rolle, 1997). But does this also apply to the "even more extreme types" who cope with particularly long or difficult distances? They may not differ from the norm or the other runners. Doesn't there have to be something to all the comments about the "crazy" and extreme athletes?

To find an answer, I compared the Big Five reference data of more than 1300 people (Rammstedt et al., 2013) with the survey results from hundreds of runners (Ufer, 2018). I then divided the runners into three groups, depending on their longest distance so far:

1.   Up to 42 km: marathon or shorter

2.   Up to 161 km/100 miles: ultramarathon

3.   Over 161 km: Extreme ultramarathon

The last category is mainly about those I've interviewed within the context of technically and climatically difficult races, sometimes lasting several days, in the desert, the rainforest, or the Arctic Circle. Media representatives and marathon runners often describe these races as extreme due to their special length and complex challenges, such as extreme heat or cold, self-sufficiency, difficult route planning, challenging terrain, and so on. For simplicity's sake, I followed this common perception and named the third category "extreme ultramarathon." But now it's getting exciting. What were my results?

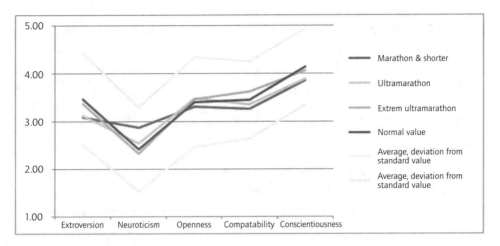

Figure 15 Personality profiles of runners

If we analyze the personality profiles of the groups in more detail, the following becomes apparent:

The values for **extreme ultramarathon runners** are initially in the standard value range and show the same characteristic pattern as the reference group (i.e., the same ascent and descent). They are relatively close to the standard profile and are the only subgroup that does not deviate significantly from the reference values in any parameter. So we can give them the all-clear: Frequent and extreme runners are not crazy.

> What surprised me, however, was this: Those who have **run marathons and shorter distances** so far differ significantly in four dimensions from the norm (except for openness). The differences in neuroticism are particularly noteworthy. According to their self-assessment, the emotional instability of those who have run marathons or less so far seems to be significantly higher, while the extroversion, conscientiousness, and tolerability seem to be lower than the norm. The latter could be of interest in the sense that high values for conscientiousness and tolerability are considered to promote performance.

To sum up: The longer or possibly more extreme the run, the closer the personality profile is to the norm (except in the case of tolerability, which is likely to have positive effects). On average, the run-of-the-mill and extreme runners seem to be just as crazy, or not crazy, as the rest of society. That's good to know, isn't it? Perhaps not something I would include in a scientific journal, but the conclusion I can draw here is: The available data could suggest that it would be crazy not to run much and extremely. The frequent runners among you should have enough fodder if someone wants to give you the "crazy" label again. And if you're not a frequent or extreme runner yet, you might consider becoming one. There seem to be good reasons to. At least, it would almost be more "normal."

7.7 WHAT HAPPENS WHEN SUCCESS MAKES YOU UNHAPPY?

Can the sunny side of life also be the dark side of life? This is where this book comes full circle. The description of mental training programs and strategies usually begins with the subject of *goals*. We like to say, "Nothing motivates more than success" or "Success is achieving your goals." But what happens when the goals you achieved weren't set by you or don't meet your needs? Does that really motivate you? Does it make you happy?

AN EXPERIMENT
Imagine you are able to participate in a personality training program at a well-known hotel, and the experienced trainer invites you and a few other guests to change clothes and meet on the running track of a neighboring athletic field in half an hour. Before you line up on the starting line, you are welcome to prepare for a few minutes, because after the starting signal you will have to run as good as you can a distance of 1200 m, or three laps. All participants are ready and the trainer holds up the starting gun. How do you prepare for the start? What is your stance?

The gun goes off and you take off. What would you be thinking at that moment? What would your movements look like or feel like? What would you do? Mentally place yourself briefly in that position. You would probably do the same thing as most other participants: step on the gas pedal and run the 1200 m as fast as possible, then, understandably, gasp for air at the finish line with more or less heavy legs. So far, so good!

WHAT'S GOOD IS IN THE EYE OF THE BEHOLDER
This experiment is actually conducted as part of a personality training program, the focus of which is to reflect the ingrained ways of thinking, points of view, and behaviors, and the influence of the group on the individual. The following questions lead to contemplation after the conclusion of the experiment: What is actually good for me? How well do I pay attention to myself? What might have been good or better for me during the experiment? How do I generally do something good for myself?

And, to come straight to the point: Could the prompt to "run as well as possible" mean something completely differentthan reaching the finish line performance oriented and as fast as possible? Maybe it would have done your soul and your body good at that moment if you had run particularly slow and relaxed. Maybe you would have enjoyed having a pleasant conversation while running or maybe you would have enjoyed the fresh air, the scent of the flowers, or the view of the landscape, if the experiment had taken place on a balmy summer evening. Following the instruction may have been good, or maybe not.

What's good for someone is ultimately very personal, and someone can be considered well off when they have a sense of what is good and feels right in a particular situation. In some situations, it could also be good to confidently emancipate oneself from requirements, demands, and expectations and just say "No."

Why am I telling you this? It's simple: It reminds me of a number of my running buddies, some of my coaching clients, and myself.

FROM RESEARCH: THE NEGATIVE EFFECTS OF GOALS THAT ARE NOT YOUR OWN
The experiment can reveal how we may lose touch with ourselves and our innermost needs and goals, and how we adopt points of view or goals that aren't in line with our own, usually unconscious, motives. But when our very own goals are displaced by the goals of, for instance, the running group or society, it frequently leads to motivational and performance blocks.

The renowned personality psychologist Dr. Kuhl even points out that the discrepancy between conscious goals and unconscious needs can be a stressor that can lower life satisfaction and well-being, and is a proven significant risk factor for mental health and a trigger for depression and anxiety, as well as psychosomatic complaints such as head and stomachaches and increased risk of infection. Especially affected are so-called state-oriented people, meaning people who worry or who worry too much about past, present, and future things and have difficulty letting go of failures, while action-oriented people are able to focus their thoughts on executing an action and more easily block out failures. Research shows that state-oriented people are more likely to set goals or take on goals that are not in line with their needs.

For someone with a highly developed competitive streak, a strict, demanding running program with an appropriate competitive event calendar would be a great fit. But would it make sense for someone who is searching for a relaxing balance to a stressful job, or seeks a pleasant social life, to power through regular interval training and prepare for a 2:50 h marathon? I often encounter people who diverge from their goals more or less unnoticed and focus on the goals of others, as part of a gradual process. And thereby risk suffering the aforementioned consequences.

One simple question might help us examine the coherence of our goals: Does what I do really make me happy? If so, that's great. If not, it is possible that we have passed up our needs. We can avoid doing so by also listening to our gut when we formulate or examine our goals. Our gut will give us reliable information about what is good for us, regardless of what our head tries to rationally ram down our throats. All we need then is the courage to follow it...

FROM EXPERIENCE: THE MENTAL COACH AT AN IMPASSE
And that is precisely what happened to me in 2014, during the desert run in Namibia. At times I was faster than ever, and in spite of modest training even ran within touching distance of the subsequent winner after the first day, during the following 2 or 3 stages. The result? A fantastic time. Personal best! Awesome success! Still, despite being an extremely strong runner, I wasn't happy. Anger and boredom arose. Any conversation within the lead group was limited to, "Which way?", "Right!", "Left!". I wasn't able to take as many photos as I would have liked, and I realized that it wasn't my desire to run through Namibia really fast and be at the front. Spending relaxing time outdoors with like-minded people, enjoying nature, discovering new places, that's where I MYSELF currently draw strength and joy. Admittedly, I didn't run that fast completely voluntarily. Like many others, I had orientation problems on the first day. I simply did not see route markers on the trail, and on the second day I attached myself to the lead group for safety reasons because the participants running behind me were so much slower than I. At least that's what I thought. Hindsight is 20/20. And so I slowed down towards the end. This experience was very timely for me, and while it was successful from an athletic point of view, it was primarily beneficial and subsequently helped me remember what is really important to me and good for me.

If you go your own way, no one can pass you.

—Marlon Brando

No matter how far you run, you will always just see your own horizon.

—Max von Eyth

OUTLOOK

And here we are at the end of our journey into *Mental Toughness for Runners*. We're really just getting started, aren't we?

We began with the Atacama experiment. As you may recall, by doing a self-test, I wanted to find out and demonstrate which performance increases could be achieved through the use of mental techniques. This experiment was extremely successful. I introduced many of the applied strategies in a realistic setting so you could try them out yourself and adapt them to your personal goals and circumstances. Keep at it and make mental training techniques as much a natural part of your training as the physical elements.

Of course I am curious to find out which suggestions will turn out to be most valuable to you. I appreciate your feedback in any shape or form. And remember: Sometimes psychology and mental training is much like the expert hairstylist who wants to cut his own hair. Occasionally things go faster and better with a little help.

If you would like suggestions beyond the book, you can find further information on the following topics on the Institute for Running Psychology website, www.running-psychology.com:

◆ Practice workshops that accompany the book *Mental Toughness for Runners*

◆ Motivational lectures for sports teams and business corporations

◆ Training to become a certified Running Psychology Coach

◆ Exciting hands-on research projects

You can of course also get in touch with me on my personal website **www.michele-ufer.com**, on Facebook, as well as the other popular social media sites. Let's stay in touch, if you like. And maybe we will meet sometime during a run and enjoy our time and one or two relaxed kilometers together. I would like that very much!

Figure 16 The test image for stress diagnostics

Mental self-coaching for executives and entrepreneurs

If you're like me, you will devour this book in no time flat. I have already tried many of the exercises myself. It is exciting to experience your own self. I am taking away a lot for my own professional life and can recommend this book without reservation to any independent business owner that may not have such a connection to running.

Thomas Biermann,
General Manager CSB & Chairman, Tax Consultant
Association Westfalen-Lippe

INTERVIEW with Michele Ufer

WHEN MANAGERS LEARN TO RUN

The book *Mentaltraining für Läufer* by Michele Ufer, internationally renowned expert on sport psychology and management psychology, came out in May 2016 (the book was originally published in German, and *Mental Toughness for Runners* is the translated version). The book introduces highly effective mental training and self-coaching strategies and has quickly become a standard work in running and marathon literature. It is geared primarily to runners, other endurance athletes, and trainers, but business executives and entrepreneurs among the readership continue to report that the presented strategies are also a valuable resource for everyday management. That is no surprise to the author.

MR. UFER, RUNNING SEEMS TO BE POPULAR AMONG MANAGERS AND YOUR BOOK IS PRETTY WELL RECEIVED. WHY IS THAT?

Michele Ufer: I recently read somewhere that running is the new golf. It's possible. In any case, running is definitely one thing: simple! It is a technically simple sport and doesn't require much more than a few minutes of your time. That's definitely practical because running can be integrated relatively easily into a full appointment calendar. And then there are the many positive effects of moderate endurance training on health and productivity. Moreover, having completed a marathon has become almost de rigeur among executives because it is associated with qualities like determination, willpower, and endurance that are also important in a job. But here is the crux—and it is also where my book comes in—although running is pretty easy and can have many positive effects, runners can absolutely stand in their own way or sabotage themselves. And they do so surprisingly often, regardless of whether their goals are health or performance oriented. Managers are not immune from doing so either.

WHY IS THAT?

Michele Ufer: While you run, you have a fair amount of time for dysfunctional thinking and behaviors that can unnecessarily complicate goal attainment instead of leading you to your goal effectively and in a relaxed manner. Of course, there are tons of running books and training manuals, but they usually focus on the sport's physical aspects and generally don't include any well-founded information about the psychological influencing factors. It is surprising, because athletes and managers basically agree that success is also a matter of the mind and the right attitude. That is precisely where my book begins and provides a key puzzle piece for increased motivation, performance, and the joy of living. These methods can then also be used in other areas of life outside of running.

LEARNING FOR YOUR LIFE AND YOUR JOB WHILE RUNNING?

Michele Ufer: Exactly! Sport as a metaphor for business is sometimes worn a little thin for my taste. But running makes immediate feedback possible about the attitude with which a person approaches challenges, how he monitors himself, and how his mindset and mental strategies affect his motivation, performance, and health. People usually don't experience this immediacy in an everyday business setting. Here running can quickly become a look in the mirror of one's own self-leadership and a playground for experimentation. It offers an excellent, safe space to try out and fine tune important mental strategies the way they have long been established in elite sports, like, for instance, effective control of emotions, thought management, focusing of attention, controlling arousal, working with mental images, and self-motivation techniques.

THE MARATHON AS A PERSONNEL DEVELOPMENT METHOD?
Michele Ufer: In a way, yes, but probably more as an informal measure. But the idea is appealing. On the one hand, running is harmless because it's only our sport. On the other hand, it is merciless because it often shows—surprisingly plainly—how we tend to handle and approach challenges. In that sense, I agree with the saying that life is an ultra-marathon.

BUT AREN'T ATHLETIC AND PROFESSIONAL CHALLENGES COMPELTELY DIFFERENT?
Michele Ufer: Of course they are. At least on the surface. There is a difference, whether we build a car, run a hospital, program new software, launch a company, hold an important meeting, build a shopping center, or run ultra-marathons through the desert. But in the end it's about one thing: achieving challenging goals as effectively as possible by being able to reliably access existing abilities and potentials. It is about finding consistent answers to the following questions and implementing them in your everyday life: How can we manage to achieve ambitious goals slightly faster, more effectively, or maybe just in general, while also keeping an eye on our health and joy of living? That's where the challenges and psychological mechanisms in sports and business aren't all that different. Many readers of my book seem to agree.

THERE ARE MANY BOOKS ABOUT SUCCESS AND MENTAL TRAINING.
WHAT MAKES YOURS SPECIAL?
Michele Ufer: One possible reason for the success of my book may be that I don't peddle secrets to success, but rather rely on solid tools. I take no stock in snappy motivational slogans along the lines of "You can do anything if you just put your mind to it" and "No limits." It might push some people for a little while, but is usually unrealistic and can even lead to burnout. All of us have different goals, qualifications, and underlying circumstances. The reader is therefore instructed to develop and implement his individually suitable mental training project plan based on a psychologically valid varianceanalysis of his own motivation and mental strengths. To do so, he is provided with many methods he can choose from and combine according to his situation.

Another possible reason for the book's success may be that I intensively tested the presented strategies many times in my own coaching work with athletes and executives and on myself during extreme or ultra-marathon races around the world, and, by doing so, I was quite successful. I exemplified that with many practice examples. There is no shortage of humor and the book examines other areas such as, for example, soccer, swimming, or chess.

WHAT EXACTLY DOES MENTAL TRAINING MEAN?
Michele Ufer: Mental training originated in sport psychology and refers to the intensive work with mental images and perceptions used in, for instance, movement optimization or preparation for and anticipation of impending challenges. I consider mental training in the larger sense to be the systematic development of mental abilities that are productive or important to the respective context. The positive effects on motivation, performance, and health can be considerable and have been scientifically proven. All good reasons to engage in the subject.

REFERENCES

American Psychiatric Association (2013). *Diagnostic and statistical manual of mental disorders (DSM-5)*. Arlington, VA: American Psychiatric Pub.

Amler, W., Bernatzky, P. & Knörzer, W. (2009). *Mentaltraining im Sport*. 2. Aufl., Aachen: Meyer & Meyer.

Bejenke, C. J. (2009). Vorbereitung auf medizinische Eingriffe. In D. Revenstorf & B. Peter (Hrsg.), *Hypnose in Psychotherapie, Psychosomatik und Medizin* (S. 630-640). 2. Aufl., Heidelberg: Springer.

Bell. K. (1980). *The nuts and bolts of psychology for swimmers*. Austin: Keel.

Benson, H., Lehmann, J. W., Malhotra, M. S., Goldman, R. F., Hopkins, J.& Epstein, M. D. (1982). Body temperature changes during the practice of Tummo yoga. *Letter to Nature Magazine*, 21 January 1982. *Nature, 295*, 234-236.

Birrer. D. & Morgan, G. (2010). Psychological skills training as a way to enhance an athlete's performance in high-intensity sports. *Scandinavian Journal of Medicine & Science in Sports, 20*, 78-87.

Bongarzt, W. (1996). *Der Einfluss von Hypnose und Stress auf das Blutbild: psychohämatologische Studien*. Frankfurt a./M: Peter Lang-Verlag.

Borg, G. (1998). *Borg's perceived exertion and pain scales*. Champaign, IL, US: Human Kinetics

Burkeman, O. (2012). The power of negative thinking. *The New York Times,* Zugriff am 5.12.2015 unter http://www.nytimes.com/2012/08/05/opinion/sunday/the-positive-power-of-negative-thinking.html?_r=2&emc=eta1

Burton, D. & Weiss, C. (2008). The fundamental goal concept: The path to process and performance goals. In T. Horn (Ed.), *Advances in sport psychology* (pp. 339-375), 3. Aufl., Champaign: Human Kinetics.

Butler, R. J. & Hardy, L. (1992). The performance profile: Theory and application. *The Sport Psychologist, 6,* 253-264.

Cuddy, A. (2012). *Your body language shapes who you are.* Ted, Zugriff am 2.12.2015 unter http://www.ted.com/talks/amy_cuddy_your_body_language_shapes_who_you_are/transcript?language=en

de Groot, A. D. (1966). Perception and memory versus thought. In B. Kleinmuntz (Hrsg.), *Problem-solving* (pp. 19-50). New York: Wiley.

de Marées, H. (1992). *Sportphysiologie.* (6. Aufl.). Tropon: Köln.

de Shazer, S. & Berg, I. K. (1997). „What works?" Remarks on research aspects of Solution-Focused Brief Therapy. *Journal of Family Therapy, 19,* 121-124.

Dutton, K. (2012). *The Wisdom of Psychopaths. Lessons in Life from Saints, Spies and Serial Killers.* London: William Heinemann

Eberspächer, H. (2012). *Mentales Training.* 8. Aufl., München: Copress Verlag.

Ehrenreich, B. (2011). *Smile or Die. Wie die Ideologie des positiven Denkens die Welt verdummt.* München: Antje Kunstmann-Verlag.

Eichhorn, C. (2002). *Souverän durch Self-Coaching: ein Wegweiser nicht nur für Führungskräfte.* Göttingen: Vandenhoek & Ruprecht.

Frey, M., Laguna, P. L. & Ravizza, K. (2003). Collegiate athletes' mental skill use and perceptions of success: An exploration of the practice and competition settings. *Journal of Applied Sport Psychology, 15,* 115-128.

Gill, S. K., Hankey, J., Wright, A., Marczak, S., Hemming, K., Allerton, D. M., Robson, P. A. & Costa, R. J. S. (2015). The impact of a 24-h ultra-marathon on circulatory endotoxin and cytokine profile. *International Journal of Sport Medicine, 36* (08), 688-695.

Gill, S. K., Teixeira, A., Rama, L., Rosado, F., Hankey, J., Scheer, V., Hemmings, K., Robson, P. A. & Costa, R. J. S. (2015). Circulatory endotoxin concentration and cytokine profile in response to exertional-heat stress during a multi-stage ultra-marathon competition. *Exercise Immunology Review, 21,* 114-128.

Grant, A. M. (2012). Making positive change: A randomized study comparing solution-focused vs. problem-focused coaching questions. *Journal of Systemic Therapies, 31*(2), 21-35.

Hagemann, N., Tietjens, M. & Strauß, B. (2007). Expertiseforschung im Sport. In N. Hagemann, M. Tietjens & B. Strauß (Hrsg.), *Psychologie der sportlichen Höchstleistung* (S. 7-16). Göttingen: Hogrefe.

Hagenah, J. (1999). *Teilnahmemotivation von Ausdauersportlern.* Unveröffentlichte Magisterarbeit. Universität Leipzig.

Halsband, U. (2009). Neurobiologie der Hypnose. In D. Revenstorf & B. Peter (Hrsg.), *Hypnose in Psychotherapie, Psychosomatik und Medizin* (S. 802-820). 2. Aufl., Heidelberg: Springer.

Hanin, Y. L. & Stambulova, N. (2002). Metaphoric description of performance states. *The Sport Psychologist, 16* (4), 396-415.

Hardy, C. J. & Crace, R. K. (1990). Dealing with injury. *Sport Psychology Training Bulletin, 1* (6), 1-8.

Hardy, J., Hall, C. R. & Hardy, L. (2009). Awareness and motivation to change negative self-talk. *The Sport Psychologist, 23,* 430-450.

Hardy, L., Roberts, R., Thomas, P. R. & Murphy, S. M. (2010). Test of Performance Strategies (TOPS): Instrument refinement using confirmatory factor analysis. *Psychology of Sport and Exercise, 11,* 27-35.

Hatzigeorgiadis, A., Zourbanos, N., Galanis, E. & Theodorakis, Y. (2011). Self-talk and sports performance: A meta-analysis. *Perspectives on Psychological Science, 6,* 348-356.

Heil, J. & Podlok, L. (2012). Injury and performance. In S. Murphy (Ed.), *The Oxford handbook of sport and exercise psychology* (pp. 593-617). New York: Oxford University Press.

Hinz, A., Schumacher, J., Albani, C., Schmid, G. & Brähler, E. (2006). Bevölkerungsrepräsentative Normierung der Skala zur Allgemeinen Selbstwirksamkeitserwartung. *Diagnostica, 52* (1), 26-32.

Hoffmann, E. (2001). *Weniger Stress erleben. Wirksames Selbstmanagement-Training für Führungskräfte.* Neuwied: Luchterhand.

Hollmann, W., Strüder, H. K., Tagarakis, C. V. M., King, G. & Diehl, J. (2006). Das Gehirn – der leistungsbegrenzende Faktor bei Ausdauerleistungen? *Deutsche Zeitschrift für Sportmedizin, 57* (6), 155-160.

Hosseini, S. A., & Besharat, M. A. (2010). Relation of resilience with sport achievement and mental health in a sample of athletes. *Procedia-Social and Behavioral Sciences*, 5, 633-638.

Ievleva, L. & Orlick, T. (1991). Mental links to enhanced healing. *The Sport Psychologist, 5* (1), 25-40.

Ika, M., Yawe, K. & Ischii, K. (1967). Muskelkraft und Muskelermüdung bei willkürlicher Anspannung und elektrischer Reizung des Muskels. *Sportarzt Sportmed, 18,* 197-203.

Jackson, S. A., Thomas, P. R., Marsh, H. W. & Smethurst, C. J. (2001). Relationships between flow, self-concept, psychological skills, and performance. *Journal of Applied Sport Psychology, 13,* 129-153.

Jacobsen, E. (1964). *Anxiety and tension control.* New York: J. B. Lipponcott.

Janelle, C. M., (1999). Ironic mental processes in sport. Implications for sport psychologists. *The Sport Psychologist. 13,* 201-220.

Janouch, C. (2015). *Trailrunning: Motivationale Zugänge und Persönlichkeitsstrukturen von Trailläufern.* Masterthesis, Universität Halle-Wittenberg

Johnson, U. (2007). Psychosocial antecedents of sport injury, prevention, and intervention: An overview of theoretical approaches and empirical findings. *International Journal of Sport and Exercise Psychology, 5,* 352-369.

Johnson, U., Ekengren, J. & Anderson, M. B. (2005). Injury prevention in Sweden: Helping soccer players at risk. *Journal of Sport and Exercise Psychology, 9,* 308-322.

Jones, N. L. & Kilian, K. J. (2000). Exercise limitation in health and disease. *New England Journal of Medicine, 343,* 632-641.

Keller, M. (2009). *Verletzungen und Überlastungsschäden im Laufsport.* Unveröffentlichte Vortragsunterlagen. Sölden.

Kogler, A. (2006). *Die Kunst der Höchstleistung: Sportpsychologie, Coaching, Selbstmanagement.* Wien: Springer.

Kolata, G. (2006). I'm not really running, I'm not really running. *New York Times.* Zugriff am 09.11.2015 unter http://www.nytimes.com/2007/12/06/health/nutrition/06Best.html?scp=5&sq=pain+radcliffe&st=nyt&_r=0

Krane, V. & Williams, J. M. (2010). Psychological characteristics of peak performance. In J. M. Williams (Ed.), *Applied sport psychology: personal growth to peak performance* (pp. 169-188). 4. Aufl., Mountain View: Mayfield.

Kretschmar, T. & Tzschaschel, M. (2014). *Die Kraft der inneren Bilder nutzen. Seelische und körperliche Gesundheit durch Imagination.* München: Südwest-Verlag.

Kudlackova, K., Eccles, D. & Dieffenbach, K. (2013). Use of relaxation techniques in differentially skilled athletes. *Psychology of Sport & Exercise, 14,* 468-475.

Kyllo, L. B. & Landers, D. M. (1995). Goal setting in sport and exercise: A research synthesis to resolve the controversy. *Journal of Sport and Exercise Psychology, 17,* 117-137.

Larson, G. A, Starkey, C. & Zaichkowsky, L. D. (1996). Psychological aspects of athletic injuries as perceived by athletic trainers. *The Sport Psychologist, 10,* 37-47.

Lessmöllmann, A. (2006). Das Kuli-Komplott. *Gehirn & Geist, 3,* 12-13.

Liebers, V. (2015). Nicht nur „mental" – Ultralauf und Abwehrkräfte. *ULTRAMARATHON, 3,* 118-120.

Liggett, D. R. (2004). *Sporthypnose. Eine neue Stufe des mentalen Trainings.* Heidelberg: Carl-Auer-Verlag.

Lutz, A., Dunne, J. D. & Davidson, R. J., (2007). Meditation and the neuroscience of consciousness: An introduction. In P. D. Zelazo, M. Moscovitch & E. Thompson (Hrsg.), *Cambridge handbook of consciousness* (pp. 499-552), Cambridge: University Press.

Lynch, J. & Scott, W. (1999). *Running within: A guide to mastering the body-mind-spirit-connection for ultimate training and racing.* Champaign: Human Kinetics.

Madisson, R. & Prapavessis, H. (2005). A psychological approach to the prediction and prevention of athletic injury. *Journal of Sport and Excersice Psychology, 27,* 289-310.

Masters, K. S. & Ogles, B. M. (1998). Associative and dissociative cognitive strategies in exercise and running: 20 years later, what do we know? *Sport Psychologist, 12,* 253-270.

McCrae, R. R., & Costa Jr, P. T. (1999). A five-factor theory of personality. In *Handbook of personality: Theory and research, 2*(1999), 139–153.

Meiss, O. (2009). *Mentale Stärken.* Unveröffentlichte Seminarunterlagen, Abano.

Merlot, J. (2008). Die Nebenwirkung der Angst. *ZEIT Wissen,* 2. Zugriff am 4.1.2016 unter http://www.zeit.de/zeit-wissen/2012/02/Dossier-Noceboeffekt

Meyer, T., Ferrauti, A., Kellmann, M., & Pfeiffer, M. (2016). *Regenerationsmanagement im Spitzensport: REGman-Ergebnisse und Handlungsempfehlungen.* Köln: Sportverlag Strauß.

Mischel, W. (2014). *Der Marshmallow-Test. Willensstärke, Belohnungsaufschub und die Entwicklung der Persönlichkeit.* München: Siedler-Verlag.

Moritz, S. E., Feltz, D. L., Fahrbach, K. R., & Mack, D. E. (2000). The relation of self-efficacy measures to sport performance: A meta-analytic review. *Research quarterly for exercise and sport, 71*(3), 280-294.

Naber, I. (2015). *Dieser deutsche Marathonläufer greift die Kenianer an.* http://www .welt.de/sport/leichtathletik/article147972984/Dieser-deutsche-Marathonlaeufer-greift-die-Kenianer-an.html

Nideffer, R. & Sagal, M. (2001). Concentration and attention control training. In J. M. Williams (Ed.), *Applied sport psychology: Personal growth to peak performance* (pp. 312-332). New York: McGraw-Hill.

Nideffer, R. M. (1976). Test of attentional and interpersonal style. *Journal of Personality and Social Psychology, 34,* 394-404.

Noakes, T. (2002). *Lore of running.* 4. Aufl., Champaign: Human Kinetics.

Oettingen, G. & Gollwitzer, P. M. (2010). Strategies of setting and implementing goals: Mental contrasting and implementation intentions. In J. E. Maddux & J. P. Tangney (Eds.), *Social psychological foundations of clinical psychology* (pp. 114-135). New York: Guilford Press.

Ogles, B. & Masters, K. (1993). The development of an instrument to measure motivation for marathon running: The Motivations of Marathoners Scale (MOMS). *Research Quarterly for Exercise and Sport, 64,* 134-143.

Perna, F. M., Antoni, M. H., Baum, A., Gordon, P. & Schneidermann, N. (2003). Cognitive behavioral stress management effects on injury and illness among competitive athletes: a randomized clinical trial. *Annuals of Behavioral Medicine, 25* (1), 66-73.

Pressman, S. D. & Cohen, S. (2005). Does positive affect influence health? *Psychological Bullentin, 131,* 926-971.

Rammstedt, B., Kemper, C., Klein, M. C., Beierlein, C., & Kovaleva, A. (2013). Eine kurze Skala zur Messung der fünf Dimensionen der Persönlichkeit: Big-Five-Inventory-10 (BFI-10). *Methoden, Daten, Analysen (mda)*, *7*(2), 233-249.

Riskind, J. H. & Gotay, C. C. (1982). Physical posture: Could it have regulatory or feedback effects on motivation and emotion? *Motivation and Emotion, 6*, 273-298.

Roland, P. E. & Zilles, K. (1996). Functions and structures of the motor cortices in human. *Current Opinion in Neurobiology, 6*, 773-781.

Saulsman, L. M., & Page, A. C. (2004). The five-factor model and personality disorder empirical literature: A meta-analytic review. *Clinical psychology review*, 23(8), 1055-1085.

Scheich, G. (2001). *Positives Denken macht krank. Vom Schwindel mit gefährlichen Erfolgsversprechen.* Köln: Eichborn-Verlag.

Schipfer, M. (2015). *Sportbindung und Sportsucht im Ausdauersport: Theorie – Diagnostik – Empirie.* Hamburg: Korvac-Verlag.

Schmid, G. B. (2010). *Selbstheilung durch Vorstellungskraft.* Wien: Springer.

Schmid, J., Birrer, D., Kaiser, U. & Seiler, R. (2010). Psychometrische Eigenschaften einer deutschsprachigen Adaptation des Test of Performance Strategies (TOPS). *Zeitschrift für Sportpsychologie, 17* (2), 50-62.

Schmierer, A. (2009). Zahnärztliche Problempatienten. In D. Revenstorf & B. Peter (Hrsg.), *Hypnose in Psychotherapie, Psychosomatik und Medizin* (S. 734-748). 2. Aufl., Heidelberg: Springer.

Schubert, C. (Hrsg.). (2011). *Psychoneuroimmunologie und Psychotherapie.* Stuttgart: Schattauer.

Schumacher, J, Leppert, K, Gunzelmann, T, Strauß, B, & Brähler, E. (2005). Die Resilienzskala - Ein Fragebogen zur Erfassung der psychischen Widerstandsfähigkeit als Persönlichkeitsmerkmal. *Zeitschrift für klinische Psychologie, Psychiatrie und Psychotherapie*, 53, 16–39.

Schwarzer, R. & Jerusalem, M. (Hrsg.) (1999). *Skalen zur Erfassung von Lehrer- und Schülermerkmalen. Dokumentation der psychometrischen Verfahren im Rahmen der Wissenschaftlichen Begleitung des Modellversuchs Selbstwirksame Schulen.* Berlin: Freie Universität Berlin.

Schwarzer, R., & Jerusalem, M. (1995). Generalized Self-Efficacy scale. In J. Weinman, S. Wright, & M. Johnston. *Measures in health psychology: A user's portfolio. Causal and control beliefs* (pp. 35- 37). Windsor, England: NFER-NELSON.

Servan-Schreiber, D. (2006). *Die neue Medizin der Emotionen. Stress Angst, Depression: Gesund werden ohne Medikamente.* 14. Aufl., München: Goldmann.

Sgherza, A. L., Axen, K., Fain, R., Hoffmann, R. S., Dunbar, C. C. & Haas, F. (2002). Effect of naloxone on perceived exertion and exercise capacity during maximal cycle ergometry. *Journal of Applied Physiology, 93,* 2023-2028.

Siegmund-Schultze, N. (2008). Schein-Op: der Placebo-Effekt täuscht auch Chirurgen. *Ärzte Zeitung.* Zugriff am 3.1.2016 unter http://www.aerztezeitung.de/medizin/fachbereiche/chirurgie/article/517816/schein-op-placebo-effekt-taeuscht-chirurgen.html

Simon, H. A. & Gilmartin, K. (1973). A simulation of memory for chess positions. *Cognitive Psychology, 5,* 29-46.

Smith, D., Wright, C., Allsopp, A. & Westhead, H. (2007). It's all in the mind: PETTLEP-based imagery and sports performance. *Journal of Applied Sport Psychology, 19* (1), 80-92.

Smith, R. E., Smoll, F. L. & Ptacek, J. T. (1990). Conjunctive moderator variables in vulnerability and resiliency research: Life stress, social support and coping skills, and and adolescent sport injuries, *Journal of Personality and Social Psychology, 58* (2), 360-369.

Soon, C. S, Brass, M., Heinze, H. J. & Haynes, J. D. (2008). Unconscious determinants of free decisions in the human brain. *Nature Neuroscience, 11,* 543-545.

Staudenmayer, S. (2014). *Die Körperbeherrscher. Menschen am Limit des körperlich Leistbaren.* Zugriff am 12.12.2015 unter http://www.zdf.de/terra-x/supertalent-mensch-koerperbeherrscher-am-limit-der-koerperlichen-leistungsfaehigkeit-35755080.html

Stegemann, J. (1991). *Leistungsphysiologie: Physiologische Grundlagen der Arbeit und des Sports.* (4. Aufl.), Stuttgart: Thieme.

Stevinson, C. D., & Biddle, S. J. (1998). Cognitive orientations in marathon running and "hitting the wall". *British Journal of Sports Medicine, 32* (3), 229-234.

Stoll, O. & Becker-Kopsch, F. (2015). *Einmal war ich in Biel.* Zugriff am 9.11.2015 unter http://www.einmalwarichinbiel.de.

Stoll, O. (1998). *Zur Reliabilität und Validität einer deutschen Version der Motivations of Marathon Runners Scale (MoMS).* Unveröffentlichter Forschungsbericht, Universität Leipzig.

Stoll, O., & Rolle, J. (1997). Persönlichkeitsprofile und habituelle Streßbewältigung bei Ultralangstrecken-Läufern. *Sportwissenschaft, 27,* 161-172.

Summers, J. J., Sargent, G. I., Levey, A. J., & Murray, K. D. (1982). Middle-aged, non-elite marathon runners: A profile. *Perceptual and Motor Skills, 54* (3), 963-969.

Szabó, P. & Berg, I. K. (2006). *Kurz(zeit)coaching mit Langzeitwirkung.* Dortmund: Borgmann Media.

Tomlinson, A. (2010). *A dictionary of sport studies.* New York: Oxford University Press.

Ufer, M. (2001). *Implizites Wissen von Führungskräften. Eine Empirische Untersuchung zur Bedeutung der Befragungsperspektive bei der Wissensdiagnostik.* Unveröffentlichte Staatsexamensarbeit, Universität Duisburg, Duisburg.

Ufer, M. (2013). Grenzkompetenz. Souveränität in persönlichen Extremsituationen steigern. In M. Sauerland, M. C. Ullrich, S. Gaukel, A. Frank & M. Ufer (Hrsg.), *Selbstmotivierung für Sportler. Motivationstechniken zur Leistungssteigerung im Sport* (S. 65-74). Balingen: Spitta.

Ufer, M. (2013). Laufhypnose. *RUNNING – Das Laufmagazin, 3,* 102-103.

Ufer, M. (2014). *Action Learning: Speed-Coaching für Teams und deren Führungskräfte.* Unveröffentlichte Workshop-Unterlagen, München.

Ufer, M. (2015). *Zur Reliabilität und Validität einer überarbeiteten deutschsprachigen Version des Test of Performance Strategies (TOPS).* Unveröffentlichter Forschungsbericht, Herdecke.

Ufer, M. (2017): *Flow-Jäger. Motivation, Erfolg und Zufriedenheit beim Laufen.* Bielefeld: Delius-Klasing Verlag.

Ufer, M. (2018). Neues aus der Laufpsychologie-Forschung.Die sind doch verrückt, oder? *RUNNING, 1,* 38-39.

Ufer, M. (2018, June): *The resilient athlete. Personality,* psychological strategies and the ability to bounce back after a crisis in endurance sport. Paper presented at the International Congress of the French Society of Sport Psychology, Lausanne

Ullrich, M.-C. (2013). Verletzungsmanagement. Wege zur schnellen Genesung. In M. Sauerland, M. C. Ullrich, S. Gaukel, A. Frank & M. Ufer (Hrsg.), *Selbstmotivierung für*

Sportler. Motivationstechniken zur Leistungssteigerung im Sport (S. 141-150). Balingen: Spitta.

Weinberg, R. S. & Gould, D. (2015). *Foundations of sport and exercise psychology.* 6. Aufl., Champaign: Human Kinetics.

Weston, N., Greenlees, I. & Thelwell, R. (2010). Applied sport psychology consultant perceptions of the usefulness and impacts of performance profiling. *International Journal of Sport Psychology, 41,* 360-368.

Weston, N., Greenlees, I., Thelwell, R. (2011). Athletes perceptions of the impacts of performance profiling. *International Journal of Sport Psychology, 9,* 173-188.

Wicks, G. R. (2009): Chirurgie. In D. Revenstorf & B. Peter (Hrsg.) (2009), *Hypnose in Psychotherapie, Psychosomatik und Medizin* (S. 641-651). 2. Aufl., Heidelberg: Springer.

Williams, J. M., Andersen, M. B, (1998). Psychosocial antecedents of sport injury and interventions for risk reduction. In G. Tennebaum & R. C. Eklund (Eds.), *Handbook of sport psychology* (pp. 5-25), 3. Aufl., New York: Wiley.

Yerkes, R. M. & Dodson, J. D. (1908). The relation of strength of stimulus to rapidity of habit-formation. *Journal of Comparative Neurology and Psychology, 18,* 459-482.

Zourbanos, N., Hatzigeorgiadis, A., Goudas, M., Papaioannu, A., Chroni, S. & Theodorakis, Y. (2011). The social side of self-talk: Relationships between perceptions of support received from the coach and athlete's self-talk. *Psychology of Sport and Exercise, 12,* 1-8.

READERS' OPINIONS ON THE BOOK

As a repeat offender in extreme sports and a profound expert and lecturer in sport psychology, Dr. Michele Ufer provides an outstanding compendium on the subject of mental training. It is not just for runners. This book is also an excellent manual for other areas of life. During the journey, we find out what happens to our body and our mind while we run, how we can redefine and achieve goals through relaxation techniques and our imagination, and how we can incidentally also undergo some positive change along the way. But the great power of this book lies in its applicability to many disciplines: sports, work, private life, etc. The book teaches us methods to influence mental processes in a performance-enhancing manner while conserving resources. Many of these things can also be used in professional life. I highly recommend this book!

—Ludger Gerbhardt, team manager at Konica Minolta

As a mountain guide and ambitious Skyrunner, I know from personal experience that the mind is extremely important—possibly critical—to the success of projects. In this book, Michele provides awesome explanations of the mental aspects of sports as well as directly implementable instructions on how to improve motivation and mental strength. These approaches are also very well suited for alpine sports and challenging expeditions.

—Karl Egloff, mountain guide and holder of multiple Skyrunning records (Kilimanjaro, Aconcagua, Elbrus)

Do you have a mental block? Does an obstacle seem too great? Is running too strenuous? Have you lost the lightness? This book isn't just ingenious, the writing is realistic and suspenseful. The exercises help you return to the roots of running. Why do I want to run? How do I want to feel when I run? What resources do I have available to me? I have gained a liberating and enormously strong clarity about my own wishes, needs, and goals. The purpose of the individual exercises is underpinned by many vivid, real-life examples. I have worked through this book more than once. Thank you!

—Kirsten Althoff, winner of the 250 km Sahara Race (4Deserts Race Serie)

Michele Ufer manages to present new perspectives on performance improvement through mental training. It is an important addition to sports medical and sport-scientific aspects. But the health-oriented recreational athlete will also be able to enhance his training with the presented methods.

—Dr. Ulrich Schneider, Chief of Sports Medicine, Hellerson Sports Medicine Clinic

And one thing becomes very evident in this book: Mental training can also be fun! The many easy-to-apply exercises make this a work I will always return to for the rest of my running life!

—Florian Reus, World and three-time European Champion in the 24-hour race

Be it for sports or other challenges, this book is a very successful overview of the effects and the training of the mind from the perspective of a runner, coach, and scientist.

—Rafael Fuchsgruber, artist manager, concert promoter, desert runner

Michele Ufer hit the mark with his book. It is a must-read for any ambitious athlete.

—Jana Hartmann, six-time German National Champion in 800 m

This book really helps to successfully master the occasionally extreme challenges in sport, day-to-day management work, and private life.

—Christoph Harreither, partner at Ernst & Young Accounting Firm

SUCCESS STORIES

The following success stories represent the value of mental training.

MY WAY TO THE DREAM RUN AND DREAM JOB

Krister Wiklund, Planning Analyst TJX Europe / 361° Ambassador

I started running in the summer of 2015. After just a few weeks, I could feel how good the movement was for my body and soul. It especially helped me reduce stress and heavy thoughts in connection with my bipolar mental illness. The runner in me was born. I bought the book *Mentaltraining für Läufer* to support my journey toward the first half marathon in Cologne in 2016.

Because of my bipolar disorder, I am well versed in cognitive therapies. I have to understand thought patterns and what role the power of thoughts plays in changing feelings and behavior. During running and in life there are always situations where you don't feel well, which can't be changed or avoided. But you can learn to perceive situations differently and to react better to them. For this Michele gives very good suggestions and provides the tools. Maybe it hurts somewhere, maybe it's exhausting, or maybe I don't feel motivated and even want to give up the run completely. The exercises from the book have helped me develop mental thinking for these very situations that steers my thoughts away from the problems and toward possible solutions. By practicing regularly, I could significantly improve the mental side of training.

I've even used the mental training for important achievements outside of running. I have used the tools for setting and formulating powerful and achievable goals to get my dream job. I used the Positioning & Resource Reload technique to find out what new professional challenge I needed. The whole process took about three months from start to finish. In particular, the book helped me to develop clear answers to the following questions: Where do I stand now? Where do I want to go and why do I want to go? And finally: What do I have to do to get there? My new boss said that he had never experienced anyone who knew exactly what challenges he was looking for and who had dealt with the position in this way. When I sat in the last interview, everything went in slow motion. I knew exactly what to say and where to go. It was as if I had released the arrow from the bow and now just had to wait for it to hit the target. A really cool feeling, and when I got the job, it was more like déjà vu. And yet I celebrated it with a fist pump and a smiling "Yes!"

Meanwhile I have three marathons and a handful of half marathons behind me, and this year I will realize my new dream, ultrarunning. This book is still my permanent companion. To change something permanently often requires a lot of mental work and perseverance, but it is always worth it.

BOOSTER FOR THE WORLD CHAMPIONSHIP

Eva Sperger, Psychotherapist, German Champion Ultratrail Run 2017

In 2017 I won the German Ultratrail Championship (DUV). To mentally prepare for the race in the Alps—a distance of 82 km with 4,200 meters altitude—I worked intensively through Michele's book. A little later, after two demotivating competitions directly before an international ultra race, the Transvulcania, I wanted to recharge my mental batteries. To prepare, I used the instructions in the book to prepare mentally, and using these mental strategies, I competed in the race full of newly won energy. The strategy of focusing on a performance goal, such as placement or process, helped me a lot. It became clear how much running is my passion and how much it can transfer to my life. The competition with its 74 km over volcanic rock was miraculously pure enjoyment and an absolute booster for the upcoming World Championship in 2018 in Spain where I achieved 17th place in the Penyagolosa Trail.

After winning the German Championship, being nominated for the national team and participating in a World Championship, I was contacted by sponsors. This raised the question of what values I wanted to represent. There is a chapter on this in the book. That helped me a lot to understand why I do this sport, which is important to me. Knowing the reason why I run and invest so much time fuels my motivation and passion.

Since then I have used the book to prepare for hard competitions and have always gained new methods for competitions. It is really fun to discover the "resource jokers," to draw on them while running, and to incorporate the resource work into psychotherapy. I am a psychotherapist and have hypnosis training. Michele's book and instructions for implementation totally helps me to learn the techniques better and to use them more for the therapy sessions!

A funny anecdote: an acquaintance once observed me reading the book and had to laugh a lot about how deep I was and how often I nodded approvingly without the presence of others. This unique combination of mental training, hypnosis, and running hits the nail on the head. Thank you very much for the great suggestions and the strength I gained from the book. In my next competition, the UTMB with its 170 km and 10000hm, it will surely motivate me again and help me prepare mentally and be a source of strength.

WHEN MOTIVATION IS STRONGER THAN ILLNESS

Frank Konkel, Ultralunner & Sales Manager

August 13, 2017, 7:13 am. After 100 miles and 25:13:42 hours, I crossed the finish line in Berlin, managing something incomprehensible for me. April 1, 2011, irrevocably changed my life. I spent a week in a clinic on suspicion of a stroke and was thoroughly examined. It was not a stroke, but I was diagnosed with multiple sclerosis. Now I had an explanation for my bad physical condition and the many pains and complaints in the last decades. Well, a bad diet, obesity, and only spectator sports also contributed to this. On the way home, I realized that I had to change my life immediately. Three years later, my daughter asks me on a hike what goals I still have in my life (at the age of 49). Spontaneously I answer, "I want to walk 100 kilometers at least once in my life." I still have no idea why I said this, but it would change my life a second time. Still on vacation, I ordered books on running training. I had already changed my diet considerably in the last few years, completely renounced alcohol, smoking became less, and only sport was missing. My goals were quickly set: 2015 a marathon, 2016 a 100-kilometer competition, 2017 the 100 miles.

I was able to learn to walk quite well with the appropriate training. In March 2015, I took part in a 6-hour run and ran a little over 54 kilometers. While the pounds were falling, the running shoes were wearing out more, the times were getting faster, the distances were getting longer. I actually had only one weakness: me! Even if feelings of happiness prevailed, the head can unfortunately put a spoke in the wheel. As negative thoughts were becoming more frequent, Michele Ufer's book fell into my hands by chance. In recent years, I had concluded that the power of thought can have enormous effects on life, so why not mental running training? Completely fascinated, I decided to try the strategies. Through mental training, it has been incredibly easy for me to motivate myself. I almost never skip a training session because I usually look forward to the inner satisfaction after the training. I got rid of my negative attitude. The negative thoughts still come today, but much more rarely and not so strongly. Usually I meet them in advance, because I am in constant dialogue with myself. On some stressful and uncomfortable days, the positive self-talk already begins after a few hundred meters and release energy immediately. So it sometimes happens that I set training records that I didn't expect. When the feet start to hurt during long runs, I recall pictures from the past, like a moment from a holiday: After hours of hiking, we passed a Kneipp pool with ice-cold mountain water. Then it happens that after some time I freeze at my feet.

After four years of ultrarunning and mental training, not only my physical condition has improved, but my whole life has changed for the better. In addition to my general fitness, I have acquired a tremendous mental strength, which is also transferred to my daily work. I always find myself setting professional goals that I would never have dreamed of years ago.

And the multiple sclerosis? My doctors said with a twinkle in my eye that it hardly had a chance to happen to me because my body had to function constantly and perform at its best and simply had no time to let the disease appear. Let's hope it stays that way. In any case, the beautiful long runs on the weekend are transferred to the whole week, to everyday family and professional life. I am very satisfied with myself and my life.

STORMY TIMES? ALWAYS A QUESTION OF ATTITUDE.

Achim Dietrich, Ultrarunner & Police Officer

At first I was skeptical about mental training techniques. But then the personal experiences of Michele and others convinced me that it is possible to improve performance and mental endurance through mental training and control.

In January 2019, my wife and I flew to Florida for vacation. I wanted to use this opportunity to run a 50-kilometer race there and set a personal record. I had set my sights on a new best time of 4:13:48. I was really looking forward to good running weather, far away from the Central European winter. But it didn't quite work out as expected. A cold front with continuous rain and squalls came up. You're flying halfway around the world, looking forward to a sunny ultra, aiming for a best time, and then that. Frustated, I began thinking, "I can't start in such bad weather," or "I can tick off the record attempt." But I started anyway, in the dark at 7 in the morning, in continuous rain, in 50 degrees. Up to kilometer 25, my pace was on record course and then I had to call on some of the motivation techniques from this book. With the rain continuing to pour, inch-deep puddles formed in the streets, and the wind whipped my face. I was feeling doubtful almost the entire time. So I used the visualization technique. I imagined how every single raindrop works like an energy drink and gives me the strength to continue running at a fast pace. I also thought that each puddle would serve as a springboard. Using another mental strategy, I concentrated 70% on my running technique: clean feet on the asphalt, knee lift. With the remaining 30%, I kept thinking about a tasty medium steak as a reward or a hot shower at the end of the run. These mental strategies made it easier for me to reach my goal, step by step. The effect was sensational for me. I finished second overall in 4:11:20. Despite the difficult external influences (weather), the motivation techniques helped me to complete the run successfully and earn a personal best.

I have also used some focusing techniques several times in my profession as a police officer and passed them on to other colleagues. As a patrolman, you are confronted daily with unexpected situations. I am often called upon to settle a dispute and restore calm. At these moments, negative thoughts only make the situation worse. Instead, I consciously stop the negative thought reformulate it as: "I know both parties, and I know how everyone ticks. I make our approach transparent to both parties and end this dispute safely and satisfactorily without much effort and violence."

Having used the mental techniques to achieve my goals means I can say from experience: they work.

MENTAL PERFORMANCE (NOT ONLY) AT THE SWIMMING WORLD CHAMPIONSHIPS

Regina Senften, Masters Swimmer from Zurich, Switzerland

I've been studying Michele's book about the 50-meter pool swimming world championships. Although I had already read some books about mental training and even attended courses, it was this book that triggered the "click" and was a huge help. Why would a swimmer consult a book on mental training for runners? Quite simple: Even a swimmer wants to be highly focused and highly motivated on the starting block. Even a swimmer wants to remain positive in competition, even if her muscles hurt and her lungs burn. And even a swimmer wants to say at the stroke: Today everything fits, body, head, and gear.

Before reading the book, I had often noticed during training that I was afraid of hard series, which we call "vomit series" in swimming. It was quite clear to me from a training science point of view that such high-intensity intervals are mandatory if you want to improve your performance. Nevertheless, my head kept me from training really hard for a long time, meaning my performance didn't increase as desired. My inner voice often said to me, "I can't do any more." "I can't swim clean anymore." "I can't breathe anymore." Thanks to this book, I finally managed to get my negative thinking spiral under control and to stay focused from in the race from beginning to end. An unbelievably great experience! Michele has taught me to let positive thoughts, pictures, music, and movies unwind, not only when pain occurs during training or competition, but always when external influences distract me or negatively influence me. Instead of complaining internally, I have put together positive mantras and mental pictures. "I swim very fluidly, loosely, and fast." "I feel totally comfortable in this element." "My strong muscles do a great job." I shot a video of a sparkling mountain stream on a beautiful summer day, accompanied by upbeat music. In training, I try to play this video sequence in my head when I notice negative thoughts regarding pain at the start of training. I rehearsed a gesture for stopping the thought and noted down very concrete result, performance, and process goals with regard to the World Cup. I have put together mantras and pieces of music that put me in a positive, confident, lively mood before the start of the competition.

That didn't happen overnight, but with time, it worked out better and better. During the last six months, I have taken the book almost daily and worked it through. In the end, I translated almost all the strategies that Michele describes for himself and his sport to me and my life and competition situation. Michele's ideas and suggestions have opened the door to a new competition experience! The intensive occupation with mental motivation paid off in the end. Everything really worked out at the World Championships: Head, body, and gear. Three new best times and a top 15 place were the reward!

I also use the techniques I have learned outside of my sport. Negative thoughts often appear on the job or in everyday life with the family. With positively formulated inner persuasion, difficult situations can be mastered better than if you constantly keep those negative things in mind. I even use my gesture of stopping my negative thoughts repeatedly outside swimming. The book *Mental Toughness for Runners* is ultimately a book for mental performance in all sports and in everyday life.

SPARTATHLON. AT THE FEET OF KING LEONIDAS.

Gunter Rothe, Ultrarunner

The 246-km Spartathlon in Greece is considered the unofficial world championship in the ultramarathon and one of the most difficult road races in the world. As a recreational runner, my goal is to arrive within the cuttoff time. Already in 2016, I had put more focus on mental preparation in addition to run training. The starting point was Michele's book. At that time, I focused on the positive transformation of all possible negative thoughts or phases of weakness occurring during the race. So, the words "not" (I can't anymore) or "none" (I have no more strength) were removed from my vocabulary and transformed everything into inspiring and forward thinking. This also included simply ignoring certain issues (pain, complaints, etc.), giving them no place in my self-talk and consciously directing my senses in a goal-oriented direction. Michele's challenge "Don't think of person .... in pink pajamas" was and still is for me a very special tongue-in-cheek example of how one can steer one's subconscious correctly. And it is always a lot of fun to say this sentence to others and ask them: and, what are you thinking about now?

Two years later: the preparations for the 2018 Spartathlon were absolutely catastrophic. Repeatedly I was slowed down by health problems. Mostly my back, then again other "construction sites." Continuous training was simply not possible. My few long runs covered a maximum of 20 km, meaning I was badly prepared for the adventure Spartathlon at the end of September with almost 900 run training kilometers. My counter-strategy was optimal mental preparation! And for that I found a lot of inspiration and suggestions in Michele's book. It became a kind of mental Bible for me. Each smaller round of running began 10 minutes before the actual running, lying on my back with my eyes closed. In my mind I already ran, breathed in the different smells (the grain was being harvested, and the air was full of harvest dust), heard the wind in the trees, and "saw" my route: paths, paths, inviting benches at the edge, blackberry bushes full of ripe delicious fruits. Later, while actually running, I rediscovered everything with all my senses. For this next time, I wanted to put together mental bricks to build a bridge from Athens to Sparta. I made a picturebook using real photos to imagines the sites and smells I'd experience during the run. All the strategies Michele so aptly describes them proved to be effective during my short training rounds. The evening before the start at the Acropolis, I went through this picturebook again, page by page, step by step. And my goal was clear: I want to make it to King Leonidas! (Michele's note: The finish of the race is reached by touching the foot of the statue of King Leonidas in Sparta.)

And then I ran. And how! I used my mental images one after the other, but it was only after more than 100 km I noticed surprisingly that my physical condition was much better than my training condition would have allowed. Michele's mental tricks were taking effect. No muscular problems, no mental crises! My head was already programmed for the next picture. But the Spartathlon 2018 was not the same as previous years. It rained continuously for more than 28 hours, and from about 220 kilometers on, the side effects of hurricane "Zorbas"—violent hurricane gusts—gnawed at my mental preparation. At this time, I started to talk to Michele in my mind. Michele: "Visualize the goal!" Me: "Okay, there he stands, the king, I want to go there!" At the same time the thoughts: "Who will be on the home straight in this weather, is it still there at all? The paramedics' tents to the left of it have surely already blown away and the flags behind Leonidas are surely only hanging as rags...Never mind! Go on! Less than 10km!" I visualized the next picture: "Finish, end, done!" My last picture in my bridge picturebook from Athens to Sparta.

Thanks to Michele for endless inspiration, many great, sometimes at first meaningless, little tips which ultimately had a huge impact, for the hint to go forward with eyes opens, fading out the performance-reducing factors, but not forgetting them—very important! Actually, it is always about reflecting on one's own strengths, about putting them in the foreground. And this reflection always begins in your head!

PHOTO CREDITS

Cover and jacket design, Layout and composition	Eva Feldmann (3rd edition adaptation: Annika Naas)
Cover photos:	©AdobeStock
Interior photos:	Pg. 10 RUNNING – the running magazine
	Pg. 18, 23, 47, 48/50, 146 www.4deserts.com - Zandy Mangold
	Pg. 12/14, 16, 33, 105, 119, 137, 188 www.michele-ufer.de
	Pg. 117 Physiomed – Petra Kober
	Pg. 164 Beyond the Ultimate – Martin Paldan
	Pg. 210 Private
	Pg. 230 Melanie Schipfer
	Pg. 24/26, 76/78, 106/108, 131, 132/134, 151, 166, 200/202, 245, 246, 247 ©Thinkstock, iStock
	Pg. 248, 250 ©AdobeStock
Interior images:	1, 2 a/b, 3 a/b, 4, 5 (photo ©Thinkstock), 6, 9, 11 a/b, 12, 13, 14, 15 Michele Ufer
Managing editor:	Elizabeth Evans
Copyeditor:	Anne Rumery